Farewell my Pashtun

Mark Frew

Farewell my Pashtun

Copyright © 2013 Mark Frew
All rights reserved. No part of this publication may be reproduced, stored in a retrieval system or transmitted in any form or by any means, electronic, mechanical, photocopying, recording or otherwise, without the prior written permission of the publisher.

The information, views, opinions and visuals expressed in this publication are solely those of the author(s) and do not reflect those of the publisher. The publisher disclaims any liabilities or responsibilities whatsoever for any damages, libel or liabilities arising directly or indirectly from the contents of this publication.

A copy of this publication can be found in the National Library of Australia.

ISBN: 978-0-9954440-4-1 (paperback)
ISBN: 978-0-9954440-5-8 (hardback)
ISBN: 978-0-9954440-3-4 (ebook)

Other books by the same author:
Michael and the Multicoloured Gospel

Dedicated to the establishment of tolerance, understanding and friendship in the twenty-first century communities we are creating and throughout the global village in which we live.

To Abdul

Chapter 1

When I first had an Afghani student in my class, I realised how little I knew about Afghanistan. In fact, all I had heard about this country was of the Russian war which had featured on the news years previously and of the recent influx of refugees as a result of the Taliban. Apart from that, all I knew of this land was that it was just a small blob on the map of Central Asia with a thin stretch of terrain like a finger pointing accusingly at China.

The first Afghani I ever met had the not-so-original name of Mohammed. He was a small, thin young man with slanted eyes which made him look as if he were Chinese but with much more facial and body hair which betrayed a Caucasian mixing. I was at first afraid of him because I was not sure if he were really a refugee or simply a terrorist dressed up in refugee clothing. However, I got used to him and grew to like him as he turned out to be quite a nice, pleasant guy.

Mohammed told me a little of the adventurous escape from his country that had been held hostage by the Taliban. Unfortunately, in the short conversation that we once had, he was totally inept in his limited English to explain to me what had transpired as he made the daring attempt to leave Afghanistan and find respite in Australia. All he told me was of the terrifying boat trip, the months in open sea without food and water and the feeling of relief to be finally established in a country that had virtually known no civil war within its borders.

I learnt from Mohammed that Afghanis were not one people but were a mixture of races. Mohammed's features, so he explained, were typical of a tribe called Hazarah and the Hazarahs were an oppressed minority in the land. But there were also other tribes competing for living space in this small region of the world: Uzbeks, who also shared their heritage with the inhabitants of Uzbekistan in the north, and Tajiks, who had a common link with neighbouring Tajikistan. Although of different tribes, all Afghanis had two things in common: they all shared a common religion, Islam, and they all spoke a common language, Dari. Dari, as I was later to find out, is simply an intelligible dialect of Farsi, or Persian, the national language of Afghanistan's western neighbour, Iran.

Mohammed didn't tell me much more about the Taliban that I had not already read about in the newspaper or seen on the news. Mohammed portrayed the Taliban as a bunch of uneducated barbarians who believed in a basic and radical form of Islam, and explained how the Taliban had tried to establish power in his homeland through brute force.

But Mohammed also provided me with new information about the Taliban. The Taliban, he explained, was a warlike group of people made up of yet another Afghani tribe known as the Pashtuns. The Pashtuns spoke their own language, Pashto, and were insistent on establishing themselves all over Afghanistan and making their language the official language throughout the land. Pashtuns were Taliban and the Taliban were Pashtuns as if the two words were simply synonyms from a Roget's Thesaurus.

I was a teacher at a special college, the Australian English Language College or AELC. This was a private college which specialised in teaching English to migrants and took in students who could not be readily accommodated by colleges which already ran the governmental Adult Migrant English Program or AMEP. AMEP was originally set up to provide immigrants with their first intensive course in learning English when these immigrants first stepped off the boat as it were. However, with the recent sudden influx of refugees, there were many more students than governmental facilities to accommodate them and so private colleges like AELC mopped up the surplus.

Because of my job, I always learnt a few words of the languages my students spoke. Well, maybe that's an understatement! I taught my language because I was crazy about learning other languages and so my classroom was more a place for sharing different languages than simply the teaching of English. Because Mohammed could not find the right words to tell me his story, I thought that if I learnt Dari, this would create the bridge between an Afghani and an Australian, and help break down the walls of suspicion between us. I thought that it would also enable me to understand first hand what had really happened that led thousands of Afghanis to flee to Australia.

No sooner had I started to learn this fascinating language than Mohammed left my class. But I was certain that there would be other Afghanis to fill his place and not make my first attempts at this language a waste of time. And sure enough, when I started the new class for the year, among my league of nations of students, came Mohammed's replacement - Faisal.

From first appearances, Faisal wasn't really anything remarkable to look at, quite the contrary. He looked about 40 years of age, was clean shaven, had a receding hairline, dark, bushy eyebrows, deep furrows in his forehead and a perpetual sad look which gave me the impression that he embraced melancholy as a lover. He had a thin, emaciated build, coarse hands which betrayed his skill as a labourer, and a pale complexion as if his body had never seen the light of day.

He was the first student to arrive at the class and, from his appearance, and by the way he skulked into the classroom, he gave me the impression that the angel of death had arrived bearing evil tidings.

But he was Afghani, one of the boat people whom the media had caused us to fear and suspect. What was he doing here in our country anyway? Was he fleeing terrorism or was he here to spread it? Should I feel sympathy for him or fear? In the global climate that makes the twenty-first century, each new Afghani student that entered my class was always at first a source of anxiety because it was a physical reminder that today there was almost nowhere left on the globe where we could find calm and serenity.

In an attempt to welcome him and make him feel at ease, I tried to make light conversation. But with each monolexic answer, I had the impression that I was achieving the opposite effect.

"So, what's your name?" I asked while I glanced down the class roll to find a name that matched the man who had entered the classroom.

"Faisal," he replied cautiously, as if I were a member of the Federal Police sent here to interrogate him, not a common teacher to educate him in the official language.

"Faisal, Faisal, Faisal," I half whispered as I ran my finger down the class list until I found his name.

I placed a cross in the roll to mark his presence. "Aha! Faisal! My first student for the evening. Welcome to the class."

Faisal did not show any signs of recognition or understanding of my attempts to make him feel welcome. He simply placed his carry bag on the desk and removed the necessary equipment that students need: an exercise book, a variety of pens, an English textbook and a bilingual dictionary.

"So," I began, in an attempt to make light conversation, "did you work today?"

"Yes," Faisal said as he eyed me cautiously.

"What do you do?" I asked.

"Carpenter," was his reply.

"Oh! Do you like your job?"

"Yes."

"Where do you work?"

"Fairfield."

"Is it far from where you live?"

"No."

While trying to make him feel at ease, I was becoming more and more anxious, thinking that I was frightening the guy. How was I to interpret this? If he were a terrorist, his clipped speech could be interpreted as his suspicion of and possible contempt for non-Muslim Anglo-Celts. However, as someone who had escaped atrocities in his own country, his short answers could also have been taken as fear of authority, which is what I represented in my capacity as a teacher.

At this point, I didn't know whether to try to continue talking or allow an uncomfortable lull in conversation to be established as two strangers occupied the same area of space. Fortunately, I didn't have to contemplate this awkward situation for very long as other students began entering the class and soon I was able to begin teaching.

Faisal remained quiet and melancholic during that first class while the other students participated in the lesson in group activities and enthusiastically called out answers to my questions. In fact, to be totally honest, I cannot remember much else about him on that first day because he seemed to disappear into the background as the other students held a prominent image in my mind.

This class began at the end of January, in the middle of what is officially the Sydney summer. This is the season I love the best because, being fond of swimming and bodysurfing, it is the time of year when I spend most of the time where there is water, either at the beach or the local swimming pool.

Sydney is a great place for those who love the water. There are swimming pools dotted about the metropolitan area which provide a variety of places to lay out the towel and relax under the sweltering sun or swimming laps which is the closest thing to the sensation of flying.

Sydney is also bordered with beautiful beaches from north to south that attract millions. Coloured towels and the odour of coconut oil, coupled with golden sands and rolling waves, provide what is needed to overcome the rigours of the daily grind of work and is definitely a way to relax and enjoy the thrill of simply being alive.

Summer is also the time when we can wear as little as necessary. It is only at work, however, where I break this tradition, donning a long-sleeve shirt and tie in order to look presentable and at least give my students the image that I am a proficient teacher. I started the tradition of wearing a tie to work because I began working at the college in winter. A tie is certainly a convenient piece of attire that traps needed body heat to cope with the biting cold. However, in summer it is totally unnecessary. I don't have to wear a tie at all, especially when many of my colleagues wear their casual jeans and a T-shirt during the summer months. But I had started the tradition and really didn't know how to break it despite the heat. It had become my uniform and, without these clothes, I would have felt that I was standing before the class naked.

As the weeks rolled by, I began to get to know the students in the class as individual beings but

Faisal was the one I knew the least. It was very difficult to work out his personality and, during the first couple of weeks in my class, I was of the impression that he was completely devoid of any.

I don't think I would have taken much notice of Faisal for the rest of the semester if I hadn't tried to get to know him. But the teaching style I try to adopt, especially as I teach adults, is to make my students more my friends than keep them at arm's length as impersonal students. Faisal was always the first to class and I decided to use this opportunity to show that I was stretching a friendly arm out to him by using his language as the instrument.

As was usual, Faisal quietly entered the class like a convicted criminal entering a courtroom waiting for a guilty verdict. He sat down and carefully took out everything he needed for the class. When he was set and the normal disquieting silence had been established in the classroom, which had now become the tradition when we were alone together, I greeted him in Dari. Faisal looked at me with surprise.

"Do you speak Dari?" he asked in Dari.

"A little," I replied in his tongue. Because this was about the extent of my knowledge in this language, I continued the conversation in English.

"I knew you spoke Dari because you're Afghani," I continued.

"Where did you learn that?" he asked with the first sign of interest.

"Oh, from a book," I said. "Really, it's a book that teaches Farsi but I know the two languages are similar. After all, I notice that you use an English-Farsi dictionary so I guess Farsi and Dari are one and the same language. Dari is your mother tongue, isn't it?" I felt quite proud of myself that I could illustrate to Faisal that I was not Anglo-centric and knew something about his country and culture. But his answer illustrated that I still had a lot to learn.

"No, Dari isn't my mother tongue. I am Pashtun. Pashto is one of the official languages of Afghanistan. Dari is the other. I speak Dari but my mother tongue is Pashto."

Faisal's insistence that he was Pashtun and that Pashto was one of the official languages of Afghanistan and, moreso, that Pashto was his mother tongue made me freeze on the spot. My former Afghani student, Mohammed, who had come across as sincere and honest, had warned me about the Pashtuns. Now I was standing facing what I was convinced was a member of the Taliban. My attempt to make this student open up and engage in a friendly conversation was squashed in an instant. What could I say? I cannot explain the fear that instantly overwhelmed me when I realised that one of these uneducated barbarians, who probably ruthlessly murdered Afghanis of other tribes, was alone with me in the one room. I was speechless and terrified. Here I was, a representative of probably everything the Taliban despised, a westerner and a non-religious, gay man. Any one of these facets about my person would have been enough for a member of the Taliban to draw a knife and slit my throat or carry out any of his savagery against me. If the Taliban could commit such atrocities against other Afghanis when they at least shared some common cultural traits, what hope was there for me?

It was a dreadful moment. I could feel the sweat form pearls of water on my forehead and begin to run like minute streams down my cheeks despite the fact that it was, after all, about 35°C in our non-air-conditioned classroom. The seconds seemed to take forever while I waited for the other students to arrive. When the other students did arrive, I was so relieved. At least there were enough men amongst my group of students who could hold Faisal down if the need arose.

From that evening on, I didn't like this student at all. I wanted to speak to the Course Coordinator and have Faisal transferred to another class, but what would have been my basis for it? Because I suspected him of being a terrorist and a member of the Taliban? But what was the evidence? I knew I had nothing really to go on except his ethnic background.

The weeks progressed and Faisal remained an illusory figure in my class. He was a quiet man who said almost nothing. But what intrigued me more was that he never laughed. In fact, he seemed to portray the image of a man who had never known happiness. To try to make it worthwhile for my students to come to class, I always entertained them with a joke or two every now and again. Although the other students would laugh or at least humour me with a smile, Faisal would sit there with a sullen look on his face as if mirth and laughter were the works of the devil.

This was yet another indication to me at the time that Faisal had to be a terrorist. This evidence was based on a magazine article I had read not long after the attack on the Twin Towers in New York. A lecturer in a German university was completely horrified to find out that one of her Muslim students was one of the major participants in this world-shaking event. This lecturer noticed two things about this young man. One was that he never smiled. Faisal fit this description well. It was even more striking now because his lack of joviality coupled with his Pashtun background only reinforced my initial impressions of his possible former terrorist involvement.

The other thing that this lecturer noticed about her student was that he was conscientious and intelligent. Mohammed had explained to me that the members of the Taliban were nothing but a bunch of uneducated barbarians, but I had completely put this aside in favour of what this German lecturer had said. Faisal also fit this description. Although a very quiet person, eventually I began to realize that Faisal was the most intelligent and industrious student in the class.

Because Faisal did not say much in class, I didn't notice his abilities. Most of the other students were relaxed and outspoken. Through our conversations in class and in their answers to my questions about the English language, I was able to gain an overall assessment of each student's ability of their mastery in the language. But Faisal said very little which to me meant that he knew very little.

However, my perspective of his capabilities came out when I asked the students to do a writing activity. While the students struggled writing in a language that was not their own, I noticed a confident ease with which Faisal mastered this language. While the other students abused the English alphabet with marks and squiggles which seemed to dance over the page and look more like Egyptian hieroglyphics or a secret code that they alone were privy to, Faisal's handwriting was clear and correct and his spelling was impeccable. But not only was his handwriting grammatical and legible, it was neat and beautiful, like the work of an artist. Even though this is a rather sexist comment, I couldn't help thinking that I had never seen a man write as neatly, as if what had been written came from a woman's hand. I couldn't help mentioning out loud to the rest of the class how beautiful Faisal's handwriting was. But Faisal showed no recognition for the compliment, not a smile, not a thank you - nothing.

Faisal was not only quiet, he was also aloof. There were other Muslims in the class, two from Iran and one from Iraq. I thought that maybe Faisal would at least befriend these students. But at the break, he would stand outside the classroom puffing on a cigarette in deep meditation. Some students would take the opportunity to go to the canteen while others formed a small group near the classroom door. While they socialised, talked and laughed, Faisal would stand at a safe distance, standing silently in deep thought with a morose expression on his face.

"He's probably contemplating a terrorist attack here in Sydney," I often thought maliciously and shuddered at the thought. This, unfortunately, was the pervading fear that overwhelmed us here in Sydney at this time. Australia went to war with the USA and Spain against Iraq. There had been a terrorist attack in New York and Madrid as a result. Sydney had to be next. Because my first impression of Faisal was that he was a terrorist, his aloofness only further accentuated this image of him. He did not want to know other people personally because this would make the attack all the more difficult. If he became personally involved with those who lived in Australia, how would he be able to blow up a building or a train knowing that it was quite possible that one of these people he knew well was inside at the time? Even my attempts to get to know him as a person were totally futile and this is how I interpreted his aloofness.

During this time, there were many television advertisements warning Australians to "be alert but not alarmed". If we suspected anyone, there was a toll-free phone number that we could ring. And we could ring anonymously. The frequency of these advertisements coincided with how frequently I saw Faisal. Was this mere chance or was a higher intelligence from another dimension purposely putting these two situations before me to show me blatantly how I was supposed to act? I did entertain the thought of ringing. But again, what was the basis of my accusation that Faisal was a terrorist? Suspicion and fear are two very dreadful emotions which, when mixed with a helpful serving of ignorance, can lead us to act rashly and naively against innocent people.

I decided to hold back a little longer. Maybe there were other reasons for Faisal's unusual behaviour. Mohammed was my first introduction to Afghanistan and I was also suspicious of him at first as well. But Mohammed was very different. He adapted to the class environment and was very open and, in a short time, I felt very relaxed with him in the class. Although he struggled with the language, he tried to assimilate and socialise with the other students irrespective of their cultural or religious backgrounds.

Mohammed did not even show signs that he was a Muslim or that he followed Muslim practices. I remember during Ramadan, the Muslim month of fasting, that he ate and drank during the day as if it were just another regular month of the year. The only association that he seemed to have with Islam was that he shared his name with the founder of this religion.

But not Faisal. Although he didn't say much, I learned quite early that Faisal was a dedicated devotee to his faith. I discovered this one day when he placed his arm on his desk in such a way that it revealed a tattoo on the downside of his forearm. At first I caught a glimpse of what I thought was simply a bluish smudge on his arm. But when I had time to observe it in detail, I could make out the name of God, Allah, in Arabic script, etched into his skin. I had had other Muslims from other countries in my class before but none of them appeared to feel any compulsion to carry a permanent reminder of God in their flesh. But Faisal did. And the Taliban was a fanatic group of Muslims who feared no-one but Allah and did everything in Allah's name. This again seemed to me further evidence that Faisal followed blindly a religion without the thought of the world being filled with people who have alternative views and ideas about the universe.

But there were two conversations we had in class which finally brought it out clearly that Faisal had to be a terrorist and was ready to set his hand against everything that was westernized and non-Muslim.

My job was to teach my students English so that they could integrate and assimilate into Australian society. I had three evenings a week for eighteen weeks to provide my students with enough English to be able to communicate in situations such as filling in forms, going to see the doctor, shopping, socialising, getting a job and so on. I thoroughly enjoyed this job, and still do, because of my interest in language and languages in general.

I still think this is a fascinating feature about human beings. One human makes noises that come from the throat and which pass through the mouth. By moving the tongue around in all sorts of contortions, the sounds change, and the regular changes of these sounds are interpreted by another human as meaning. This becomes all the more fascinating when I observe people who speak to each other in a language I don't understand. One human makes funny sounds that have no meaning to me but do to another human being, who knows how to interpret these strings of sound, and as a result, he or she reacts in a certain way, whether laughing, showing surprise or moving to do something.

Because of the limited knowledge that my students had of the English language, conversations were confined to subjects that were real and concrete and of the every day. Well, they were supposed to be. I was warned by colleagues to avoid topics on politics and religion. Why it was particularly pointed out not to discuss these topics in class I could not quite understand because it was general common sense to avoid these topics when talking to fellow Australians.

I don't know how the topic was raised but I can assure you that I was not the one who raised it. There seemed to be one thing about politics that my students suddenly wanted to discuss: democracy. Was democracy really the best form of government? Today we throw the word around and preach democracy as being the best and purest form of government in the same way that religious idealists promote their religions. Any country that does not follow the principles of democracy is looked upon in much the same way as followers of a particular religion view those outside their faith. I wasn't sure whether to stop the conversation immediately or let the students talk. A political discussion was likely to create a lot of heat but at the same time it made the students enthusiastic enough to practise their English, forcing them to grope for words in the

English language to express what they wanted to say.

During this conversation, even Faisal spoke. It was the first time I saw that he was so passionate about anything or showed any signs that he was more than just barely alive. But he was critical of democracy. Was democracy really a good form of governing a country? Should everyone really have a right to vote and have a say as to how their country should be run? The class suddenly became a parliament in session. Each student had something to say about the virtues of democracy and how they were happy to be in Australia in a country where they were free.

But Faisal was different. He was critical of democracy. His belief was that democracy was not a good form of government at all. I was horrified and angry, and immediately stopped the conversation before I could allow him to substantiate his claim. How could such a person, who fled his country which knew no democracy, seek asylum in a country which was protecting him and based its politics on the same principles that he despised?

But this was further evidence of his terrorist leanings. Faisal was here to upturn and overthrow everything that Australian society represented: freedom of speech, equal rights and antidiscrimination. I was therefore convinced that if Faisal had his way, a theocratic society based on the principles of Islam would become the established form of government in this country.

Because this discussion of democracy ended up being too sensitive an issue, I told my students that we would not discuss politics in class again. It had made my blood boil when I heard Faisal say that democracy had its faults. I hadn't even allowed him to support his argument and yet I had already come to the conclusion about what type of person Faisal was, based purely on his comment.

The weeks rolled on, the hot weather continued and my fear of and hatred for this strange man in my class became firm and steadfast. I couldn't wait for the end of the semester to see him leave my classroom, never to be seen again. An enemy of democracy was, as far as I was concerned, an enemy of mine.

That Faisal was a strict Muslim and wanted all to be converted to his religion was only further borne out in yet another discussion. Again, as it was with the discussion on politics, I don't know how we got onto the topic but I certainly wasn't the one who started it.

My class was made up of followers of four major religions: Christianity, Islam, Hinduism and Buddhism. This was a beautiful cocktail of beliefs that only needed a spark to get the fire going. There was no need to discuss religion in the class because the belief in God was certainly of no assistance when filling out a job application form or buying a packet of sugar. So how it began, I will never know. Just as it is with bushfires, the ignition of the fire is always hard to trace but the effects are all too evident.

I was discussing a topic that I thought was quite innocent when suddenly the class was in an uproar as all the gripes and contentions that the religious have against each other were suddenly let out in a moment. All I could hear was a babble of noise, see lots of red faces and students half standing, half sitting in their chairs as they yelled at each other across the room. I knew it was over religion because within this thunderous cacophony I managed to hear the words "God" and "prophet" besprinkled with "stupid" and "unbelievers". I was immediately filled with fear because I thought there would be an outright riot in my class. The adrenalin just pumped liberally into my body and I jumped on the teacher's desk and began jumping up and down screaming, "Quiet! I said, quiet!" while I bashed the back of the duster against the whiteboard.

This had the desired effect. The class suddenly went from explosive chaos to tranquil silence. I was fuming and I let my feelings out to the class.

"If you students ever do that again, I will make sure that you don't ever come back to my class. While you are in this college, you will treat each other with respect as human beings. Leave your religions at home."

There was utter silence in the room and the red hostile faces turned slowly white with shame. Some students bowed their heads and were too afraid to look me in the face. Except Faisal. Once the silence had been established, Faisal looked at me with that clinical expression as if he had never experienced an emotion in his life and asked me, "What do you mean, leave our religions at home? Don't you carry your religion with you?"

I wasn't sure what surprised me the most, the fact that Faisal actually spoke to me more than one word or that he strung a whole two sentences together in English without a fault in grammar.

"No, I don't carry a religion with me because I don't have a religion. I don't believe in religion and what just happened in this classroom explains why. Religions are supposed to bring harmony and equality but look what it has done here."

I wasn't sure if the students understood all the words I used. But I knew my comment, if understood, would probably incite a rebuttal in defence of my students' beliefs. So before they had time to reply, I simply concluded my statement with, "And I don't want any talk of religion raised ever again from this time on. Now, let's get back to what I was talking about earlier."

With that, the class slowly returned to normal. It took some time for the smoking embers to be completely extinguished but eventually the class returned to its original state. But the students were good at the end of the class because, before leaving, each apologised for the disruption

Faisal, however, was the last student to do so. When all the other students had left, and while I was packing up my things to go, Faisal stood outside the door waiting for me. When I had locked the door and turned around, I saw Faisal, the pale faced angel of death, waiting pensively to talk with me.

"Yes, Faisal," I more grunted than said, "what do you want?"

"I'm sorry for the class this evening. You're a good teacher and I want to be in your class. We were not good students today. I'm sorry."

"That's okay, Faisal," I replied as we began walking down the corridor. "I just hope it doesn't happen again."

There was a short silence as we clip clopped down the corridor on the polished wooden floors when Faisal began to speak again.

"So, you don't believe in God?" he asked. "Are you not Christian?"

"No, I'm not. I don't believe in any religion," I replied.

Faisal stopped for a second which, in turn, made me stop.

"Then," he continued, "how did the world get here? Who made it?"

I looked into Faisal's expressionless, melancholic face.

"Faisal, what did I tell you in class? I don't want to talk about religion. Leave your religion at home."

"But I can prove to you that God exists," Faisal continued. "You're a teacher, yes?"

I wanted to end the conversation there but Faisal was cunning enough, so I imagined at the time, to use my profession as an argument for his belief and so the curiosity drove me to allow the conversation to continue.

"Yes," I replied.

"Do you give tests at the beginning or at the end of the course?"

I thought this was one of the stupidest questions I had ever heard. But I had to listen to what he was getting at and so I answered him.

"Naturally, I give them at the end of the course. It would be silly to give a test at the beginning of the course because you know nothing of the subject that I would be testing. That's why you come to class. I teach you certain things and then I give you a test to see how well you have understood what I have taught."

"That's why there has to be a god," Faisal replied. "Our life is a test and we have to learn to do good things here in this life. If there is no god, we don't know what we must learn. We would then fail when we go to the next life. But we have a textbook, like the textbook we have in class, to tell us how to live life properly, so that we know how to pass the test in this life so that we can go to the next life."

Faisal didn't have to say much but I understood fully what he was trying to say. Being a Muslim, he believed that God gave humans the Koran which is like a textbook for life. The Koran tells us what is the right and wrong way to conduct our lives, just as an English textbook tells us what is the right and wrong way to speak and write English. If we don't follow the textbook correctly and take on what it teaches, then when we do an exam, we are more than likely to fail. So it is with the Koran. However, failing an English test is not like failing to do the right thing according to the Koran. If the students failed the test in my class, they would have to do the course all over again. But with the Koran, if you failed the test, you simply went to hell in the next life.

I was angry at Faisal for once again raising the issue of religion when I had expressly told him not to do so. But I was also intrigued by his ability to express in good English this rather complex idea. I marvelled at the way he used the present perfect "have taught" when I had only days earlier taught it in class, and he had correctly used the word "would" to express a supposition.

I was just as amazed at how similar his argument was to what I had learnt when I was a Christian. My whole image of Islam was a religion filled with hostile, angry religious zealots with chips on their shoulders running around carrying out jihad against non-Muslims. But the idea of a book being life's textbook was identical to the Christians' argument for the Bible.

But further, Faisal talked about doing good. But what is doing good anyway? My interpretation of doing good is making sure that people around me are adequately fed and clothed, and free to do whatever makes them happy as long as they are not harming other people. Did Faisal mean this or did he mean in light of the pervading view of Muslims that doing good according to a Muslim was to raise a Fatwa against anyone who criticised their religion in any way, blowing up buildings and innocent people who lived or worked within them?

That was my understanding of Islam and never would I adopt a faith so dangerous and radical. I was angry that Faisal had made even the slightest attempt to convert me to his faith. After all, he had fled his country because of Islamic extremists and he was now protected within a country that held to democratic, non-religious principles. I liked living in Australia and being Australian because of this. I loved my country also because I was at liberty to live openly as a gay man and had Australian law to protect me. God was rather irrelevant within this peaceful and tranquil society. I was sure that Islam was totally against homosexuality as it was against the freedom of women and, more importantly, the freedom of thought.

I dismissed Faisal with a further comment that I didn't ever want to talk about religion again and then walked away. I was so cut up with anger at this man that I didn't even say good-bye as I walked off. I could no longer stand the sight of him, his very presence was symbolic of all the troubles that had begun the twenty-first century, and he was a living reminder of my fight against religion and final acceptance of my homosexuality.

And Faisal was a Pashtun, therefore a member of the Taliban. He was intelligent and a stranger to mirth. He criticised democracy and was a passionate Muslim. And he tried to convert me to this violent, closed-minded religion. Faisal, therefore, had to be a terrorist. Why had we let these refugees into the country in the first place, to completely destroy the freedom that Australians had so vehemently fought for and which we currently enjoyed?

I wasn't going to allow Faisal to change anything about my life in Australia. I was happy with my life the way it was. If he wanted to be a non-democratic Muslim, he should stay in his own country. He had no business being here. It was time to make a phone call.

Chapter 2

The following day, the Course Co-ordinator, Azizah, called me into her office. She had heard the sudden riot in my class and needed an explanation.

Azizah was a lovely woman and I was so happy that she was my boss. She was a short, dumpy woman of Middle Eastern extract. She was Egyptian and she was Christian. She was also a just and fair person. I admired her a lot. She was an excellent boss who ran our department with an efficiency that I thought only the Germans could master. Her name, Azizah, was so appropriate because it was the Arabic word for "dear" and she was in every way a dear friend. One of the reasons why I enjoyed my job so much was that I could talk to Azizah about anything honestly and openly. She was aware that I lived a life that was contrary to her Christian upbringing but her only concern was that I was a proficient and respectable teacher. However, I also knew that she cared for me and the other teachers as if we were the members of her extended family. I admired how well she was able to unite and keep her staff together and promote a congenial atmosphere that made coming to work a real pleasure.

What made Azizah a wonderful boss to work for was that whenever I was called into the office, I knew that, no matter how serious the problem was, she was there to resolve it, not to find blame. There was no trembling or a knot in the stomach as I walked through the door. This was so different from other working environments where my former bosses tended to be like corporate dictators. In comparison to my previous places of employment, I noticed that fewer problems ever arose because of Azizah's more gentle and open approach.

"Take a seat, Michael," Azizah said with half a smile on her face. "So, what happened last night in class? I heard quite a ruckus coming from your room last night."

"The topic of religion got raised. Everyone got heated and started arguing."

"'Arguing' would be an understatement!" Azizah replied and smiled. "Why did you raise the topic of religion in the first place? You know it will only end in disaster."

"I didn't raise it," I protested. "I was simply teaching the students how to entertain Australians if the students ever invited them to their homes. I started describing the typical things that Australians would usually eat at a party and the next thing all hell broke loose."

Azizah laughed. "I guess what must have happened is that you trod on some students' toes if you mentioned foods which are against their dietary laws. Or did you mention that Australians, in general, drink alcohol?"

"I can't remember exactly, now. Everything happened so suddenly. But if I did mention foods that my students are not allowed to eat because of their religion, surely they must understand that Australia is generally considered a Christian country and Christians eat practically anything - as long as it's not poisonous."

Azizah laughed again. "OK, don't worry about it. I will come to your class tonight and have a word with them. They have to learn that we are in Australia and this is not acceptable behaviour. Don't take it too much to heart. Try to avoid any topics that may dance around sensitive issues. I know it's not always possible but do try your best."

"Thanks, Azizah," I replied and was about to get up. But then a thought came to mind. I was sure I knew who started the argument.

"I think Faisal was the one who caused the argument," I said.

"Faisal? Who's Faisal?"

"He's my Afghani student," I said and then thought a little more. Should I say it or not? I had enough evidence to support what I was about to say and so I began.

"Azizah, this Faisal I just mentioned. I'm a bit worried about him. I don't know how to say this in any other way but I think he's a terrorist."

Azizah's face changed from a smile to a serious, concerned look.

"Why? What makes you say that?"

"Many things. Over the last number of months he's been in my class, I've observed his behaviour. I find he acts in a rather suspicious manner. And he's Muslim."

"Just because he's a Muslim doesn't necessarily mean that he's a terrorist," Azizah said sternly.

"Yeah, I know, Azizah. I have three other Muslim students in my class, Reza, Mustafa and Khadija. But Faisal acts differently. He's not like them."

With that, I followed through with all the evidence that I had built up that proved that Faisal possibly had a terrorist past: his Pashtun background, his lack of expression, his intelligence, the tattoo, his criticism of democracy and his attempt to convert me to his religion. While I explained, Azizah sat listening intently. I noticed through her facial expression that I was winning her over to my judgement. When I had finished, Azizah sighed with a hint of worry and fear.

"I see. I'll have to make a note of that. I appreciate that you have shared this with me. As you are aware, it is AELC policy to report any student who we suspect. I will make a note of that and follow it up. What was his name again?"

I told Azizah his name and she wrote it down on a piece of Post-it Note™ paper and stuck it to her desk.

"Okay, Michael. Thanks for that. I will come to your class this evening and have a word to the students."

"Okay, thanks. By the way, I was going to ring that toll-free number they advertise on TV if you suspect someone is a terrorist," I replied and stood up.

"Well, there's no need to now. I can look into it, okay?"

"Yes, thanks," I replied. But before leaving, I turned back to Azizah and added, "Can't Faisal be transferred to another class?"

"I'm really sorry, Michael," Azizah said with another laugh. "It's a bit late, now, to move students around. Unfortunately you will have to put up with him. Don't worry. It won't be long before he's no longer in your class. Try not to let it bother you."

But it did. I loved my job and I had always loved my students. But Faisal I hated. His whole existence annoyed me. He was like a fly that had dropped into a bowl of delicious soup. While the fly takes up a very small area of space in comparison to everything else, it becomes the complete centre of attention.

What even annoyed me more was that Faisal was always the first student to arrive in class. I liked to have the classroom open fifteen minutes before the class started to allow those who came early somewhere to go. It was also an opportunity to reward early students by giving them extra feed-back on their work. But Faisal never asked questions. There was always an ugly silence until the other students came. While he sat and did whatever he did in his notebook during this waiting period, mapping out strategic bombsites or whatever would-be terrorists did in their English as a Second Language class, I would shuffle papers around my desk in an attempt to look busy. In the end, to get around this, I began to come to the classroom later and later.

Learning a language is not an easy thing. I speak several of them now with varying degrees of proficiency. I know what it is like to clumsily string a row of words together and the strain it can be on the brain.

The first language I ever learnt was German. I studied it at school and had decided that I would not waste this knowledge by letting it slip by but rather tried to find a means of keeping my proficiency in this language. I was a frequent visitor to second-hand bookshops and bought loads of books in German for fifty cents each and then would struggle to read the contents. It was hard work at first. Sometimes it would take me over an hour to simply read a page and then I had to do some brainless activity such as washing up or watching television to relax my mind. It was a real struggle and there were times when I wanted to abandon the whole idea. But I was glad I kept it up. I can now read a novel in German almost as comfortably as I read a novel in English.

Reading in a language is one thing but trying to speak it is yet another. To improve my speaking ability, I became a member of the Goethe Institute, a special organisation which promotes German language and culture. The first time I went there, the woman behind the counter garbled something in this staccato language and my only reply was, "Bitte?" Then, when I made an attempt at replying, the woman looked at me unimpressed as if she thought I were a secret agent sent there to make a complete mockery of the language.

What made German so difficult at first was not only its harsh pronunciation but also the word order. When I was only a beginner, speaking German was like mental callisthenics where I had to take an

English sentence in my mind, completely juggle the words around in a very different and, what I thought at the time, totally illogical order, find the equivalent words in German, and then say what I wanted to say. Conversations were very stilted at first and many of the Germans at the Goethe Institute were too impatient to have a five minute conversation that consisted of me struggling to ask a question and then the answer being repeated many times over, slower and slower each time until I understood what was being said.

However, I was fortunate to find a sympathetic ear when I met a guy called Stefan. He was patient enough to help me struggle with this language until I reached a point at which I was relatively competent. I cannot say that I now speak German flawlessly but I speak and understand it enough to engage in conversations for hours without the slightest feeling of mental fatigue. Unfortunately for me, Stefan went back to Germany but I still at least keep in contact with him via e-mail.

Since then, I have learnt several other languages. The most difficult and intriguing was Mandarin. I went to TAFE to learn this language. My goodness, what a complicated language this is for an English-speaker to learn! The obvious difference between Mandarin and English is the writing. While an English speaker has only 50 odd symbols to learn to be able to read and write, Chinese uses something like 6,000 which all have to be committed to memory. I still don't know all the Chinese characters and am not sure I ever will.

Reading Chinese characters is hard enough but trying to write them with the same skill and artistry as a native speaker is even more complicated. Every time I teach my students to write in English from a language that doesn't use Roman letters, I have the patience of Job when I reflect on my introduction to Chinese characters. Fortunately my Chinese teachers were patient enough to turn my pictographic attempts at their language to look less like stick figures from a kindergarten child's art book to something that was vaguely pleasing and, more importantly, understandable to a Chinese eye.

But while reading and writing are within themselves a challenge, there are no words to describe how different this language is from English. Because German is a European language, there are underlying similarities between German and English. But Chinese and English are vastly different. Whenever I speak Chinese Mandarin, I feel as if I'm using a completely different mind.

But my language learning experience paid off when I began teaching English as a second language because I can now pass on this experience to my students. One thing I constantly stress to my students is that learning a language is not merely something that happens in the classroom. I can explain certain points of grammar and how to express ideas in English but a lot of the work has to come from how the students use the language out of class. I often gave the example of Chinese because I used to live near a corner shop whose owner was Chinese. He was an adorable old man, the typical, stereotypical, wise-Confucius-looking old man, with small, perfectly circular glasses and a pencil-lined beard and moustache. Every day I would go to that shop to buy general everyday items and make an attempt at the language. The man behind the counter was abso-lutely thrilled that an Australian had taken the trouble to learn his language and he was all the more helpful in improving my linguistic ability.

My students had to do the same. It was a hard step to make but they had to do it if they wanted to successfully operate within the Australian community.

One of the offshoots of learning a language that I discovered was that learning another way to move my mouth and tongue to create meaning was only one facet of language learning. Language is not simply a tool to get things done. Each language is embedded within a culture and by learning a new language I discovered not only another way to speak but also another way to think and view the world. Knowing two languages is like holding two universes in one's head. In fact, I have learnt from experience that being bilingual not only means we increase the number of people we can communicate with but that it also improves lateral thinking. This is because bilingual people have two ways of viewing the world and hence the saying, "two heads are better than one" is fulfilled in the one person.

I explained to my students that understanding the language was, therefore, not simply understanding what Australians say but also understanding what Australians do, what Australians consider appropriate behaviour and what was considered taboo. This was necessary to avoid cultural clashes which are just misunderstandings of the speakers' intent on both sides of the cultural barrier.

Again, I learnt this particularly when I was learning Chinese. In Australia, we overwork the words "please" and "thank you" in a way that the Chinese find rather bizarre. But the Chinese also express these polite epithets non-verbally by a tap on the finger or on the table which passes imperceptibly by an Australian which is why the Chinese come across as rude and impolite. But the Chinese, like Australians, are just as thankful for services rendered although they express their gratitude in a completely different way.

The most difficult part about keeping a language alive is meeting people who speak the language in question. For my students, so I explained, this meant that they had to make friends with Australians. Learning a language therefore had to become more than just a classroom subject. Language learning requires social interaction and I knew that this was the ultimate aim of my job, to help these new Australians integrate within the greater Australian community.

Not long after stressing this point, I noticed a change in Faisal's behaviour. Because I was a smoker at the time (but thankfully have since abandoned the habit), I used the break as an opportunity to top up on my falling level of nicotine which was now further necessary while one of the Taliban's henchmen shared the same area of space three times a week.

But one evening, instead of just standing alone in deep contemplation, Faisal made an attempt at communicating. I had just stepped out of the classroom when Faisal walked slowly over to me to offer me a cigarette. I wasn't sure what to do at first. The first thought that passed through my mind was to say, "But I don't want one of your scabby cigarettes, you stupid, little terrorist. What? Do you think I'll look on you sympathetically when you bomb the Harbour Bridge just because you offered me some trivial piece of paper filled with tobacco?"

But it was the first time he demonstrated an act of humanness, the sharing of something in common. I cautiously removed the cigarette from the packet as if it were a detonator on a grenade. While I rummaged in my pocket for a lighter, Faisal presented his before my face in such a swift movement that, when he lit it up, I jerked my head back as if it were about to explode.

Faisal looked at me through his sullen eyes but it was the first time that they became round and wide.

"I just wanted to light your cigarette," he said in Dari-accented but yet grammatically perfect English.

"I'm sorry." These were the only words I had to say in reply. I took a deep puff and then let out a large cloud of smoke. Faisal spoke again.

"You don't come to class early now," he said.

"No," I replied. I was embarrassed. Faisal was the only person who came to class early so what reason could I give him that wasn't the real one? My mind worked overtime until I was able to say something.

"I...I stopped coming early because no-one gets here until 6 o'clock. So I thought I might as well come at 6 o'clock as well."

"But I come early. I get here at five thirty so I can talk to you."

Talk to me? Whenever in the past did we ever engage in conversation when we were alone together? The only time we ever had what could be defined as a conversation was his attempt to convert me to Islam. That only made it even more difficult for me to want to engage in dialogue with him. What topic of conversation could we share that would encourage me to come early?

For a moment, there was a further awkward silence but I felt I had to say what was on my mind.

"Look, Faisal. I'm not religious. I respect the fact that you're a Muslim. I respect other people's beliefs but I'm not a believer. This is something that you'll have to learn about Australia. People have different beliefs and, to get along together, we have to respect these differences."

Faisal looked morosely at me as if he hadn't quite understood what I had said. His face had returned to its traditional unemotional, blank expression. There was yet another deathly pause and I was going to make an excuse that I had to attend to something when Faisal spoke again.

"You said that we must meet Australians to practise our English. But how can I meet Australians? When I go to a nightclub or a bar, no-one wants to talk to me. Look at my face. I'm not good-looking and when people meet me for the first time, they don't want to talk to me simply because of my looks. But I watch you teach. You are a good teacher. I know you are a good man, too. And you know me now. You are the only Australian I know. I know you want to learn my language, too. So we can help each other."

Nightclub? Bar? Faisal goes to nightclubs? I thought. I tried to picture Osama bin Laden fronting up to a city nightclub, sipping on cocktails or swigging down a schooner, pinching a woman on the bum or swivelling his hips to the music. This was, after all, my image of Faisal, despite the fact that he wore western clothes and was clean shaven.

Faisal's appreciation of his own looks and how people reacted to them was precise. This was my initial impression of him as well, a not-very-good looking man with a dull expression on his face which appeared to advertise, "Keep away! Keep away! Unclean! Unclean!" My whole perception of the man as a terrorist had all begun with his appearance.

And he thought I was a good man! Yeah, right! It is hard enough in Australia to meet open-minded people who can accept that a homosexual man is no different to anyone else, let alone be a good person, even though this entire sexual phenomenon is openly talked about here. Faisal came from a country where even women struggled to prove that they, too, were human. So, if he knew how I really lived my life, would he still think of me as a good man?

However, Faisal knew I was non-religious but he still said I was good. This in itself was striking. Not only did I admit to him that I was not Muslim, I confessed that I did not ascribe to any religion at all. This is what led Faisal to at least try to make me see the possibility that God exists. But I told him I wasn't interested in religion and he still thought I was good.

I really didn't know what to say. My mind was in utter confusion. Who was this Faisal after all? Did he really mean what he said or was this simply a means to get to know me and therefore become more familiar with the Sydney infrastructure? There was a long pause but then I finally made a reply.

"Okay, all right. If you come early, I'll be here. And I would be grateful if you could help me learn Farsi," I said mechanically.

"Thank you," Faisal said quietly. It was the first time he ever expressed appreciation for anything I said.

But the whole situation disturbed me. I suddenly wanted to get away from this man so I made the excuse that I had to attend to something in the staffroom and would be back before the end of the break. But when I got to the office, I just sat there leaning my chin in the cup of my hand and my elbow on the desk. Many thoughts were dashing through my mind. My initial image of this strange man was now called into question. Or was it? I couldn't quite make up my mind.

It was a stinking hot evening that evening. The classroom was not air conditioned but we had ceiling fans that made an attempt to cool the room. Really, they seemed to just blow the hot air around. Maybe it was the way that Faisal troubled me that made me feel hotter than usual. It was always uncomfortable wearing a tie in the middle of the sweltering heat but this night I felt as if my tie were choking me.

When I got back to class, I tried to teach but my tie felt as if it were chafing my neck. It was becoming unbearable. I had never taken my tie off ever in front of my students. I knew that to do it at that moment would have made me feel as if I were stripping down to my underwear. But the more I taught, the more uncomfortable it felt and the feeling of choking began to overcome my feeling of embarrassment. But before I removed my tie, I thought it was polite to ask the students their permission.

"Sorry, class. But do you mind if I take my tie off? It's just too hot."

At this point, I really didn't care whether or not the students were happy for me to take off this long piece of material wrapped around my neck. Even if they were offended, I was going to take it off anyway.

While I struggled with the knot, each student in the class replied one after the other that this was okay. But while I slid my tie over my neck, Faisal, who was the last to give his permission, expressed his opinion with the words, "With a tie or without a tie, you're still Michael."

As soon as he said these words, I felt as if the entire universe stood still. Those words plunged deep into my heart. What did he say? "With a tie or without a tie, you're still Michael".

The beauty of language is that this is the only way an idea in our heads can be put into the mind of another. But words are like vessels, coming in different sizes and shapes. Sometimes they are small to express small ideas and sometimes they are huge to carry volumes of meaning.

These ten words that Faisal said to me on face value expressed a simple idea, that my clothes don't change my person. We can change our clothes a thousand times in a day but the person inside these clothes remains the same. But I could see an entire philosophy behind these words. Irrespective of who I was or what I believed, these were only external trimmings which did not change my person. Despite the fact that I was not religious, that I ate pork and drank alcohol, and possibly he meant further, although I had never told my students this, despite the fact that I had sex with men and not women, I was still Michael.

I stood their stupefied for what seemed an eternity. The words went round and round in my head like a whirlpool. I had never heard the belief in tolerance towards all people so beautifully and succinctly expressed. But these words came from Faisal's mouth, Faisal, the Pashtun, Faisal, the member of the Taliban, Faisal, the terrorist.

When I got home that evening, I sat on the balcony of my flat with a glass of wine and stared out into the darkness. The conversation at the break that I had with Faisal and those words, "with a tie or without a tie, you're still Michael" were swimming around in my mind. I was beginning to realise that my entire perception of this man was all wrong. It was a paradigm shift. If Faisal believed in tolerance, then he could not be a terrorist, and therefore he could not be a member of the Taliban. The Taliban blew up Buddhist statues because these stone objects were symbols of a completely different way of viewing the world that the Taliban could not tolerate. One cannot believe that "with a tie or without a tie" a person remains the same person, and then obliterate those things that another person holds dear.

But also, Faisal said he went to nightclubs and bars. Did this mean that he drank alcohol? How can anyone go to a nightclub and not drink? Muslims are forbidden to drink alcohol, so what would he be doing at a nightclub?

Not only so, nightclubs at this time of year are full of women who wear the bare minimum, exposing legs, shoulders, back and face in opposition to Muslim belief. From what I had heard about Islam, if a man saw a woman, apart from his wife, naked or close to being naked, he was committing a grave sin. What I had read about the Taliban in Afghanistan was that women were shut up in their homes and the windows of their houses painted over so that a man could completely avoid the sight of a woman. If Faisal frequented nightclubs, this would then be very peculiar and, in the vast extreme, hypocritical behaviour for a Muslim extremist.

And Faisal said I was a good man. But I was completely different in culture and belief. The Taliban, so my former Afghani student, Mohammed, had told me, committed the cruellest acts of violence against Hazarahs, Tajiks and Uzbeks, who were all still Afghani and Muslim. A person cannot commit such atrocities if they consider these people good. So, if Faisal thought I was good, surely there were people who came from the other Afghani tribes who shared a common language, culture and religion that Faisal also considered good.

I began to think about all those facets that made me believe that Faisal was a terrorist and tried to fit these into this new view of him. First of all, the tattoo. Because he carried God's name permanently in his flesh, did this really mean he was intolerant of other religions? Azizah is a Christian and she constantly wears a cross on a chain around her neck to declare her belief in Christ. But that didn't make her intolerant or a Christian extremist. She didn't go around killing non-Christians or treat non-Christians with spite. She was a wonderful woman towards all people. But she strongly believes that Jesus is her god and carries a permanent reminder of her belief wherever she goes. Was it possible that Faisal's approach to his religion and his toleration of those outside of his faith was the same as Azizah's?

And what about Faisal trying to convert me to Islam? Was that really so wrong? My mother is a Christian and she tries from time to time to convert me back to the faith. My mother does this because she loves me and doesn't want me to go to hell in the next life. She is totally convinced that this is what will happen if I don't believe. But this doesn't make her a fanatic or an extremist. She still welcomes me when I visit, eats and drinks with me, and gives me little presents from time to time despite the fact that she knows what life I lead. Although her insistence to reconvert me is utterly annoying, I know that from her point of view, it is a sincere form of her love and concern for me.

Then what about Mohammed's explanation that Pashtuns were Taliban? Was it possible that Mohammed was wrong? I tried to imagine World War II and what a Frenchman would have said if he had escaped occupied France and landed in Australia as a refugee. What would his views of the Germans be? Most probably the only Germans he knew were Nazis which led him to the ultimate conclusion that "German" and "Nazi" were synonymous. The word "German" refers to a nation of people whereas "Nazi" refers to a political party. We know that many Germans were put into concentration camps as political dissidents under the Nazi regime and their Germanness did not save them. Was this then the same with "Pashtun" and "Taliban"?

But what about Faisal's criticism of democracy? I had never given him the opportunity to express his views. Was it possible that democracy, like all forms of government, has its weaknesses that we, in so-called democratic countries, simply overlook?

And what of his melancholic nature? If he was happy to be in Australia out of the grips of the Taliban, what on earth could make him feel so sad here? He was now free to pursue his life in any way he liked and it appeared that he was enjoying the fruits of this freedom by frequenting nightclubs.

A new image of Faisal was now forming. Those words "with a tie or without a tie, you're still Michael" expressed a philosophy that I embraced. Those words alone convinced me more than anything else that Faisal was not a terrorist after all, that my original picture of him was incorrect. Faisal was, therefore, most probably the victim of the horrors going on in his country which led him to flee to Australia and ultimately end up in my classroom. It was the first time that I felt some sympathy for the man. I thought to myself that I needed to start afresh with my approach towards him and try again to establish some sort of amicable relationship with him. And so, after a third glass of wine, I decided it was time to go to bed.

But when I was in bed and Morpheus was about to wrap his gentle arms around me, a terrible thought crossed my mind which made me sit up in horror.

"Oh my God!" I gasped into the darkness. "I have to talk to Azizah!"

Chapter 3

As soon as the alarm went off the following morning, I was out of bed and getting ready for work. I glanced at the kitchen clock every five minutes waiting for the little hand to point at the number 8. Azizah was usually in her office by then. I didn't have to be at the college until 8.30 but I wasn't going to wait till I got there. I had to ring Azizah first thing. I was terrified that Azizah may have already notified the authorities and investigations were underway. It would have mortified me to know that I had accused an innocent man of any wrongdoing. It was possible that I was convicting Faisal of being a terrorist when I was now beginning to realise that I had misunderstood him. What if he had fled Afghanistan after all to escape terrorism only to fall into the hands of some ignorant Australian who was now pushing him back into it? I would not have been able to live with myself if that had happened.

After a shower and a shave, I made myself a cup of coffee and sat on the balcony, puffing on one cigarette after another as if smoking had some influence on accelerating the pace of time. Eventually, the clock struck 8 o'clock and I began nervously punching in the numbers of Azizah's work telephone number, holding the receiver against my ear in desperation. I could hear the dial tone chirp away while I tensely waited for Azizah's voice to answer it.

"Hello, Australian English Language College. Azizah speaking."

"Hello, Azizah. It's me, Michael," I said in panic as if the words were tumbling over each other to try to get out of my mouth as fast as possible. "Have you followed up about Faisal?"

"No, I'm really sorry, Michael. I haven't yet. I totally forgot about it. But don't panic, my note is still here in front of me. I'll do it today, Okay?"

"Don't!" I screamed. "Please, don't do anything!"

There was a slight pause and then Azizah replied.

"Is everything all right, Michael?"

The sudden relief overwhelmed me and I just slumped into the closest chair.

"Azizah, I think I've made a mistake. I don't think Faisal is a terrorist. I think my whole analysis of him is wrong. Please don't notify anyone. He's a good man."

I was just as surprised as Azizah with my last statement. I hardly knew the guy and I was already declaring that he was good. It didn't feel as if I had said the words, they came out of my mouth almost involuntarily.

Azizah laughed. That was another feature of Azizah that I loved, always laughing in a moment of crisis.

"This is really a big change of events! Only recently you wanted him out of your class and now you say he's a good man! Something certainly has happened between you and Faisal since then that I have entirely missed."

"Yes, he said something which made me realise he cannot be a terrorist," I said, my heart still pounding against my rib cage. I tried to explain the two events that led to my change in opinion, the conversation at the break and those eternal words he said in class afterwards.

"So, you're sure that he's *not* a terrorist this time?" Azizah asked.

"Yes, yes. Please don't notify anyone. Please just ignore it. Anyway, he's coming to class half an hour earlier than the rest of the class to talk with me to practise his English. So, I will have an opportunity to find out if he really is a terrorist. But I don't believe he is anymore. I think he's just an ordinary guy. So, please, just ignore what I told you about him the other day."

I heard Azizah sigh at the other end of the phone.

"That's good, then. I didn't feel comfortable doing it in the first place. It's not nice to have to ring up about one of the students. But I trust your judgement. I'll just tear up the note. Okay?"

"Yes, thanks, Azizah! Thank you so much. I'll see you a little later."

I hung up the phone and sighed with relief. It was like a burden removed from my shoulders. If Azizah had told me that she had already acted on my request, I would not have known how to face Faisal when he fronted up to class. What would I have said to him: "Hi, Faisal. So, how's your day been? Good?

Well, I've just made it better because the college is notifying the authorities as we speak and you'll probably be chucked out of the country and shipped back to Afghanistan into the hands of the Taliban before you can say 'boo'. So, what topic would you like to talk about to improve your English?" The mere thought of this possible scenario sent a shiver down my spine. But I was relieved that it was now only hypothetical.

I worked at AELC on a casual basis. At the time, teachers were only offered casual contracts which meant there was no job security, which is something that always hung over my head. But I loved the job anyway. There was no other job which gave me such satisfaction. I remember that Confucius had once said something to the effect that you should choose a job that you enjoy doing because then you will never work a day in your life. I knew that this was priceless advice. I enjoyed teaching my language so much that half the time I was totally unaware that I was fulfilling an employment objective, not enjoying my time in a hobby.

Because I was a single man, I accepted irregular hours of work. I had a number of morning classes from 9.00 to 1.00 and then the three evening classes that Faisal attended from 6.00 to 9.30, except Thursday evening when the class finished at 9 o'clock. These irregular hours didn't worry me at all. During the summer months, at 1.00 I went to the local swimming pool, did my laps and then lay on my towel soaking up the sun before showering and then going back to class for the evening. In winter, I simply went home and relaxed on the lounge with a good book.

Thursday evening I finished class at 9.00. I didn't leave, however, until 9.30 because a colleague of mine, Khatyn, who I gave a lift home, finished at that time. Khatyn was a great colleague. Out of everyone I worked with, she was the one I felt the closest to and I guess it was because we both seemed to fall outside the societal norms: I was gay, and she was an unmarried mother with two teenage children. She was also a vegetarian not because of religious reasons but because she did not like the idea of killing animals.

Khatyn was not just a colleague but had become a great friend. From time to time, I would pay her a visit because she lived conveniently close to me and we would spend the afternoon chatting about whatever came to mind.

Khatyn had two charming teenage kids, a daughter and a son. Her daughter, Kylie, was an 18 year old girl who was going through a Gothic phase, wearing black clothes, dying her hair black and wearing black lipstick. This caused problems at her school because the teachers insisted that black was not a suitable colour to apply to lips. Although Khatyn herself did not like her daughter dressing up in such macabre clothes, she maintained that it was not harming anyone. Khatyn always complained back to the school that black, after all, is just another colour and was as good as pink and red as the traditional colours to enhance the lips.

Her son, Brendan, was a tall, well-built, six foot tall 19 year old who looked older than his age. Poor Brendan was very homophobic and it took him quite a long time to come to terms with the fact that a male friend of his mother played flippy-flop with other men. Greeting him with a handshake was both annoying and amusing. He always stood at a safe distance and presented his hand with reluctance as if I might consider shaking hands as an overt sign of consenting to a roly-poly in the hay. If ever I was visiting Khatyn and only the three of us were there, if Khatyn left the room leaving Brendan and I alone together for any length of time, Brendan would shuffle his feet and visibly show his discomfort until Khatyn returned.

Because of the extra thirty minutes that I had to kill each Thursday evening, I usually had to find something to do in the staff room while I waited for Khatyn to finish so I used this opportunity to send emails or chat on the Internet.

It was a Thursday evening when I came to class at 5.30 to spend my first half an hour of dialogue with Faisal to help him practise his spoken English. I really didn't know what to talk about when he came so I felt rather apprehensive while I waited in the classroom for him to arrive.

I will never forget that first evening together. When he walked in the room, he greeted me with the Arabic greeting, "Salaam walaikum" to which I replied accordingly. But what struck me was that for the first time he smiled. That simple smile completely changed his entire appearance as it was not just his mouth that smiled but his eyes sparkled and his entire countenance shone as well.

"Thank you for coming early," he said as he took up his traditional position in the classroom. But this time, he simply placed his carry bag on the desk and left it unopened.

"I was nearly late," Faisal continued. "My boss wanted me to stay back another hour but I told him I had to go to class."

I was impressed by his diligence and willingness to come to class. I knew it was a drag for the students to carry out an occupation during the day and then spend another three or so hours in the evening in class three days a week before finally getting home. I was doubly impressed by the way he spoke to me. No longer were his answers monolexic, they were complete sentences which completely changed his entire persona. It was so striking this change in him. I found it difficult to believe that the Faisal I was now talking to was the same Faisal at the beginning of the course.

"You're a carpenter, aren't you," I said and this allowed a conversation between the two of us to develop.

"Yes. It's hard work but I like the job. I work contract."

"How long have you been working there?"

"Ever since I came to Sydney."

"Oh, really? When did you come to Sydney?"

"In February last year. Before then, I was working in Victoria picking fruit."

Picking fruit? I knew that fruit picking was a seasonal job and that it was very hard work. It was a popular job taken up by young travellers here in Australia on working holidays or alternatively by people who could not get a job doing anything else. Faisal came across as quite an intelligent man so this information came to me as a shock.

While I thought on this, Faisal continued. "My boss's name was Michael also. Ever since I came to Australia, all the Michaels I've met have been good men. I liked my boss, Michael, very much. I can say that I loved him. That's why I knew you were a good man."

I wanted to say to him, "Now, hang on a minute. You *loved* your boss, Michael?" But I knew it was totally inappropriate to say so. I didn't know much about the Afghanis so maybe it was possible for a man in his culture to say that he loved another man. This is certainly not the case amongst macho Australians. Australian men may have strong affections for other men but to use the word "love" to express this would either be followed by a punch in the mouth or a bonk in the bed. It certainly was never used to mean something to the effect of, "I like your personality and your company very much beyond what words can tell". Maybe love could be expressed much more freely within Afghani society.

"So, are you still in contact with him?" I asked.

Faisal's face showed yet another expression, a frown. This guy obviously had emotions and feelings just like everyone else after all.

"No. Before, we rang each other all the time. But now, if I don't ring, he won't ring me. Later I thought that he didn't want to be my friend anymore."

"So, why did you come to Sydney, then?" I asked.

"I heard that Sydney was a big city and there were more opportunities for work. When I arrived here, I discovered it was true. I got a job when I got here. And a good job."

"You work in Fairfield, don't you?" I asked.

"Yes."

"Is that where you live?"

"No, I live in Auburn."

"Do you like living in Auburn?"

"It's okay. It's good because it's close to my work and my class."

"Don't you ever talk to the neighbours to practise your English?"

Faisal smiled for the second time when I asked this question. "I live in a flat. My neighbours in the next flat are Iraqi, there is a family downstairs who are Turkish, my neighbours on the other side are Iranian and my neighbours above me are Chinese. There are no Australians in Auburn. They don't speak English very well so I can't practise with them. I live with my friend and he doesn't speak English."

I wanted to say, "Now, wait a minute. You loved your former boss, Michael, and now you live with another man you call '*my* friend'. Is there something about yourself you want to share with me? You'd be in good company." But I kept silent on the issue. It was difficult enough for me when I told people about my lifestyle in my own culture so I guessed that it would probably be difficult for him coming from a completely different background. In any case, it wasn't necessary to know. I had no particular feelings for him.

We had quite a casual conversation about general topics and I marvelled at Faisal's ability to express himself very well in English. I had been of the opinion that he was the least of all the class to be conversant in English and yet he was much more advanced than everyone. If he didn't practise speaking English, how was it that he spoke it so well?

6 o'clock soon arrived and the rest of the class came in dribs and drabs, and so the conversation came to an end. But not only had Faisal changed outside class, this change was now obvious in the classroom as well. For the first time, Faisal was more open and more willing to participate. Not only did he participate, any question I asked about anything we had done in class, Faisal was the only one who knew all the answers. Whenever I asked questions about certain grammatical points, the other students humphed frustratingly because they had forgotten what I had taught them. But Faisal could recite to me the answer precisely even if it was something I had taught my students months earlier. This metamorphosis in Faisal's character was both pleasing and disturbing. It further accentuated how much I did not understand the man at all.

When 9 o'clock arrived, the class disbanded. I locked the door behind me but instead of going anywhere, I decided to have a cigarette. After all, I had to wait till 9.30 when Khatyn finished before I could leave. So I had time to kill. Faisal was the last to leave the class and when he saw me take out a packet of cigarettes, he stopped and watched me.

"Are you not going home now?" he asked.

"Not yet. I'm waiting for a colleague of mine. Why?"

"I don't have to go home straight away. Can I talk with you more?"

There was no reason why he couldn't. I didn't have much else to do.

"Yeah, why not," I replied and offered him a cigarette.

Faisal took one, lit it and began smoking.

"You know," he began, "you can ask *any* question you want about me."

I looked at Faisal with suspicion.

"Any question?"

Faisal nodded.

"Can I ask you a personal question?" I asked half jokingly.

"Yes, of course," he replied.

Why did he invite me to ask anything I wanted to know about him? This was the strangest thing to say. But Faisal had been a strange man all the time I had known him so I was beginning to believe that strangeness was a common denominator in his character. There was one question I wanted to ask but didn't dare ask it. It would have been revealing about me and if I had misinterpreted him, it would have spelled disaster. But there was another personal question I had in mind that I wanted to know about him.

"Tell me, Faisal. Do you drink alcohol?"

Faisal blew out a cloud of smoke and smiled. I absolutely loved his smile because his smile made his eyes sparkle.

"Yes. I drink beer."

I thought carefully before I asked the next question because I knew I was moving onto tender ground. But he told me I could ask any question I wanted and the invitation was open.

"How can you drink alcohol if you are a Muslim? Doesn't Islam teach against the drinking of alcohol?"

Faisal accepted this question without flinching.

"Yes, we're not supposed to. I started drinking beer when I came to Australia. I know I shouldn't. But my friend drinks alcohol. Because of him, I drink alcohol."

He had answered my question. I knew that Muslims were forbidden to drink alcohol. But who was I to judge him? If I required my students to respect other people's beliefs, who was I to tell him that he should not act against his own religion? As long as what he did in his life was not affecting those around him, it was his business what he did with his life, not mine.

I tried to restrain myself from asking the next question. In Australian culture, it is taboo to ask people their marital status because for those who are not married, like me, the answer can be quite embarrassing because not everyone is accepting of so-called alternative lifestyles. But I had to know. This man who loved his boss and now lived with a man whom he called a second time "*my* friend" may have had more in common with me than he realised. It was not due to any physical feelings I had for him for I had no physical feelings for him. It was more of a comfort zone, that if he were like me, it would have been easier for the two of us. So, I just let the question fall from my lips.

"Tell me, Faisal, are you married?"

"Yes."

I was taken aback.

"Well, why don't you live with your wife?"

Faisal looked down at the ground before looking up to speak to me. From his reaction, I thought that maybe there were personal questions he preferred, after all, that I didn't ask. I regretted having asked it at first but I was glad later that I had.

"My family is still in Pakistan. I have a wife and six children."

Afghanistan, Pakistan, these were two separate countries. Faisal was an Afghani refugee so where did Pakistan fit into the picture? Why was his family in Pakistan? If his family is in Pakistan and not Afghanistan, why did he flee to Australia? Had he been lying to me when he said he was Afghani? But Faisal was able to give me a plausible answer to this question.

"Yes, I am Afghani. But I fled to Pakistan when the Taliban came to Afghanistan."

"Then, why didn't you stay in Pakistan?" I asked puzzled.

"Because the Taliban came to Pakistan," he replied.

There was a moment of silence. We heard nothing in the news about the Taliban entering Pakistan. The Taliban situation was entirely an Afghani affair, that's why Afghanis fled to Australia. I didn't know any Pakistanis and no Pakistani had ever been a student in my class. This, then, meant to me that Pakistan was a safe haven for those who fled from the terrors within the Afghani border.

"Hang on," I said. "You're an Afghani but you were living in Pakistan when the Taliban threatened your life. I thought all this stuff about the Taliban occurred in Afghanistan."

When I made this comment, Faisal's expression resumed the original, expressionless dullness that I had been familiar with earlier in the year. He looked thoughtfully at me for a moment and then spoke.

"I will tell you the story from the beginning."

Faisal offered me another cigarette which I dutifully took. We both lit up which was like the signal to begin his story. Little did I realise that my inquisitiveness was akin to asking Faisal to release the white rabbit that I, like Alice, would follow into Wonderland.

Faisal began by explaining the situation of Afghanistan prior to the Taliban. First there was the war between Russia and Afghanistan in the 1970s. During the war, Faisal fled to Pakistan for a short period of time. During his short sojourn in Pakistan, his marriage was arranged with the daughter of another man who had also fled Afghanistan momentarily to seek protection in Pakistan. Although the war continued, there was a time when the intensity of the war subsided which allowed Faisal and his wife to return to Afghanistan. On return to Afghanistan, Faisal and his wife settled in a small village within the environs of Kabul city.

Here Faisal lived and raised a family, and this situation continued up until around the year 1996. At about this time, he enrolled in an architectural course at a major university in Kabul. However, the war renewed its intensity and so, after one year of study, Faisal was forced to leave the university. Because the war now involved the entire country, Faisal was called in, like all his compatriots, to fight.

Faisal became a high ranking member of a political party called Hezbe-Islami which was a political party in opposition to the government. The Hezbe-Islami was a political party with an Islamic political platform and was in opposition to the government of the time, a secular government that was backed by Communist Russia.

Faisal did not join the Hezbe-Islami party for any particular personal convictions. Rather, Faisal was offered a position in Hezbe-Islami because his two elder brothers had held prominent positions in this party. One brother had been killed during the Russo-Afghani war. The other brother was arrested one evening during the mid 1980s by Afghan local intelligence under the command of the KGB. This second brother was taken away and was never seen again.

Because of his brothers' exceptional qualities as commanders, it was naturally assumed that Faisal also possessed these qualities. So Faisal was reluctantly dragged into the party as a prominent member.

"There were two things I wanted to do in life," Faisal said. "I wanted to study at university and play sport. I completed a year at university studying to become an architect. I also played a lot of football and I was very good at it. But, because of the war, I had to leave both of them. I didn't want to have anything to do with politics or this party. But, because of my brothers, I had no choice."

I was stunned at what he said. What a dreadful position to be in, not being able to pursue a course at university. I reflected back on my own university studies. I had completed a degree and then done a postgraduate. At any time, I could go back to university and do further studies. Nothing prevented me from doing this. In fact, all Australians have the freedom to get as much education as they physically and economically can cope with.

And not being able to play sport. This was a part of my life. Swimming was my number one sport that I engaged in almost every day of the week. Sport was such a popular pastime among Australians and we didn't know life could be any other way.

I felt so sorry for his situation. The life I led I took so much for granted and had never realised until this moment just how lucky I was. I thought my free life was the same everywhere. I was beginning to realise that I had been living in a comfortable shell, protected from the rest of the cruel world for all this time.

Faisal then continued. The Hezbe-Islami party was not only in opposition to the government at the time, it also was in opposition to a new political party that was beginning to form just outside Afghanistan's border, a political party called the Taliban. The Afghani nation didn't take this political party seriously. However, in 1996, the members of the Taliban set out like an army from Quetta, a Pakistani town just south of the Afghani-Pakistani border. No-one believed that the Taliban would come to anything so the rest of the country just looked on indifferently.

However, it was a lightning strike. It was not long before the Taliban had reached Kabul. Kabul, as Faisal described, is a city built on a river which cuts the city into two. One half of the city was controlled by the Hezbe-Islami party and the other by the then government.

Faisal didn't believe the Taliban would reach Kabul and he expressed openly what he thought of this party. But contrary to his expectations, the Taliban besieged Kabul. Faisal's open criticism of the Taliban in itself put Faisal in danger because, as far as the members of the Taliban were concerned, if you didn't support the Taliban, you were executed. Faisal's open criticism of the Taliban was like openly advertising to all Afghanistan his opposition to this party and therefore this put his life at risk.

Faisal explained that the members of the Taliban were an ignorant, uneducated group of people, just as Mohammed had said. But he also explained that they were also very strong. They needed weapons and it was easy to get them. All the Taliban had to do was go to someone's house and demand the occupants to hand over their guns. It didn't matter to the Taliban whether or not these people actually possessed a weapon. People learnt early that if they said they did not have a gun, the Taliban would arrest and kill them. So, to get around this, those harassed by the Taliban would tell the members of the Taliban that they had a gun but it would take a day or so to retrieve it. They would then go out, buy a gun and then present it to the members of the Taliban who would then leave them alone.

The members of the Taliban knew that Faisal, apart from speaking condescendingly about them, held a relatively prominent position in the Hezbe-Islami party and had replaced his brothers. Thus, the Taliban decided that Faisal was in possession of 300 rifles that would no doubt supplement the Taliban's forces. One night, the Taliban captured one of Faisal's nephews and interrogated him about the rifles. Faisal's nephew knew that these 300 rifles didn't exist but he also knew the consequences if he tried to reason or negotiate with the members of the Taliban. So, he told the Taliban that Faisal had the 300 rifles somewhere and with that the Taliban let him go.

Faisal's nephew eventually passed this news onto Faisal. Faisal saw he was in a difficult position. He realised that he could not scold his nephew for telling a lie to the Taliban because his nephew would have been killed for telling the truth. But Faisal was now in a predicament. It was one thing to go out and buy one gun for the Taliban but where was Faisal going to find the money to buy 300 rifles?

Faisal's life was now in the balance. The Taliban had surrounded him and, if they caught him, his life would be over. He could no longer stay safely in Kabul or Afghanistan and so he managed to flee to Peshawar in Pakistan. Faisal thought that the Taliban would eventually collapse or other political parties would fight against them and re-establish the former government in Afghanistan. But the months passed and he realised that this was not the case. As a result, he sent a message for the rest of his family to come to Peshawar.

The Pakistani government allowed Afghani refugees to settle in Pakistan and set up refugee camps around Peshawar city. However, Afghani refugees were issued identity cards which only allowed them protection in and around Peshawar city. Afghani refugees were not free to wander off to other parts of the country. If ever they were caught in other areas of the nation, they would be arrested and imprisoned immediately.

These refugee camps in and around Peshawar city started out simply as an agglomeration of tents but gradually developed into significant suburbs with small shops and schools. The refugee suburb where Faisal lived was inhabited by members of the Hezbe-Islami party. Faisal acted as a desk clerk while he remained under the auspices and protection of Pakistan.

While in Pakistan, Faisal questioned the Hezbe-Islami party politics. Through a friend of his, he joined a new party called the National and Islamic Council of Ethnicities of Afghanistan. Faisal became relations officer of this party. The National Islamic Council of Ethnicities of Afghanistan originally wasn't taken seriously by Afghanistan or Pakistan. But with the passage of time, the Council became a significant body organised into a proper system. The initial objective of the Council was to enlighten the people's minds about the Taliban, to show them the real image of the Taliban and what the Taliban really was.

Faisal and various members of the Council began to wonder whether the Pakistani government would allow them to have a movement of this nature on Pakistani territory. After all, Pakistan recognised the Taliban as the legitimate ruling party in Afghanistan. This was of concern to many of the Council members, wary of how the Pakistani government would react towards the members of this Council. A Pakistani official was brought to the Council and the official stated that the Pakistani government had nothing to do with the Taliban.

The members of the Council grew confident that things were going to be okay and decided to start a program to overthrow the Taliban regime, starting with an unarmed uprising in Nangarhar province, a province in the east of Afghanistan. They were of the opinion that if they carried out this uprising and similar unarmed uprisings within Afghanistan, they would be able to overthrow the Taliban. They thought that if they could get one district under the Council's control, this would set up a domino effect, resulting in other areas unshackling themselves from the grip of the Taliban.

Although now dissociated from his original political party, Faisal said that he still maintained an amicable relationship with some members of the Hezbe-Islami party who had close associations with his murdered brothers. Faisal discussed the Council's ambitions with these members of the Hezbe-Islami party. The members of Hezbe-Islami said that any uprising against the Taliban was welcome but the Hezbe-Islami party would not get involved but would take on an independent stance.

Despite the Council's attempts to operate clandestinely, the Taliban eventually became aware of the Council's existence and the planned uprising but the Taliban was not clear of the details. Those who held prominent positions in the Council soon had their names on the Taliban's black list. However, Faisal explained that the Council members' hatred for the Taliban and their desire to see the downfall of the Taliban was the impetus which gave the Council members the courage to carry out the planned uprising.

The night before the uprising, the leader of the Council was arrested. The news spread to the other members, and Faisal and all the other Council members went into hiding. Faisal never found out the details of the arrest but he suspected that Pakistanis had been arresting Taliban opponents despite the reassurance of the Pakistani official who had claimed that Pakistan held a neutral stance regarding Afghani affairs. Faisal was of the belief that the Taliban instructed the Taliban consulate in Peshawar to dismantle the Council.

The Council obtained information about the Taliban through an informant stationed at a place near the Afghani-Pakistani border. This informant, although a high level commanding officer of the Taliban in Nangarhar province, regularly passed on confidential information about what the Taliban was doing. However, when the informant passed on a secret letter stating that the Taliban had drawn up a list of Council members to be captured and executed, a list which included Faisal's name, the informant was caught, was subsequently arrested and was never seen again.

Faisal explained that this caused fear among the Council members and so they all had to go into hiding. Faisal said that he tried to keep a low profile because he did not want to be seen by many people.

However, in September, 2000, an article appeared in the English language newspaper of Pakistan, *The Nation*, which talked about the Council. This article exposed the members of the Council and specifically named certain members, including Faisal, as being on the Taliban's hit list. As a result of the article, Faisal became completely fearful for his safety and realised that the only course of action that now remained was to get out of Pakistan. Faisal said that he was afraid that he would be arrested by the Pakistani government because of his affiliation with an anti-Taliban organisation, especially as the

Pakistan government had recognised and were in favour of the Taliban as the legitimate governing body in Afghanistan. Faisal had not been safe in Afghanistan and now Faisal realised he was not safe in Pakistan either. He no longer had any other options - he had to get out of Pakistan.

I stood there dumbfounded as he related the story. I wanted him to go on. But at that moment, Khatyn appeared.

"Are you ready to go?" she asked.

"No, I'm not ready to go!" was what I wanted to say to Khatyn. I wanted to hear the rest of the story. This was so gripping. For the first time I heard from an occupant of the country what had happened during the Taliban regime. Here was someone who was a living testament to the horrors that had occurred in Afghanistan that we only heard second or third hand through the media. But at the end of the news bulletin, we simply turned the channel over to light entertainment as if the news were just a movie. But real people were living out this horror as a part of their daily lives. And Faisal had witnessed it all and had been an integral part of it.

I didn't want to leave but I knew both Khatyn and I had to go home.

And so a second night was spent on the balcony, sipping glasses of wine and contemplating who this strange man, Faisal, really was. But things were confusing me about him. There seemed to be two sides to him, a man who frequented nightclubs and therefore supported the freedom experienced by Australians but also a politician in direct opposition to the government of his country and a religious devotee. This man was becoming a real enigma. I really didn't know what to think of him. Nothing made sense. I had two feelings for him, one a sense of fear, the other, a strong sense of sympathy.

However, he had at least confirmed one point, if he were telling the truth. If he was fighting against the Taliban, then it was a Pashtun fighting Pashtuns. Pashtuns were simply a race of people, just another tribe, just as I had surmised.

Fortunately we still had a few weeks of this class before the course finished. This meant that I still had the opportunity to form a proper image of who this man really was.

Chapter 4

From that Thursday to the following Monday, time seemed to pass very slowly. For the first time since Faisal had come to my class, I couldn't wait to see him again. What he had begun to tell me was like reading a thriller. I just couldn't stop thinking about it.

The following Saturday after this conversation, I spent the day at the beach. I watched the crowds out on the beach on this beautiful, sunny day, soaking up the sun and riding the waves. What Faisal had told me the previous Thursday night made me view this scene through different eyes. We were so lucky and we didn't know it. This paradise that we enjoy we take so much for granted. We are totally oblivious to the privilege we have of living here. I watched families and friends in groups together, relaxing, reading, laughing and playing on the beach as if we were living in heaven.

We are so lucky to have been born here and to have grown up in an atmosphere of peace. War and oppression are two dimensional phenomena depicted through a small box in the corner of our living rooms and seem as unreal as a horror movie. For the first time I saw this whole scenario in a different light.

I put my feet in Faisal's shoes and tried to imagine what it was like to live in a country where I was bullied around by people who told me how to think and live. Further, I tried to imagine living in a country where speaking my mind was flirting with death. I began to realise why the nations of the world flocked to Australia. I don't believe Australia is necessarily heaven on earth but compared with Faisal's experience, it was certainly close to it. From that day on, I stopped taking the good life for granted. Every day when I wake up, despite what happens to me during the day, I enjoy what really is an easy life in comparison to the horrors that Faisal and other refugees have had to endure.

The following Monday finally arrived. Faisal and I had agreed to meet at 5.30, half an hour before class started. But I was in the classroom at five o'clock and waited pensively for him to turn up in the hope that he could come even earlier than before. But he arrived at 5.30 as we had agreed. He explained to me that he could not come any earlier because he could not leave work earlier.

When he arrived, he was again a completely different person to the one who had initially come to my class. It was as if he had been born again and a new life began to surge through his body.

"Salaam walaikum," I said as he entered the class.

"Walaikum salaam," he replied as he took his place at his desk.

"How was your weekend?" I asked, while burning inside to hear the rest of the story.

"Okay," Faisal replied. "I didn't do much. On Saturday I just stayed at home and listened to music. Yesterday I just visited friends."

"Do you miss your family?" I asked.

Faisal sighed. "I think about them every day. I have a temporary protection visa so I can't go back to see them and they can't come and see me. My wife is also trapped at home and I depend on my nephews to do everything for me."

"Why? Is your wife threatened by the Taliban?"

Faisal went silent for a moment. Each time he went silent, I realised that his mind was clicking over because to answer what seemed like an easy question was quite a complicated affair.

"You need to understand that Afghani culture and Australian culture are very different. My wife cannot go out on her own without a man to accompany her. I have two sons but they are too young to do this. So, my nephews have to look after her."

I was beginning to realise just how complicated Faisal's separation from his family was.

"How long have you been here?" I asked.

"Three years."

He had not seen his family for three years. Here was this man, trapped in a country, waiting for a decision by the government to give him the right to not only settle down in freedom but also to be reunited with his family. I was not a family man but I could imagine what it would be like to live away from those one loves dearly and unable to protect. I could feel my heart sink and a lump form in the back of my throat. I had to suppress this feeling before I could utter another sentence.

"So, how did you know how to get out of Pakistan?"

Faisal sat back in his chair.

"A smuggler helped me to come to Australia."

I was amazed once again at his English and that he knew the English word "smuggler". Maybe it was one of the first words in the English language that he had to learn.

"But how did you get in contact with the smuggler? I mean, I'm sure smugglers don't have a sign at the front of their houses advertising their occupation. How do you get in contact with them?"

Faisal looked at me with a stern expression on his face. I thought I was asking a question far too sensitive for him to answer. But then he spoke.

"You have to realise that the way we do things in Afghanistan and Pakistan is very different to what happens here. People talk. And people know other people. So, soon you find out who can help you. I had a friend in Pakistan who knew a smuggler. He told me that this smuggler could get me out of Pakistan."

This was the part that I wanted to know. All we knew of boat people was their final arrival in Australia in ships that should have been destined for the scrap heap but to which these people clung as their last ditch at survival. But I had to know the story from the beginning. How did he get here?

And so Faisal began this part of the story. This friend of Faisal's invited the smuggler to his place and met Faisal. This man was Pakistani. This smuggler explained to Faisal that, for seven thousand US dollars, the smuggler could ensure that Faisal got to Australia. Australia was a better destination than the UK and the USA because it was closer, cheaper and less risky. Faisal explained that he knew very little about Australia before he got here and had no idea what to expect.

Faisal had nothing to lose. He had a family to support and the only way he could do this was to save his own life. In a very short time, he packed a few belongings, photos of his family, a few clothes and then set off. I tried to picture this event, Faisal kissing and hugging his wife and six children in turn before being escorted onto a bus and leaving his family behind, not knowing when or if he would ever see them again.

Faisal explained to me that his first destination was Lahore. He had to go by bus. It was a long rickety journey on a packed bus that seemed more like a cattle truck. This was frightening enough but what was more frightening was that Faisal was now travelling outside the protection zone that Pakistan offered. He had to hope that no-one during the trip asked for any identification because, having left Peshawar and its environs, he was now travelling illegally. However, eventually he arrived safely in Lahore. He was met by another man who seemed to know him and who took Faisal to a hotel where Faisal stayed for several nights.

At the hotel, Faisal met many other refugees in the same plight. There were about seven of them. All of them were told to remain in the hotel because it was too dangerous to venture out. If at any time they were arrested, they would be put in prison and there was nothing neither the smuggler nor anyone could do to get them out. Faisal went on to explain that the smuggler didn't say this out of any feelings of altruism but simply because each refugee held a dollar value. The smuggler was not paid for his services until the refugees arrived safely at their final destination.

Staying at the hotel was no holiday. Although a hotel like any other, Faisal could not enjoy its services. There was very little to do but sit around in the room or walk around the hotel precinct to make time move on. Each day was filled with fear, tension and boredom.

Eventually Faisal got word that this group of refugees would be moving to another hotel. This move was at least a breath of fresh air. But as Faisal explained to me, it wasn't because of any sympathy by the smuggler. It was a wise move by the smuggler to move the refugees on to prevent raising any suspicion about them.

Again, the weeks moved on and the tension and boredom continued. Faisal was told not to contact his family under any conditions, to prevent him from being traced. This only intensified his feelings of apprehension because he had no idea of how his family were getting on without him. It also concerned him that his family did not know whether or not he was okay.

Finally the refugees got word that they were moving on. From Lahore they were sent to Karachi on the Pakistani coast. Again, they were told to stay in a hotel where all their food and lodging would be provided for by the smuggler. They were to remain in the hotel until they were given further instructions. They were instructed not to leave the hotel under any circumstances because again they could be arrested by the police at any time. If the local police arrested anyone of them, the smuggler would wash his hands of the affair. The days and nights were tortuously long because while he was in Pakistan, Faisal did not feel safe.

After weeks of waiting, another man turned up at the hotel. This man presented Faisal with a false passport. This was what Faisal needed to continue his travels beyond the borders of Pakistan.

Faisal, along with the other Afghanis, was shuttled on to a plane destined for Hong Kong. He was told that when he arrived in Hong Kong, he was to take another flight to Singapore.

"Weren't you scared?" I asked, trying to imagine myself doing all this travelling under such circumstances.

Faisal laughed sheepishly. "Of course, I was scared. At any moment along the route, I could have been arrested. I was frightened the whole time. It was difficult for me to eat and sleep. But I kept thinking of my family. I knew I was doing this for my family and this is what gave me the courage to carry on."

I thought of Faisal and what he did. How many of us here in Australia would risk our lives in such a way for a family member?

"And so, what happened next?"

Faisal then explained that he was told to catch another flight to Jakarta. When he arrived at the airport, he was not to go through immigration. He was told to simply wait at the bottom of a set of stairs which led to the immigration desk and not move. Someone would meet him and sort everything out so he could pass through the airport without problems. Faisal explained that this was even more frightening. How would he explain to any of the airport authorities why he was not going through immigration but was simply hanging around? Who or what would he be waiting for?

When he arrived at Jakarta airport, he did what he was told. But while he waited, he was completely frightened. I tried to imagine being there, my heart pounding inside my chest and my hands feeling clammy. Faisal explained that whenever an airport official or soldier passed by, it sent chills down his spine because at any moment he could have been arrested and placed in prison. If he were placed in prison, his attempt at survival and the survival of his family would have been severely jeopardised. But through all of it, he prayed to God to get him through for his family's sake.

Eventually, he saw a man walking around carrying a placard. It had Faisal's name on it. Faisal approached the man and said he was the man whose name was written on the placard. This man then told Faisal to follow him and he was led through another section of the airport and finally he was in Jakarta.

There was some sense of relief that he had finally made it through Jakarta airport safely. At the airport there was a special bus waiting for him and all the other Afghani refugees as if they were tourists being picked up by a shuttle bus. He was taken to a hotel and told to wait until he was given further notice. Faisal told me that he asked this stranger how long he needed to wait. The man's only reply was that he had to wait until the time was right. This man gave the same instruction as Faisal received in Karachi: don't leave the hotel under any circumstances because the Indonesian police could arrest him at any time. If he was arrested, the smuggler could do nothing for him.

Here Faisal was, in a strange city, in a country in which the locals spoke a language he did not understand, trapped in a hotel for a time period that he didn't know would end. Throughout the entire time, he thought of his family.

The days turned into weeks and the weeks into months. Several times he tried to get in contact with the smuggler. When he succeeded in contacting anyone in relation to the smuggler, this person would simply tell him that he had to wait until the time was right. Faisal guessed that they had to wait for the boat and the weather to be suitable for the voyage at sea.

Finally the big day arrived. Faisal told me that there were five buses loaded with people. Different smugglers with a different number of people banded together and placed these people on the buses. The buses headed for their final means of transport, the boat that would sail out of Jakarta and make it into the headlines of Australian newspapers.

Faisal explained to me that he was fully aware of the dangers of this last trip. He had heard of boats getting lost and the occupants being trapped on these wandering artificial islands without food and water for months. He had heard of boats sinking and the occupants drowning, making their last attempts at freedom a waste of time.

But the night before their departure, Faisal told me he had a dream. In the dream, he and a few of the people escaping from Afghanistan were trapped inside a house while there was a lion outside, pacing the house to get in. But despite all its attempts, the lion could not attack those inside. Faisal interpreted this dream to mean that, although they would be surrounded by danger during this last leg of the voyage, they would reach their destination safely.

Eventually, the boat left the shores of Jakarta and went out to the open sea. For two and a half days, the boat sailed on this vast expanse of water. After about 60 hours, they sighted Christmas Island and in doing so, the Australian officials came to greet them. Their welcoming comments were, "You are now under arrest!"

"Were you scared when the Australian authorities said that?" I asked.

Faisal smiled.

"No. We were relieved. We knew that as soon as the Australian authorities told us we were under arrest, we were safe. This was the most relieving experience of the entire journey. At that point, I couldn't help crying."

Faisal cried? When he mentioned that, I could feel the tears welling up in my eyes. I was sharing the fear and the relief that he had experienced in his attempt to save his life. But I didn't want Faisal to know that his story affected me so much, so I acted as if I had to blow my nose and then quickly wiped my eyes.

But Faisal cried. Faisal was a human being like everyone else, who expressed emotions, who had feelings. This was not the same Faisal I had met at the beginning of this course.

"So, then what happened?" I asked.

Faisal explained to me that he and all these refugees stayed on Christmas Island for two days. There had been about 200 people on the boat. But they weren't all from Afghanistan. Some were from Sri Lanka, some from Iran and some from Iraq. At the end of their two day stay, they were placed on QANTAS flights and flown to Adelaide.

"You flew QANTAS?" I asked. I tried to imagine the interior of a commercial liner like QANTAS filled with men dressed in Central Asian garb, the peerhan and the turban that is so characteristic of this area of the world that is more typical of those walking the dusty roads of Afghanistan, being attended to by flight attendants in modern, western dress. It must have been a sight to behold!

Faisal then explained that they arrived in Adelaide tired and exhausted. All the refugees were marched out of the airport by a special tunnel prepared for them which led directly to special buses. From Adelaide, they made the long journey to Woomera in the centre of the state of South Australia.

I thought about that journey. I had been to Woomera years before on a holiday trip with my parents. Our destination was Alice Springs and

Uluru but to get there we had to travel to Port Augusta and then drive up the Stuart Highway which passed this oasis. I remember this long drive in our air-conditioned car and the view outside, the flat, sweeping desert where only small shrubs and bushes dared to grow. This landscape seemed to just go on forever and ever out towards the horizon and beyond. It must have been difficult inside a bus full of people sharing the same plight, not knowing what was happening back home.

Woomera detention centre was the destination. This detention centre had made world headlines. I only knew of this detention centre through the media and now I was hearing about it first hand from someone who had occupied it for some time.

When Faisal got to this point in the story, the other students began to come to class. This was becoming frustrating. Each time Faisal told a portion of his story, he would arrive at a climax and then he was forced to keep the rest of the story for another evening. It reminded me of Scheherazade, reciting the stories that made the famous *One Thousand And One Nights*, who, to spare being executed by her husband, ended the story each night at a high point which forced her husband to suspend the execution in order to hear the rest of the story the following evening.

Everything had changed with this class now. In January, every other student held a prominent image in my mind and Faisal faded into the background. It was now April and everything was the reverse. Faisal was the prominent figure and the rest of the class was like a haze in comparison. But not only so, the other students began to appear rather dull and boring while Faisal became fascinating and interesting.

I was struck by this turn of events. My initial impression of this strange man was based on what my former student, Mohammed, had said and my general appreciation of refugees as described through the media. But because I was forced to have some sort of regular dealing with Faisal throughout this time, I had gained the opportunity to find out what he was really like as a person. It is so easy to form an initial impression of a person and yet this initial impression can be so wrong. However, little did I realise that this change in my perception of the man was the beginning of a long adventure.

Chapter 5

"Who was that guy you were talking to?" Khatyn asked as she got into my car at the end of one Thursday evening.

"Oh, it's Faisal. My Afghani student," I replied as I sat in the driver's seat and pulled the seatbelt over my shoulder.

"He's Afghani?" Khatyn asked. "He doesn't look Afghani."

I turned on the ignition of the car and began to back out of my parking spot.

"He doesn't look Afghani? What do Afghanis look like?" I asked.

"You know. They look Chinese but are hairy like Middle Eastern guys."

"Hairy like Middle Eastern guys?" I asked and gave Khatyn a strange look.

"You know what I mean. The Chinese have almost no hair on their bodies. These guys have slanted eyes like the Chinese but also have hairy arms and legs and the evidence of facial hair like you."

"So, they're hairy like Australians, too, then."

Khatyn laughed. "I didn't mean that Middle Eastern guys are gorillas. What I meant was that because they come from that part of the world, they seem to be a mixture of the two major peoples in that area, Chinese and Middle Eastern."

I began to speed off on our journey home.

"Well, I guess he's Afghani. He's not Pakistani because he's pale skinned and all the Pakistanis I've ever met have had a much darker complexion. In fact, I can't place his features into any culture I've seen before. But he said that he was Pashtun."

"What's that?" Khatyn splatted.

"Apparently there are different tribes in Afghanistan. The Chinese looking ones are from a tribe called Hazarah. Pashtuns are just another tribe in Afghanistan."

"Ooh! You've really done your homework, then," Khatyn exclaimed. "He seems like a nice guy, though. He has soft eyes. And I think he likes you."

That last comment felt like a punch in the gut.

"He likes me? What do you mean?"

"I can see it in his eyes, the way he looks at you. He has great admiration for you. I think he might be in love with you."

"In love with me?"

"Oh, Michael, why does that bother you? What? All of a sudden, you don't like men?"

I changed down a gear as we approached a T-intersection.

"No, that's not the point. He's a married man."

"Doesn't mean a thing," Khatyn replied. "Probably in his culture, he was forced to marry. I'm certain they don't have Gay Pride in the centre of Kabul city."

What Khatyn was saying was making me feel quite uncomfortable. I didn't see or feel any signs that Faisal had any physical feelings whatsoever for me. I was simply his teacher giving him extra attention outside normal class hours.

"Well, I hope he's not."

"Why not?" Khatyn asked. I hated her questions.

"Because I don't think he's physically attractive. To me, anyway. I mean, I don't have any feelings for the man. He's a nice guy and he's my student, and that's that."

"Well, don't lead him on, then," Khatyn said and laughed. "He might send the Taliban onto you and blow up your tower."

I knew that Khatyn was joking but the mention of Faisal's involvement with the Taliban unfortunately made me react violently.

"He's not a member of the Taliban. He's the victim of it. I'm sick of everyone viewing these people as terrorists," I said almost screaming.

There was suddenly utter silence in the car. Khatyn just looked out the window of the passenger side. I regretted my violent outburst and touched Khatyn on the knee.

"I'm really, really sorry, Khatyn, for that. I didn't mean to snap at you like that."

Khatyn touched my hand. She was silent for a moment and then said quietly, "I was joking around. I didn't mean anything by it."

The conversation stopped for a moment and then Khatyn added, "Michael, you're a very easy-going guy. So, your reaction was really surprising. I think you seriously like him. I think you might be in love with him, too."

"Pfeh, don't be ridiculous, Khatyn. He's just a student of mine, nothing more, nothing less."

"Michael, there's nothing wrong with that. If you love him, you love him. We've only got two weeks left of class and then he won't be your student anymore. You will be free to go out with him if you want."

I slowed down as we approached a roundabout.

"But I don't want to go out with him. I have no feelings for him," I said.

Or did I? Was there something Khatyn knew about Faisal and me that I was totally unaware of? Females of the human species are blessed with a woman's intuition and seem to suss things out much quicker than men ever can. Did Faisal have feelings for me? Was that the real reason why he wanted to come to class earlier than usual, why he had opened up to me and told me things that I thought were secrets that refugees refused to indulge? And Khatyn was right about his marital status, that it meant nothing. Being married said nothing about someone's sexuality – for those who cannot admit it, it is just a convenient way of hiding it. And I was sure that in Afghani society, homosexuality was strictly taboo as it was during my parents' generation. I was to find out much later that not only was homosexuality taboo, what the authorities did to homosexuals caught in the act was so horrific that the thought still makes me want to vomit.

I dropped Khatyn off, wished her good night and then drove home. Yet another side of Faisal was forming. He told me that he loved this other Michael he knew and he lived with another man at the moment. He also did suddenly change his entire approach to me mid-year from being completely evasive to becoming open. But this just meant he liked me as a friend, surely. If he were gay, he would not have spoken so tenderly about his wife and family.

But what about my feelings towards him? Didn't I feel something for this man? Didn't I wait pensively for time to pass so that we could be together alone for half an hour before class? Didn't the weekend seem to snail by until I came back to class Monday evening? But I wasn't physically attracted to him. So what really were these feelings I had for him?

Being a teacher at a college like AELC is a lot different to being a teacher at primary or secondary school because the students of tertiary education are adults and therefore they are of about the same mentality and maturity as I am. This means that, as much as they come to class to learn English, the classroom becomes a social event. I remember Khatyn once comparing the beginning of a new semester with a new class to a night out on a blind date because we start the new class wondering what the students will be like, whether we will like them or not. Over the months of teaching, a teacher-student relationship develops. In my classroom, it is not like the relationship between a parent and a child. Rather, the teaching style I adopt is one in which the relationship between teacher and student is something like that between an older and a younger sibling.

It is very difficult, then, when the end of the semester arrives and class comes to an end. Because I develop such a good social relationship with my students over eighteen weeks, the last day is a very sad one for me. When the class is disbanded, it's as if a whole group of friends decide to completely abandon me and this leaves me feeling very empty inside. However, I always have to keep reminding myself that these students are, after all, merely students and at the end of the semester, my task is complete and the students now move on.

My feelings towards Faisal, however, had grown much stronger than those I had ever had for any other student. So, on the last Thursday night class, I almost felt torn apart knowing that this was the last day I would see Faisal.

The class held a big party and there was plenty of food and drink. We played music from a variety of different cultures and many of the students got up and danced.

At the end of these festivities, the class disbanded, but Faisal stayed behind to have one last cigarette with me. While we puffed away out on the balcony, I decided to let my feelings known to Faisal.

"I'm really going to miss you, Faisal," I said. "Where are you going to go from here? Are you going to enrol at TAFE?"

"Yes, I want to continue my studies. I know I must learn more English."

Faisal then took a drag on his cigarette. He leant on the balcony railing and stared out into the distance. He then turned to me and said, "But can't I see you again?"

I paused for a moment. Isn't that what I wanted also, to see Faisal again? I hesitated for a few seconds before giving him an answer.

"Well, of course," I finally replied. "Whenever you're free, you can give me a call. Maybe we could have a coffee somewhere."

"Are you free this Saturday?" Faisal then asked. "I want to invite you home to meet my friends."

Wow! Faisal didn't waste time at all! At first I was going to turn the offer down but then I reflected on the idea. It was now the end of this course. Faisal was no longer my student and no longer a student of AELC, and therefore my relationship as his teacher had really come to an end. A new alliance could now be drawn up. And there was no real reason to wait. This new relationship could start as soon as we both left the college that evening.

"Sure, why not. What time would you like me to come over?"

Faisal suggested a time. We then exchanged telephone numbers and Faisal gave me his address. As we parted ways, I shook his hand and told him I was looking forward to seeing him the following Saturday.

However, when I woke up that Saturday morning, I don't know why I suddenly felt so nervous. Faisal had asked me to be at his place at about midday and told me that it wasn't necessary to bring anything. I didn't feel comfortable coming empty handed. It is customary in Australia to at least bring a bottle of wine or some alcoholic beverage when you visit someone. Faisal had told me that he and "his friend" drank alcohol but Faisal had mentioned that I would meet other friends that day as well. What if some of his other friends were stricter Muslims and looked on alcohol much more severely?

I don't know why I felt so apprehensive about what I should wear and how to act. I think it was all because we had it drummed into us at school about our multicultural society and the importance of not offending people from different cultures that made me so self-conscious about the way I should present myself on our first encounter. When I look back on it now, it was totally unnecessary. After all, these people had left their country to come to Australia and no doubt expected Australians to dress and act very differently to what they were used to in their country of origin. I really needed to simply relax and be myself. But I couldn't.

So, the first problem to be resolved was what to bring. A nice bottle of Cabernet Sauvignon or a 24-pack was totally out of the question. But what else could I bring? Flowers? Totally inappropriate! Chocolates? What if they don't eat sweets?

I tried to imagine what these friends looked like. My only impression of what Afghanis looked like was through Mohammed and Faisal. Since I had met Faisal, I had done an Internet search on Afghanis and saw photos of Afghani men dressed in the *peerhan*, the extremely long shirt that falls below the knees over their *toombarn*, the wide, puffy trousers that are held up not with a belt but with a cord tied in a knot.

I imagined them all with long, bushy beards flowing down from their heads, capped with a *karakool*, the traditional Afghani hat that looks like a thick-crusted version of the French beret.

I pictured myself arriving at their flat to see camels parked outside, hot and thirsty angry-faced Muslim men in traditional Afghani dress lying around the loungeroom on pillows, smoking hashhish from hookahs. What in the world would you bring as a present for these people? A leather saddle? Sandals? Grooming brushes? A bottle of water? Although I felt uncomfortable with the decision, I decided that, irrespective of whether or not this would create a low impression of me on first contact, it was better to act dumb and not take anything at all. Faisal had told me not to bring anything in any case. At least, once I had evaluated the situation, if ever I returned, I would find out what to bring the next time around.

And what should I wear? We were now at the tail end of autumn and the weather had become cooler. Should I wear my jeans, a T-shirt and joggers? No, too daggy. Wear a tie? Too formal. My sports jacket? Too flashy. It took me what seemed like hours to finally decide to simply wear a pair of good jeans, a blue and white chequered shirt, and my brown leather uppers that I usually wore when I went out.

I paced around the flat as the time ticked by. When the moment came to leave, my palms became sweaty. Why was I so nervous? What did I expect of these people? My whole image of these people was a group of sabre-wielding fanatics bent on nothing else but holy war. I got in my car and it was the first time I drove at a respectable speed, about 10 km below the speed limit. I was sure that any driver behind me was completely frustrated at my driving.

I finally arrived in Faisal's street and drove slowly down, looking for the number of his set of flats. I parked the car and slowly walked into the building and up the stairs until I came to a door with the number of his flat on it. I paused. What awaited me on the other side of this wooden barrier?

I knocked on the door with three raps, almost silently. I waited pensively for the door to open, hoping it would be Faisal who would reply. When the door opened, there he was with a beaming smile. Faisal was dressed in a dark-green T-shirt and black tracksuit pants, much more casual attire than I was wearing and what he usually wore to class.

"Salaam Walaikum. Please come in."

I walked through the door. I noticed that Faisal was bare foot and that there were shoes on the floor near the door. So I dutifully took my shoes off even though I was not requested to do so. But there was no-one else there.

"Are you alone?" I asked.

"Yes. My other friends will come soon."

Faisal led me down the hall which then entered a large combined lounge and dining room. The flat itself looked like a typical Australian residence but the furniture, or lack of it, was so different. Around the walls were placed mattresses upon which I guessed everyone else would later sit. The floor was covered in Persian rugs so much so that I felt as if I had entered a miniature palace of Ali Baba.

"Please sit down," Faisal beckoned and pointed to the mattresses. I guessed that was where I was supposed to sit and so I obeyed silently.

"Tea?"

"Yes, please," I replied. Faisal disappeared into the kitchen and then returned with an ornate silver tray upon which were placed two glass mugs, a large thermos and a dish with an assortment of nibblies. Some of them were recognisable, particularly the nuts and the lollies. But there was one I had never seen before, sugar-coated almonds, which I found out later was what the Afghanis call *nookle*.

Faisal placed the tray before me and then sat down himself.

"Sugar?" he asked.

"One."

I noticed that milk was lacking on the tray. I usually drink tea with milk but I decided to follow his tradition and do without it. Faisal then passed me my cup and then took a sip from his.

I was so nervous that I didn't know what to say. I looked pensively around the room and it struck me how bare it was. It was not cluttered with lounges and armchairs, a dining room set, coffee tables, lamps and little statues and figurines as is usual in a normal Australian home. The only common denominator between an Australian home and Faisal's home was a TV set and DVD player which seemed so out of place in this otherwise bare interior.

The TV was on and the volume turned down. But I recognised from what I saw on the TV screen and the sound of the music that was being played that it was typical Indian music.

"Are you hungry?" Faisal asked me.

"A little," I replied.

"My friends will be here soon. One friend is making food for us."

I wasn't really hungry at all. My stomach was all knotted up with fear. Faisal's attempt at small talk did ease me a bit until I heard a noise at the door. This brought my fear to a crescendo. Suddenly, three middle-aged men walked in holding pots and plastic bags. Each kicked their shoes off and walked into the living room placing their loads on the floor.

There was an exchange of *Salaam Walaikums* between Faisal and these three men. Despite my nervousness, I watched with admiration the way these men greeted each other. They shook hands, then gave each other a good hug and then placed their hands on their chests while they exchanged typical formulaic expressions of greetings which I had learnt from my Farsi book. But I had never before seen the involved gestures that accompanied these greetings. Was I supposed to greet them in this way?

Faisal then introduced me to each of them and I was just as amazed at how they simply extended their right hand for a simple hand-shake in the Australian way.

"Hello, my name is Zaker," the first one said in good but heavily Dari-accented English. Zaker was a middle-aged man with a neatly clipped moustache and dark brown short hair. He was a little taller than me, rather plump, and he was wearing a blue chequered shirt and brown corduroy trousers. If I had not known he was Afghani, I would have simply assumed that he was southern European.

"*Salaam, man Parviz hastam,*" Parviz said, introducing himself in the same way as Zaker but in Dari. "*Shoma Dari sohbat mikonid?*" I understood, in my limited Dari, that he was asking if I spoke Dari. Parviz looked somewhat younger than Zaker, had dark black, curly hair, light skin and was clean shaven. He was wearing a white T-shirt and jeans which covered what appeared to be a gym-toned body. He had the most unusual eyes, large but not quite round, which reminded me of images of statues from Mesopotamia that I had seen in books about the ancient civilisations of Assyria and Babylonia. I had never seen features on any living person before.

I replied in Dari that I spoke very little of his language. He then replied, to my relief, in broken English that he did speak English a bit.

"*Salaam Walaikum. Man Sattar hastam,*" the last of the three arrivals greeted me, telling me that his name was Sattar. I was amazed at Sattar's hands when he grabbed mine in his. They were large, like paddles, like no hands I had ever seen before. He had large feet to match which seemed so disproportionate with the rest of his body. Sattar had shoulder length, wavy brown hair with streaks of grey which betrayed his age. He was fairly well-built with a bit of a belly which protruded from his red T-shirt which proudly displayed "Australia" across his chest.

Sattar concluded his introduction with "no English". I realised, then, if I was going to communicate with Sattar, I would have to use my very limited Dari. This seemed a very awkward situation to be in.

Once the formalities were over, the four men began exchanging words in Dari that I could not understand and then began preparing the living room for lunch. A place mat which looked simply like a large plastic tablecloth was placed on the floor and then the food placed in the centre of the plastic sheet.

Having lived with people of almost all the nationalities of the world in one city, I thought I had seen all the food that was imaginable. But here I was introduced to yet another form of exotic cuisine. On one large metal dish was rice. I have always known rice to be pure white but this mountain of rice was a mixture of white and brown with sultanas mixed in with it. On another dish was what appeared to be rissoles swimming in a light pool of gravy. In a plastic container was something that looked like Chinese dumplings but covered with lentils and yoghurt over the top, a preparation of food which I later discovered was called *munto*.

To accompany the food were two types of bread: Lebanese bread, which I was familiar with, and Afghani bread, which was much thicker. In fact, when the Afghani bread was removed from the plastic packet, it looked like large strips of human skin.

Faisal motioned me to sit down on the floor while the food was placed in the centre of the tablecloth and portions of bread distributed among those there to eat. Everyone then sat down around the tablecloth on the floor with crossed legs. Sattar grabbed behind him a plastic bag and pulled out two long-neck bottles of Victoria Bitter beer. Sattar passed me one of the bottles.

"*Shoma beer mikhorid?*" he asked.

I was very nervous and did not understand what he said. Sattar noticed immediately and then rephrased the question in English.

"You…drink…beer?" he asked in slow English.

"Yes, thanks," I replied. Zaker disappeared into the kitchen and came back with five glasses. As he offered beer to everyone there, I began to laugh within myself when I thought of the image of these people before I arrived and what I was observing around me. Here we were, five men, sitting on the floor, having lunch together. We were sitting on the floor eating food, something I had never done before in someone's home. But apart from that, we could have been five mates from the local rugby club having a meal and drinking a beer to occupy a Saturday afternoon.

I watched the way the others ate before I tried. Each took a piece of bread and then, with the bread, grabbed at the food, the rice, the rissoles or the munto. The idea of rice *and* bread being used for a meal was particularly peculiar for me because we had either one *or* the other, not both.

The taste of the rice was okay. It tasted rather oily and I later discovered, when Faisal showed me how he made it, that both oil and sugar were used in the cooking which gives the rice its brown appearance. I found this much too oily, especially for our warm climate, but could understand that rice made this way was quite suitable for the ice-capped regions of Afghanistan from whence this method of preparing rice came.

The rissoles, which they call *gofta*, tasted just like rissoles in gravy and I was happy that there was some food there that resembled something I had eaten before.

The munto, however, was what I thought was the most delicious of all the food there. It had an unusual taste that I cannot compare with any other food that I have ever eaten. However, it looked just like Chinese dumplings but coated with a generous layer of yoghurt and black lentils and a helpful sprinkle of a green herb which I later discovered was mint. I was aware that the Chinese have a type of food called *mantou* which looks similar to what we were eating and so I guessed that munto was simply brought to Afghanistan from China in the very distant past and then readapted to suit the Afghani palate.

But most of all, the Afghani bread was absolutely beautiful. It was soft and melted in the mouth like freshly baked scones. I was quite happy to eat the Afghani bread on its own.

I was still too nervous to communicate and just allowed the private conversation the four Afghanis held between themselves in Dari to develop. There were occasional smiles in my direction at least to acknowledge my presence. We were on two sides of a cultural barrier, feeling nervous about the other side. Suddenly, Zaker addressed me.

"Do you like the food?" he asked. Zaker spoke with near to perfect English but it was heavily accented, an accent I had never heard before.

"Yes, it's not bad. I particularly like the munto. And the Afghani bread. It's beautiful."

"If you were in Afghanistan," Faisal threw in, "the bread there is better. This is nothing."

If this was nothing, I thought, this nothing was absolutely delicious. I couldn't imagine it being better.

"Are you Australian?" Zaker then asked, changing the subject and making the first attempt to get to know me.

"Yes."

"Where were you born?"

"I was born here in Sydney. I've pretty much lived all my life in Sydney, although I have travelled and lived overseas for a bit."

"Oh, that's good, that's good," Zaker said, and after dragging out the last 'good' I could tell he wasn't sure what else to ask me. I suppose, like me, he really didn't know what was okay to ask and what was taboo. So, I decided to open him up a bit.

"So, you're from Afghanistan, no doubt," I said. "Where in Afghanistan are you from?"

"From Kabul."

I didn't know whether to ask this next question but decided to ask and see what resulted.

"How did you come to Australia?" I asked.

"By boat, like everyone else!" he said and laughed. But his laugh wasn't out of embarrassment nor did it betray a feeling of a social stigma. His laughter expressed quite a neutral tone, as if it were obvious that most Afghanis in Australia were, after all, boat people originally. I began to realise that this was no secret. The Afghanis came here by boat. Mohammed, the first Afghani I ever met, was open about it, Faisal was open about it and now Zaker was open about it. Obviously, the Afghanis did not feel stigmatised about their situation and seemed quite happy to speak about it freely.

"Where did you meet Faisal?" I then asked.

"Here in Auburn. I live on the other side of Auburn station. There are many Afghanis here in Auburn."

At this moment, Faisal began speaking with Sattar. But when he spoke, there were certain sounds that he made that sounded peculiar. My Dari was still limited to a few words and set phrases but for some reason, I had the impression that Faisal was speaking yet another language because the sound of the language between Faisal and Sattar sounded very different. Sattar then spoke to Faisal and Faisal laughed. Faisal laughed! It was the first time ever that I had seen and heard this morose figure laugh!

"What did Sattar say?" I asked Zaker.

"I don't know. I don't speak Pashto."

What? Aren't all these people Pashtun? Pashtuns were the hated tribe in Afghanistan, the leaders of the Taliban, the tribe that was the source of all the troubles in Afghanistan that forced Afghanis of other tribes to flee to Australia. I had assumed, obviously wrongly, that all Faisal's friends were Pashtun.

"Aren't you Pashtun?" I then asked Zaker.

"No, I'm Tajik. Both me and Parviz are Tajik."

Hang on, I thought. Mohammed had insisted that it was the Pashtuns and the Pashtuns alone who were the source of all the evils in Afghanistan. Pashtuns were against all the other tribes in Afghanistan. But here these people were, two Tajiks and one Pashtun, sitting down and having a meal together. So, that left Sattar. What tribe did he belong to?

"Sattar's father is Pashtun and his mother is Uzbek. That's why Sattar speaks Pashto," Zaker replied.

This was suddenly getting all confusing. If the Pashtuns hated all the other tribes and the Pashtuns were the source of all the evils in Afghanistan, how could a Pashtun and an Uzbek agree to marry? I was familiar enough with central Asian custom, where it wasn't simply a choice between two people to marry. There had to be an agreement between the parents-in-law and the extended families from both sides before such a union could be accepted.

Putting this into a more familiar context, in my grandparents' generation, it was unthinkable for a Catholic and a Protestant to marry because these were two sides of a warring faction. So if a Catholic and Protestant fell in love, they would most probably not have married despite how much they loved each other. Such a union would have created so much pressure on the couple from the rest of the family that the marriage would not have survived. However, today most people in Australian don't really care. Was this the case with the Afghani tribes, that former tribal barriers were now passable?

If, then, Tajiks, Uzbeks and Pashtuns could sit in a little flat in Auburn and eat, drink and have a laugh together, was it possible that they did this in Afghanistan? Was it possible that Mohammed was wrong? Was it, therefore, possible that Mohammed had distorted the story?

There was a lot of nervousness on both my side and theirs, and I could feel it by the way they avoided talking to me. They all talked to Faisal with occasional glances at me. I felt rather uncomfortable myself but just watched this strange conversation continue. But every now and again, Faisal would move his hands in my direction with an almost frustrated look on his face. Eventually I realised that Faisal was insisting on them to talk to me.

It took some time for the ice to finally melt. After we had eaten and everything cleared away, more beer was brought out and everyone sat around either on the floor or on the mattresses. I could hear Faisal's insistence again to make them talk to me and soon Zaker came over and sat next to me.

Although a rather stilted beginning, the day moved on quite well. Zaker opened up a bit and began telling me about his work and his life in Australia. He explained that he was happy to be in

Australia but still held a temporary protection visa which I would forever hear referred to as the acronym, TPV. He also told me of his family waiting for him in Afghanistan, of his wife falling pregnant just before he set out on his epic journey and how he found out in the detention centre that he had become a father for the fourth time.

Once Zaker had blazed the trail, Parviz wanted to join in with the conversation. Parviz worked as a taxi-driver. His story as to how he came to Australia was no different to Faisal's or Zaker's. He also had a family waiting for him in Afghanistan and he was still waiting for a decision by the government before he could finally see his family again.

Now that the ice had melted, Sattar wanted a piece of my attention as well. But Sattar could say only a few words. I made an attempt in my limited Dari to try to communicate with him but it was totally futile. He eventually became frustrated and distanced himself from me.

But the afternoon progressed very well. It was relaxing for everyone. Faisal had allowed everyone to speak to me and get to know me. After these formalities were over, Faisal himself came and sat by me and chatted. He first taught me a few new words of Dari and began to show me how to write the letters of the alphabet while in the background the other Afghanis chatted and laughed in the language I was trying to become familiar with.

Faisal then asked me questions about my life in Australia. But it was really strange. There were times when he would hold my hands or grab my leg while we were in conversation. If he was in love with me, he appeared to make it no secret in front of his friends! I was extremely nervous about this entire situation. What did his friends think of us?

The afternoon dragged on into the evening. At one time, these guys began playing a card game that Faisal told me was called *Char Wali* which loosely translates as *Four Knights*. I tried to follow the game. It was something like a mixture of Rummy and Poker but I couldn't quite follow the rules.

Evening came and we ate dinner. We then talked some more. At one time, a DVD was put on to play an Indian movie. This movie was not really put on to watch but as background entertainment while they talked more. At times, the guys came over and entertained me with small talk and then later in the evening, Faisal and I chatted once again alone.

At about 10 o'clock that evening, Zaker and Parviz decided to leave. Only Sattar, Faisal and I were left. I told Faisal that I felt a bit tired and wanted to leave as well.

"Do you really have to go? But you can sleep here if you like," he said almost imploringly.

"Where would I sleep?" I asked.

"In my room," he replied, as if it were assumed.

Faisal seemed like a nice guy but this was just too much. If he wanted me, which he seemed to be indicating, I wasn't prepared to take up the offer. I began to feel extremely uncomfortable. What really were Faisal's feelings for me? If he were in love with me and wanted to spend the night together with me, I didn't share these feelings for him. There was no physical attraction, at least for me. Had I been, however, leading him on as Khatyn had suggested?

This was the right time to leave and so I did. Sattar wished me goodnight and Faisal accompanied me to my car. Faisal thanked me profusely for the visit. But before I got into my car, Faisal grabbed me and hugged me tightly.

"I'm glad I met you. God brought me to you," he whispered in my ear.

My emotions were really stirring up inside me. I enjoyed the physical display of affection from him but I didn't want it to go any further than that. But it appeared that Faisal did. At least by leaving at this point in the evening, it prevented any awkward situation from developing.

I got in my car and drove off, waving to him as I left. But once inside my flat, my emotions swirled around inside me like a whirlpool. I knew there was an attraction for him but it was not physical. Sure, by my nature, I easily fell in love with men. But I had always assumed that my attraction for a man had to have a physical element accompanied by any other attachments. But I was not physically attracted to Faisal. However, I could still feel that I did have some strong feelings for him. What were they? How could I love a man and not want to spend the night together with him?

But most fundamentally, who was this man? And who were these people? What was all this about the Afghanis really about? Prior to this time, with all my reading and my contact with those who came from other countries, I thought I had a good overall grasp of what the world was all about. But these people from Central Asia illustrated to me that there was a gap, an empty space, in my understanding of the world.

Chapter 6

The first of June marks the beginning of the Australian winter. Although really only an arbitrary demarcation between autumn and winter, winter seemed to arrive as punctually this year as a diligent student to class.

An icy wind blew across the Sydney basin and was accompanied by grey clouds which hung oppressively from the sky, threatening the area with rain. Outside the trees were almost completely bare and lifeless as if nature had entered a state of hibernation, except for the native Australian plants, such as the mighty eucalyptus tree, which, despite all odds, hung on to its leaves with a tenacity of its own. People walked the streets completely covered, grasping the collar of their coats against their necks to hold in as much body heat as possible against the blast of the cold.

Each person has their own appreciation of the seasons. Winter is the season I like the least. I hate the feeling of being cold. I hate the short daylight hours. To me, winter is the most depressing time of year and I am glad that in Sydney we only have to endure three months of this morbid season. The description of hell as a hot and fiery place would only be more of an encouragement for me to sin if I were a believer, and this description of hell was obviously furnished by someone who hated the hottest season of the year.

Because Sydney has such a short winter season, central heating is not a common feature, at least not in the outer suburbs, but more of a luxury in blocks of flats. So, for me to keep warm, I had a large oil heater which efficiently heated the entire flat although it did take some time to do so. I did not have an electric blanket for no other reason than that I didn't like them. So, getting into bed was a real trauma. Dressed in an old sloppy-joe, cotton tracksuit pants and woollen socks, I would brave the crispy, icy sheets and wrap myself in the blankets until my body heat had successfully warmed my fabric cocoon.

Fortunately I enjoyed my job because it at least gave me an incentive to get out of bed in the morning, despite the temptation to press the snooze button several times. Despite the cold, I would jump in the shower, get changed and then zoom off to work. I still enjoyed my job. However, now that Faisal was no longer in my class, the students I had at that time were just students, people to whom I held an obligation to improve their English. There was nothing special about them.

After that first Saturday I had spent with Faisal at his place, I couldn't get this strange man off my mind. I wanted to see him again. I could not understand what it was that attracted me to him. I was attracted to Faisal but at the same time was afraid of these feelings because I did not understand Faisal's feelings for me.

The week passed and I made no attempt to communicate with Faisal at all. I just felt too uncomfortable about the situation. But sure enough, when Friday arrived, I received an sms on my mobile phone. It was a laconic message in typical abbreviated English which is now common with mobile phone communication: Where r u? U cum 2moro?

It took me ages to reply. The emotions that Faisal engendered within me both positive and negative made me balk at replying. Yes, I wanted to see him, but no, I did not want to form any more than a good friendship with him. He seemed to be a nice guy but I didn't want anything more than that. But I couldn't keep him waiting forever and so I replied that I would come in the afternoon.

The following day was a dismal, wet winter's day. The sky was grey and let down from the clouds a pitiful, indecisive drizzle as if the weather felt an obligation to drop water to the earth but, in its reluctance to do so, settled on a compromise. Everywhere was wet, the roads, the pathways, the trees, the windows, everything held a depressive dampness about it.

I came to Faisal's place wrapped in a thick Macintosh which protected me from both the wet and the cold. When I entered Faisal's house, I did not want to remove my shoes because I knew as soon as I took my shoes off, the coldness of the place would eagerly wrap itself around my feet. But it was Faisal's home and his custom, and I knew I had to honour what happened in his house. I made a mental note that the next time I came, I would wear thicker socks.

Faisal greeted me with the usual Dari-cum-Arabic greeting which was this time accompanied by a solid, manly bear hug. I responded hesitantly but politely in order not to offend him.

Faisal brought me into the loungeroom where I had sat the week before and offered me a place on one of the mattresses.

"Are you comfortable there? Would you prefer a chair?" he asked.

I replied in the negative. I know that it is normal in the Australian culture to sit on chairs in someone's home. However, I quite enjoyed the concept of sitting, or probably more precisely, reclining on the mattress. This was one of the things I really enjoyed about Faisal's place and the entire Central Asian custom, the excuse to lounge around on the floor. There was something more relaxing about laying around at floor level that was less restrictive than sitting erect and rigid on a chair.

"Tea?" was Faisal's next question which I found out to be one of the traditional questions he would ask me on any of my visits, as customary as the welcome and formulaic expressions that make an Afghani greeting. I replied in the affirmative and soon Faisal returned with the ornate silver tray and the assorted nibblies that went with it.

"Are you cold?" Faisal asked as he observed me holding the collar of my Macintosh.

"Yes, very!" I replied. "I hate winter and can't wait for spring."

"Would you like a heater?" he asked.

I nodded in the affirmative. Faisal disappeared into one of the rooms and returned with a little air heater that was no bigger than a shoe box. He plugged it into the wall and soon it was gently humming away. I felt rather sorry for Faisal that this was all he had to keep him warm during the winter months.

I began to ask myself whether or not the bare interior of Faisal's house was due to a lack of the general luxuries that Australians take so much for granted in their cluttered homes or simply a reflection of the custom of his homeland.

Faisal walked around barefoot. Just the sight of this made my feet feel cold as stone. I asked him if he could cope with this. Faisal just laughed.

"Winter here is not that cold," he replied. "In Afghanistan, it snows in winter. I like the cold and miss the snow. I don't feel the cold so much here in Sydney."

I am aware that "cold" and "hot" are, after all, very relative terms. As far as I am concerned, when the temperature drops below 20°C, to me, this is cold. In some climates of the world, people live quite happily in temperatures that dive below zero degrees.

"What about summer? Is it hot in Afghanistan? It must be the beginning of summer now," I asked.

"No, not like Sydney. It's very hot here. In Afghanistan, or where I lived in Kabul, it's quite cool, like the weather in spring here."

"And is that where your family is now?" I asked.

"No," Faisal replied in a way that indicated that I should have known that. "They're in Peshawar, in Pakistan."

Yes, I had forgotten. Faisal had told me that before. But I knew I had forgotten because I still could not equate the Afghani problem with Pakistan.

"And how are your family? When was the last time you spoke to them?"

"My family are fine. I spoke to them last night on the phone."

"You have six children, is that right?" I asked, more as confirmation than as gaining new information.

"Yes, four girls and two boys. My youngest, Ziba, was born when I was in the Woomera detention centre. I have never seen her. But I speak to her often on the phone. She is now three years old."

My heart sank when I heard that. What a tragedy all this was, to leave your family under such terrible circumstances and not even have the opportunity to witness the birth and growing up of your own child. Despite the fact that I have no paternal instincts, I could easily empathise with Faisal.

"Have you seen a photo of my family?" Faisal asked.

I replied in the negative. Faisal disappeared into his bedroom and returned with a collection of photographs. He began with the first one which was a photo of his six children, two older daughters, followed by two sons, followed by two younger daughters. They all stood dressed in traditional Afghani apparel but were as cute as children in any nation can be.

Faisal then explained each child to me from the eldest to the youngest. When he reached the youngest, I could see a glint form in his eye as if he were about to shed a tear. It appeared that he tried not to let his emotions show too much. The spectacle caused a knot to form in my stomach.

"This is Ziba. Ziba means *beautiful* in Dari. I named her Ziba because of a little girl called Ziba that I met in the detention centre. She was such a pretty girl and I remember asking her name. When she told me her name, I thought it was the most beautiful name I had ever heard. So, when my last daughter was born, I decided to call her Ziba, too."

The detention centre. We had heard so much about detention centres on the news. It was the first time I had met someone who had been an occupant of these infamous places.

"You were in the Woomera Detention Centre, weren't you," I asked hesitantly.

"Yes," Faisal replied without any hint of hesitation.

"Can I ask you about the detention centre?" I asked cautiously. Again, I didn't know what questions were better left unasked but at the same time I was filled with curiosity. How often do we meet those who have had to spend time in detention centres and know what it is all about? But Faisal just replied without showing any signs of discomfort.

"You know, I said you can ask me any question you want. I have no secrets."

"Well, tell me about the detention centre. What was it like?" I asked.

Faisal smiled and leaned back.

"It was like a prison."

When he said that, I reflected on the story he had told me that began with his fleeing Pakistan to his arrival in Australia. He had fled Pakistan to save his life and arrived in Australia only to be looked on as a criminal. And his crime was simply that he sought refuge in Australia to save his life and the life of his family. I wondered what Faisal thought of Australia as a country when viewing things in this light. Australia is a humanitarian country and yet, when refugees arrive here, we simply plop them in a prison, which we euphemistically call a *Detention Centre*, before we decide whether we owe them protection or not. We seemed to have regressed back to the convict era of the late seventeen and early eighteen hundreds, back to the time when those who arrived in this country were placed under similar conditions.

However, at the same time, I could also understand this from an alternative perspective. We didn't know who these people really were. It had taken about two hundred years to finally create the stable and free society which makes it so pleasant to live here, and we didn't want people to come and upset this peaceful society.

"A prison?" I asked, returning back to the topic of conversation. "What was it like?"

Faisal pulled out a packet of cigarettes and offered me one before taking one himself. He then lit mine before lighting his, took a puff, let out a cloud of smoke and then began.

The Woomera detention centre, so he explained, was a large complex, surrounded by large wire fences that made an escape almost impossible. This image of the detention centre I was aware of because I had seen the detention centre at Woomera, at least on the outside, when it was shown on the news on TV.

The Woomera detention centre was divided into five sections and each section had its own names: November, India, Mike, Main and Oscar.

On arrival to the Woomera detention centre, the refugees were carted off into the section called *November*. I tried to imagine what drove a person to call a section of a detention centre in this manner. If someone arrived in the 11th month of the year at the Woomera detention centre, they would be in *November* in November which has a rather quaint poetic ring to it.

Faisal described *November* as being a large building of about 100 metres by 60 metres and housed up to 400 detainees at a time. It was a new building when he arrived and he guessed it was a new addition to take in the sudden influx of refugees that were arriving at this time. It was a large area with bunks and I imagined, according to Faisal's description, that it was like a large scout hall or army barracks.

Faisal was then interviewed at the end of a month's stay, the interview taking only about an hour. During the interview, he was asked many questions as to why he had come to Australia and it was an opportunity for him to finally tell the Australian authorities his plight.

After the interview, Faisal explained that he did not return to *November* but was then sent to another section called *India*. This made a lot of sense, and Faisal confirmed this, because there was no contact with the other inhabitants of *November* to tell them what was said. So there was no conferring or advice about what the Australian authorities were willing to hear as a plausible reason for the sudden arrival in Australia.

Faisal explained to me that *India* was a much smaller section which took about 300 to 400 people. *India* was made up of a series of cabins which held a maximum of 15 people per cabin, each cabin containing a series of bunks. Faisal explained that he stayed in *India* for only 10 days at the end of which he was provided with a lawyer so he could make a case in order to apply for a protection visa.

After his interview with the lawyer, Faisal was then sent to another section of the Woomera detention centre called *Mike*. *Mike* was a little bigger than *November* but like *November* was an open hall with bunk beds to provide sleeping quarters for the inhabitants.

Faisal waited a month in *Mike* before he had his final interview. During this time, the Afghani detainees had a lot of free time to discuss with each other what they planned to say at the final interview. Rumour had it that anyone who claimed Pashtun ethnicity would almost automatically be rejected. Those, therefore, who were Pashtun were advised to deny their Pashtun background in any way they could.

But Faisal refused to do so. Faisal was insistent on telling the truth of his story. Surely, he thought, the Australian authorities would accept his story because Australians believed in justice and truth.

In his final interview, Faisal was asked many questions. When the interviewer asked about his nationality and background, Faisal confessed right at the beginning that he was one hundred percent Pashtun. With that, the interviewer's entire composure changed from one of friendliness to an indifference bordering on hostility.

The interviewer asked question after question and Faisal answered each question confidently and truthfully. Not only did he answer the questions directly, he told the interviewer that, for many of the details that he presented, it was possible to obtain documentary evidence to back up his claims. The most convincing point was the article in *The Nation* newspaper.

Faisal told me that at one stage, in the middle of the interview, the interviewer asked him, quite out of context of his line of questions, if Faisal were a terrorist. Faisal told me that he laughed at the question and answered in the negative. The interviewer then continued his questioning.

At one stage during the interview, Faisal himself asked the question why Pashtuns were rejected. The interviewer explained that Pashtuns as well as any other Afghani tribe were equally accepted or rejected based on their cases. Faisal replied that it was rumoured that the Pashtuns were not favourably looked upon and that he was advised to deny his Pashtun background before coming to this interview, although he refused to do so. Faisal explained that the interviewer then changed his composure and was in deep thought before he finally replied.

"I know the situation in Afghanistan," the interviewer said. "I realise that things are much more complicated than what the average Australian realises. But you have to understand that the first wave of Afghani refugees were Hazarahs and they claimed that all the problems in Afghanistan, the Taliban, the war, everything, was a result of the Pashtuns. This story has been gobbled up as untainted truth because no-one knew any better. Now it is difficult for Pashtuns to be recognised as refugees here."

When Faisal told me this, I was horrified. But at the same time, I knew I was just as guilty. Didn't I hate Faisal in the beginning simply because of his Pashtun background? And what was my reasoning? Because Mohammed, the first Afghani I had ever met, told me that the Pashtuns were the problem. I had no reason to question Mohammed because I knew nothing of Afghanistan myself. And I also had accepted his story without question because I had trusted Mohammed was telling me the truth. To be fair to Mohammed, he may have been telling the truth based on what he knew, probably because all the Pashtuns he had ever met were members of the Taliban or at least Taliban sympathisers.

It is so strange of human nature that we accept the first thing anyone tells us about a person or a situation before making any further enquiries, and this forms the basis of whatever further judgements we make on the issue. I know that if I had not been forced to see Faisal three days a week at AELC, I would have dismissed him as a Taliban sympathiser simply based on his Pashtun background and would have continued to perpetuate this belief without making any further research on the matter.

Faisal then went on to explain to me that, at the end of the interview, he was free to return to the barracks. But before he left, Faisal had one question to ask. Why had the interviewer asked if he were a terrorist? The interviewer thought for a moment and then replied. "I asked you that to see your reaction. It was fifty percent a joke but also fifty percent serious."

"But why had he asked you that question? Was that a standard question?" I asked puzzled.

Faisal laughed. "I don't know. I don't know what it was that made him ask me that."

Again, a sense of guilt overwhelmed me. I had built up an entire image of Faisal the Terrorist and I had much more time to prove this incorrect. It appeared that this interviewer had also originally taken on this perspective of the man but fortunately was able to discern the truth of the matter within a simple interview. It had taken me months to finally change my opinion.

This was something I just could not tell Faisal at this time (although later I finally told him and we still joke about it). How could I tell him that I had also, for many months, contemplated the idea that I had among my students a Taliban supporter and a potential terrorist? And I wondered what led the interviewer to this conclusion in the interview. I was sure that his mere physical appearance and his clinical composure projected to the interviewer the same false message that I received of him. But the interviewer must have also been a remarkable man and the right person for the job to have been able to discern in this one interview what Faisal's real situation was.

Faisal had told me of five sections of the detention centre but had only explained four. There was one last one, the section called *Oscar*. Faisal explained that *Oscar* was used as a punishment cell for those detainees who acted out of line. Sometimes the detention centre detainees got out of hand and acted violently towards other detainees and so were sent to *Oscar* for a cooling off period.

By this stage, my cup was empty and Faisal offered me more tea. The heater had done an excellent job heating the room and I felt it was now warm enough to remove my Macintosh.

I made myself comfortable again and then proceeded with my questions.

"Just as an aside," I asked, taking a different tact in the conversation, "what were the conditions like?"

Faisal smiled and looked at me a bit mystified.

"Sorry? I don't understand," he said.

I rephrased my question. "I mean, what was the food like, for example?"

Faisal smiled again. "Oh, it wasn't bad. For breakfast we had Cornflakes, or Weetbix, or whatever, butter, eggs, cheese. Breakfast was really good. Lunch and dinner weren't good. Sometimes we ate things that we didn't know what we were eating. We would look at each other and then lift the food with our fork or poke at it with our fingers to try to find out what it was. So, sometimes we wouldn't eat it."

I had to laugh at the way he said this, the expression on his face and the tone of voice. I asked him to describe the food but he couldn't. I can only surmise that he probably had mashed potato or broccoli or even baked beans. After my first meal with Faisal, I realised that our food, which we take so much for granted and as being so normal, was just as foreign to him as gofta and munto were to me. If the situation in our respective countries were reversed and I had fled Australia for Afghanistan, I can imagine being in an Afghani detention centre, trying to imagine what this strange Afghani food tasted like and whether it was worth eating or not.

Faisal explained that life in the detention centre was rather boring. He passed the time playing cards or chess, playing volleyball, eating and sleeping.

"One thing I couldn't wait to do when I left the detention centre was buy my own lighter," Faisal added and pulled out his lighter to emphasise the comment. "In the detention centre, we weren't allowed to have lighters."

I didn't need Faisal to explain why. After all, although a lighter is a convenient contraption for lighting cigarettes, it was easily converted into a dangerous weapon where the entire detention centre could be set alight.

Faisal explained to me that he was allowed to smoke. However, if he wanted his cigarette lit, he had to ask one of the ACM men who would avail him of a lighter. But this was not always easy to acquire. Someone made the ingenious discovery that, if they broke one of the fluorescent lights and exposed the filament, all the smokers would have an alternative means of lighting their cigarettes.

"Who were the ACM men?" I interjected.

"ACM. This was the company who looked after us in the detention centre."

"What does ACM stand for?" I asked inquisitively.

"I don't know. It was just written on their shirts."

I found out later from another Afghani that the ACM men were contracted to carry out the job of looking after the refugees in the detention centres.

Faisal then told me a story of how one of his fellow detainees managed somehow to fall into the possession of a lighter. This was then used by everyone to light their cigarettes. Faisal explained that they had a special rule, that no-one could light a cigarette with the lighter if someone else was smoking because they could easily light their cigarette with the smouldering embers of someone else's cigarette. This helped to preserve the duration of the lighter.

However, eventually, the gas in this lighter was used up and another one was needed to replace it.

But how were they to gain the possession of another lighter without being detected? Faisal explained to me that all the smokers were on the look-out whenever they saw an ACM man to determine the shape and colour of the lighter these men possessed. As soon as someone spotted an ACM man with the same type of lighter as the empty one in their possession, they would then find a means to make an exchange between empty and full lighters.

Faisal explained that, after a meal, before leaving the eating hall, there was an ACM man who stood at the door with a lighter and on this particular day one of them had a lighter of the exact same shape and colour. An ingenious plan was set up. Two smokers stopped on their way out and asked to have their cigarettes lit. During the cigarette-lighting formality, the lighters were exchanged, Faisal and his fellow detainees obtained a new lighter and the ACM man was none the wiser.

Faisal explained to me that during his time in the detention centre, new friendships developed. All these refugees were held here under the same plight, not knowing what the future held for each other as well as for themselves.

But Tuesdays and Thursdays were days filled with anxiety. On the morning of these days, the loud speaker would bellow out the applicants who were successful in receiving their TPVs. In the afternoon of these same days, those who were rejected were called out over the loudspeaker and then they would then have to make the choice whether to stay indefinitely in the detention centre or sign the paper that said they wanted to be sent back to their country of origin.

"How long were you in *Mike* before you received your TPV?" I asked.

"About two months. This is a day I will never forget."

I sat back and waited for him to continue. Again, I could see his eyes begin to water as he adjusted himself on the floor to put himself in a better position.

"I remember waking up on that morning. It was about 7.30. The ACM man knocked on my door. I shared a room with Salim. Salim is another Afghani friend who lives on the other side of Auburn. Anyway, the ACM man came in and asked if Salim was in this room. I replied yes and pointed to Salim. The ACM man then told him that he was granted his TPV, said 'congratulations' and told him to get prepared to go. Salim was shocked and didn't know what to do. I told him to go and have a shower and a shave and say good-bye to his friends and I would pack his things together.

While I was packing his things together, another ACM man came. This was about half an hour later. When he came in the room, he said my number and my name and I replied that that was me. This ACM man then said to me the same thing, 'congratulations' and whatever. I was told to gather my things together and then go to the gate that leads out of the detention centre."

There was a slight pause and Faisal then took a deep breath.

"This was so hard. You have two feelings. You are happy because you are finally leaving the detention centre but at the same time you have to say good-bye to your friends. I remember saying good-bye to Sattar."

"You knew Sattar in the detention centre?"

"Yes, that's where we met. I asked him if he wanted me to contact his family and say everything was all right and if he needed anything. I showered and shaved, packed all my things, and then me and Salim went to the exit gate. I remember going through the exit gate and into freedom. It was a great feeling to leave the detention centre. But even though it was a great time for me, I also felt sad. I remember looking back into the detention centre and could see Sattar far away, watching me through the bars as I left. It was the second time that I cried. I just couldn't stop crying."

I could feel my throat constrict and the water welling up in my eyes. All this was a terribly emotional story. While Faisal related to me the story, I felt as if I had been whisked back to this moment and was viewing everything through his eyes as if I were watching a documentary. But while I was becoming all emotional, Faisal's eyes sparkled and his whole countenance changed to cheekiness.

"Do you want to know what's the funniest thing?" he asked.

"What?" I replied, not knowing what the joke was.

"Do you know when I left the detention centre?"

"No," I replied, not understanding the import of his question.

"It was a very significant day. It's an important day for everyone in the world."

An important day for everyone? Maybe for him and now maybe for me. But how could it be an important day for everyone in the world? I just looked at him perplexed and then he laughed as he said it.

"It was the 11th September, 2001! See? That's proof that I'm not a terrorist!"

With that, the door burst open and Sattar came in. He was carrying a load of plastic bags filled with vegetables and food so I guessed he had just come back from the shops. He kicked off his shoes at the door and as he walked into the loungeroom, he beamed a smile and said a long, drawn out Sa-laaaaam walaikuuuuuuuum, put the bags on the floor and gave me a big bear hug. He then began garbling on in Dari, the gist of which was to welcome me and to ask how I was. I replied in the simple Dari I knew that I was fine.

Sattar then greeted Faisal with the commonplace greeting ritual that I had now become familiar with. Sattar and Faisal exchanged a few words, none of which I understood but from the sound of the language, I could tell they were speaking Pashto.

Sattar disappeared with his load into the kitchen and then returned to the loungeroom with a cup and sat on the floor cross-legged. Faisal poured him some tea while Sattar reached into his coat pocket and then pulled out a letter which he then gave to Faisal.

Faisal opened the contents of the envelope and I recognised it to be a Jobsearch Centrelink form.

"Is that yours or Sattar's?" I asked.

"It's Sattar's. But I have to fill it in."

"Why?" I asked.

"Because Sattar doesn't speak English. He can hardly speak a word of it. And he doesn't even try to learn it. He's just a lazy, couch potato."

Faisal said this last sentence with a bit of annoyance. But I was amazed that he knew the expression "couch potato".

"Where did you learn that expression, 'couch potato'" I asked curiously.

"At AELC. One of the teachers taught us this."

I was amazed how well Faisal picked up words as if his brain were a linguistic sponge.

Faisal then placed Sattar's Jobsearch Centrelink form on the floor, pulled out a pen and began ticking the appropriate boxes. When he arrived at the section which asks the names of companies where the applicant had been looking for work during the fortnightly period, Sattar pulled out of his pocket a collection of business cards. But I wondered how in the world Sattar would ever be able to get a job if he could not speak English.

When Faisal had completed the form, he passed it to Sattar to sign. Sattar gave an imploring look at Faisal with sad, puppy dog eyes. But Faisal muttered something in Pashto in an overtly angry tone as if a stern father were telling a lazy son to do his homework. Sattar took the pen and the form, and then scratched something in the section which demanded his signature.

Faisal turned to me and said, "Sattar doesn't know how to read or write."

"I guessed that," I replied. "If he can't speak English, I doubt that he could write in it."

"No," Faisal corrected me, "he can't even read or write in Pashto or Dari."

Sattar couldn't read or write at all? We were living in the twenty-first century, in the age of mobile phones, computers, Internet, with knowledge available through the written word at the push of a button, and Sattar could not read or write even in his own language.

The spoken language is in itself a fascination for me but the written word is an amazing invention which has been passed down to us for at least the past six thousand years that provides us with a window outside our space-time dimension. It is through the written word that I know what is happening outside of Auburn, or Sydney, or even Australia – I just have to read the newspaper. It is through the written word that I have access to the wonders of the past, of Ancient Egypt, the Roman Empire, the Chinese dynasties or the lost civilisations of the Americas. It is through the written word that I am aware of the universe outside the lonely planet we live in, reading about new discoveries in the heavens through magazines and books. It is through the written word that I can discover the philosophy of Socrates, the belief of the Indians or the Theory of Relativity. Without the written word, I would have a vague, shadowy view of the universe, past and present, in as much the same way as a blind man cannot appreciate a magnificent scenery or the infiniteness of the starry night sky. Sattar was totally illiterate which meant that his understanding of life and time was limited through his senses and his memory.

I felt sorry for Sattar but Faisal did not share my sympathy. There was a hint of annoyance at Sattar's illiteracy and I guessed that it came from the fact that Faisal had to act as interpreter and do everything for Sattar so that Sattar could operate within Australian society.

Once again we heard the door open. Zaker and Parviz entered, followed close behind by yet another Afghani called Karim. Karim was a very tall, thin, handsome young man who looked like he was in his late teens. Faisal, Sattar and I stood up to greet the three visitors. Karim was the first to begin the ritual, initially greeting Sattar and then he turned to me. Karim looked at me and hesitated for a few seconds. Before he had a chance to say anything, I began greeting him in the Afghani fashion. I did this to see if Karim could still determine whether I was Afghani or not. Karim responded accordingly and then continued on to greet Faisal.

The formulaic greetings were followed with an animated conversation and laughs of surprise and joy. I watched for a moment as Faisal and Sattar both hugged Karim once again. Something important had happened and I was curious to know what the cause of all the excitement was. I waited until everyone had sat down before whispering in Faisal's ear to explain the source of the joy.

"Karim just got his PV!" Faisal replied quite loudly.

Karim looked over at me.

"Aren't you Afghani?" he asked in almost perfect English.

"No, I'm Australian."

"Michael is my teacher," Faisal added.

"I *was* your teacher. Now I'm your friend," I corrected him.

Karim got up off the floor and moved over to sit next to me.

"I didn't think you were Afghani because you don't look Afghani. But because you spoke Dari when I came in, I thought I was wrong! Wow! I'm impressed! How do you know how to speak Dari, then?" Karim asked.

"Faisal is teaching me. Faisal is *my* teacher, now."

"That's very good," he replied and then he began to engage in dialogue with me, asking if I were born in Australia, where I lived and so on.

Karim didn't stay long. After our conversation together, he invited everyone to his place for a party to celebrate his acquisition of permanency in Australia the following Saturday night.

Had I not met Afghanis, I would never have known what it was like to belong to a community where one of the major achievements in life was obtaining this treasured possession: a permanent visa. This later became a constant theme in conversation, who had been granted their permanent visa, when they received it, how they had received it, what they had said in the interview that convinced the authorities that they were bona fide refugees and so on.

Although I would get to know many Afghanis within the Afghani community in Sydney, there was only one person whose permanent visa was important to me and that was Faisal's. Because of this, I was about to enter into the most trying experience of waiting and finding out just how difficult and complex it is to obtain this valued prize.

Chapter 7

We human beings are strange creatures who, for most of the time, are quite happy to follow a life of regular routine. But then, from time to time, we must burst out of this blandness to do something entirely out of the ordinary. In order to do this, we choose various days of the year as a moment to stop work and completely change our behaviour, the things we eat and the clothes we wear, before returning quite happily to our regular routine lives.

Some celebrations are national. For example, in Australia, we begin the year with the New Year celebrations, then we celebrate Australia Day on the 26th January, followed by Valentine's Day on the 14th February, followed by Easter, although this bounces around March and April in accordance with the position of the moon. Then we celebrate ANZAC day on the 25th April, Mother's Day in May, as if our mothers suddenly become important on this day when during all the other 364 days she seems to fade from existence. We celebrate the Queen's Birthday strangely enough on the second Monday of June when her real birthday is on 21st April, not to mention that Western Australia, Queensland and New Zealand celebrate the Queen's Birthday on another date. Then we celebrate Father's Day, when suddenly we remember after all that we have a father and can forget this fact for the rest of the year. Then we celebrate Labour Day in October, which ironically means that we have a day off from work to celebrate work! We then celebrate Melbourne Cup day on the first Tuesday of November, although only the Melbournians are lucky enough to get the entire day off while the rest of Australia simply pauses to listen to this horse race of a couple of minutes in the afternoon before resuming work. Finally we celebrate Christmas, irrespective of whether or not we believe in Jesus, only to begin the entire cycle all over again.

We also celebrate milestones in life's journey. We celebrate the birth of a child, and then each subsequent birthday, with a special emphasis on our 18th or 21st birthday, 30th birthday, 40th birthday, 50th birthday and any birthday that ends in zero up until the time we step into our grave and those we leave behind greave together at the wake, which is, in a way, a celebration with a sad focus.

We also celebrate special occasions such as marriage and anniversaries. We have house warming parties to celebrate the move into a new residence and if we have studied at university, we have a graduation party.

On a cultural level, celebrations can tell us a lot about the importance that different cultures place on certain events and, on a personal level, it tells us the significance that certain events have on the individual. I remember reading once in the Bible about the parable of the woman with ten drachmas. After losing one, she searched her house thoroughly until she finally found the missing money and, being of such significance to her, she decided to celebrate.

Celebrations, overall, are a way to share with those around us that we have achieved something of significance or reached a certain goal and hence we want to share the happiness of our success with those around us.

It is not surprising, then, that a new moment of celebration was born in the twenty-first century for refugees - obtaining the long sought after permanent visa.

Karim invited me to attend his permanent visa acquisition party and once again I wasn't sure what to wear or what to expect. I suspected that it would be an all-out Afghani affair and I would most probably be the only non-Afghani attending. Because of this, I decided to go to Faisal's place first and then accompany him to the party.

Karim lived in Park Road, a major road in the south of Auburn. He lived on the top floor of a set of apartments and, before Faisal and I had entered the building, we could hear where the party was being held. This only heightened my anxiety because I realised I was about to enter a room filled with people from a completely different culture who spoke a completely different language.

Different people have different reactions to crowds of unknown people. I know one person who can enter a room full of people he has never met before and feel quite comfortable, moving among the gathering with ease and meeting everyone before the evening is over. By contrast, I am immediately filled with anxiety when I enter a room full of unknown people, even if they are of my own culture. The very idea, then, of going to this party with people from a completely different culture filled me with an overwhelming fear and I decided to stay close to Faisal.

Faisal and I climbed up the stairs that led to Karim's apartment and we could hear the noise echoing throughout the stairwell. I wondered how the neighbours were taking all of this! When we arrived at the door, Faisal knocked so gently and I was sure that no-one would hear with all this background noise. But sure enough, the door opened, and we were greeted by a tall, quite well-built, very hirsute, and to me, a very good-looking Afghani. I was completely struck by his very handsome features. His skin was tanned and healthy looking, he had a beard that was neatly trimmed and had pale blue eyes.

This man introduced himself as Jamal, and I realised by the way Faisal introduced himself and me that this was the first time that Faisal himself had met him. He gave Faisal a big hug with the usual Afghani greeting. Jamal then took one look at me and, much to my disappointment, instead of hugging me, he extended his hand for the conventional Australian handshake.

"How are you?" Jamal asked me in perfect but slightly accented English. "Please, come in and sit down."

Faisal and I walked through the door, kicked off our shoes and then walked into what I suppose was the living room. There before us was a crowd of men, some sitting on lounges, some sitting on the floor. There seemed to be nowhere left for Faisal and me to sit. Karim was sitting over on the other side of the room and when he saw us, he came over and gave both of us a warm welcome. He then brought us over to one of the lounges and asked the occupants to prepare some space so that Faisal and I could sit down.

I was terrified! I felt as if everyone was looking at me as if I were an alien from another planet. It was all very disturbing. This room was filled with only middle-aged men. I don't know what troubled me the most, the fact that I was in a room filled with people from a completely different culture or the fact that it was a men-only gathering. Despite the fact that I am gay, any party I ever go to within my social context has a healthy mixture of both sexes and of all ages.

Karim asked if we wanted a drink. I asked what he had to offer.

"We have pepsi, beer, wine or scotch. I suppose because you're Australian you will want a beer!" Karim replied.

"I'd prefer a wine, if that's okay," I replied. Faisal mentioned that he wanted a scotch and pepsi.

I was quite stunned that alcoholic beverages were offered. This was a room full of Muslims who were supposed to abstain from alcoholic beverages and yet it appeared that everyone was drinking.

It was a strange mixture of men. Some were wearing western clothes, such as jeans and shirts, while others were wearing the traditional Afghani garb. But what was the strangest of all was that there were some men lying on other men or men with their arms around another man, something that I had only ever seen in gay bars.

Karim disappeared and soon after, another small, South East Asian-looking Afghani came over with the required drinks. His name was Ahmed. Ahmed had a small, spindly sort of physique with overly hairy arms, features which combined made him look like a chimpanzee. When he introduced himself, his smile revealed a mouth full of teeth which gave me the impression that he had a piano stuck in his throat with the keyboard projecting below his upper lip.

Ahmed greeted Faisal in Dari and then greeted me in English. I was beginning to realise that most Afghanis could tell in an instant just from my physical appearance that I did not come from their part of the world.

Karim returned and sat on the floor next to me. He placed his arm right over my leg quite casually in a rather personal way that only another gay man would do in my culture. I was amazed that he felt quite welcome to invade my personal space so casually when we hardly knew each other.

"So, Mr Michael. Welcome to my home. Please make yourself comfortable," Karim said. I thought to myself that Karim had already made the first step!

Karim then asked about my week at work. It was very difficult to hear what he was saying with all the background noise that I had to place my ear right down to his mouth to hear him.

After exchanging a few pleasantries, Karim signalled Jamal to come over so he could introduce us.

"This is Jamal," Karim said.

"Yeah, I know. We met him at the door," I replied.

"Are you comfortable?" Jamal asked.

"Yes, yes, quite," I replied but inside I was feeling tense and was just happy that Faisal was seated next to me for protection.

"Mr Michael is Faisal's teacher," Karim explained to Jamal.

"Oh, right," Jamal replied in such a tone which indicated to me that he finally figured out why an Australian had come to the party.

"I live with Jamal and that guy over there, Ahmed," Karim added, pointing to Ahmed.

"Would you like a drink?" Jamal asked.

I picked up my glass from the floor which was hiding behind my leg to indicate that I had already been served.

"Are you hungry?" Jamal then asked.

"A little," I replied.

"We're gonna eat soon, anyway. Do you like Afghani food?"

"It's different," I replied in the usual non-committal Anglo-Celtic way.

Jamal intrigued me. I found him a very handsome, well-presented middle-aged man. He had beautiful unblemished skin although with some signs of crow's feet around his eyes which betrayed his age but which did not take away from his overall handsome features. He was slightly balding and had a carefully trimmed beard. He was wearing an elegant shirt with what looked like a good pair of jeans as if he was fully aware of good western style. But, despite his accent, I could tell he spoke a good level of English, and not only good, grammatical English, but his statement, "we're gonna" for "we're going to" illustrated his familiarity with English colloquialism.

"So, how long have you been here in Australia?" I asked Jamal.

"Two years, now," he replied.

"Two years? You speak very good English for someone who has been here for two years."

"Thank you," Jamal replied and blushed. "I learnt some English in Afghanistan before I came here."

"That explains it, then," I replied. "Where in Afghanistan are you from?"

"From Kabul," he replied.

From Kabul. Every time I asked an Afghani where in Afghanistan they came from, they always said they came from Kabul. The population of Kabul must have suddenly decreased drastically when the Taliban came if this was the case. I imagined, then, the Taliban arriving in Kabul and finding it completely deserted with a note on the window of an abandoned shop saying, "Gone to Australia". It seemed that Afghani refugees only came from this city and this city only. I was sure that Afghanistan was much bigger than that.

"Are you Pashtun?" I asked Jamal.

"No, I'm Karzel-bash," he replied.

"You're what?" I asked with surprise.

"I'm Karzel-bash. It's another tribe. It's only a small tribe in Afghanistan. My tribe comes from Mazar-i-Sharif in the north of Afghanistan."

"But you just said you come from Kabul," I replied a little perplexed.

"Yes, I was born in Kabul. But my parents were born in Mazar-i-Sharif but moved to Kabul," Jamal explained.

Yet a new tribe and a new town to add to my understanding of this part of the world. I was about to ask another question but then Jamal excused himself and left.

Karim then resumed a conversation with me. I asked him what his plans were now that he had his permanent visa. He explained that he was going back to Pakistan to see his wife and two children, and then start the process of sponsoring them so they could live together reunited once more. I was quite surprised when Karim said he had a wife and children because he looked like he was still a teenager. However, he later told me he was 28. I told him that he should continue taking the pills that gave him his eternal youthfulness but he didn't understand what I meant and I told him not to bother about it.

While engaged in conversation, I noticed Ahmed sitting on the other side of Faisal with his hand on Faisal's leg in full conversation in Dari. This struck me as very odd. Ahmed was obviously Hazarah, and here were a Pashtun and a Hazarah together in friendly conversation. How could this be? Mohammed had told me that the Pashtuns were hated by the Hazarahs because of the formers' supposed involvement in the Taliban. And yet, here were two men on what was supposed to be two sides of an impassable barrier, having a drink and casual conversation together.

Very soon after this, Karim excused himself and stood up. By the sudden movement of the crowd, I could tell that dinner was about to be served. A number of the Afghanis cleared a spot on the floor and spread newspapers in almost every conceivable space. The food, which I then realised was being cooked outside on the balcony, was brought in and placed in various places to be in easy reach. Packets of Afghani bread were then brought out, opened, and the large, flesh-like bread broken into smaller pieces and distributed around in much the same way I imagined Jesus breaking and distributing bread during the Last Supper.

The food served on this occasion looked like long stretches of minced meat cooked on metal skewers. Each person took one skewer and, holding the skewer in the left hand, took some bread with their right hand and broke off a portion of the minced meat. I have to admit that I found this unusual way of cooking minced meat quite a convenient way to eat and was also very tasty. Around the floor on the newspapers were also bowls of what looked like a conventional Australian salad, a mixture of slices of tomato, cucumber and lettuce.

There was a lot of conversation going on and what sounded like Indian or Arabic music playing in the background. Although Karim, Jamal and Ahmed had made me feel welcome, I noticed other men on the opposite side of the room staring at me as if I should not be there. This made me feel very uncomfortable indeed.

At the same time, when I scanned the room, I could also tell by their facial features that there was a mixture of Afghanis from every tribe, Hazarah, Pashtun or otherwise, all packed in together quite comfortably in this little living room in Auburn. This was not making much sense at all, unless what I had originally been told was not true.

I found the idea of using newspaper spread out over the floor quite a convenient way to serve as a tablecloth. Once everyone had finished eating, the bowls of salad and the remaining skewers were collected from the floor and then the newspaper gathered up and placed in the bin. For such a large group of people, there was little washing up to do afterwards!

After this clean up, Faisal and I resumed our positions on the couch. The drinking continued, but the more they drank, the more boisterous everyone became. The whole atmosphere was becoming too rowdy like any drunken party.

Suddenly Faisal placed his hand on my leg to catch my attention.

"Are you comfortable?" he asked.

"I'm okay," I lied.

"Do you want to stay longer?"

I could tell by the way Faisal asked this question that he himself was not comfortable and wanted to leave. This was a welcoming invitation and, just to be assured of my assumption, I asked him back, "Why, are you ready to leave?"

I could tell by a flicker in his eyes that Faisal wanted to say yes, but at the same time, he did not want to spoil it if I were quite comfortable to stay. So, to completely confirm my suspicions, I added, "If you're ready to go, then let's go."

Faisal did not need any more encouragement. He stood up and then walked over to Karim to say good-bye. Karim walked back with Faisal over to me.

"You're leaving?" Karim asked. "Just stay for another drink."

"Thanks, Karim, but I'm a bit tired. I've had a long week. I had a great time and I enjoyed meeting your friends."

"Are you sure?" Karim insisted.

Faisal then said something in Dari and Karim appeared to be content.

"Okay. Thank you for coming," Karim then said to me and this time he gave me a good, solid hug. I replied with a handshake and a pat on the shoulder to congratulate him once again for obtaining his permanent visa.

While Karim was saying farewell to Faisal, Ahmed came over.

"You leaving?"

"Yes, I've gotta go," I replied a little frustratingly, wishing that I could leave without having to give a reason. Faisal, once again, came to the rescue and said something in Dari which appeased Ahmed.

"You come any time, you hear?" Ahmed said in his not-so-grammatical English. "You welcome every time."

Faisal and I were making our way to the door when I heard a deep voice call behind us, "Are you leaving?"

I turned to see big Jamal towering over us with half an imploring, half disappointed look on his face. But I could also tell that he was quite drunk. His light blue eyes, which had earlier looked like polished sapphires, were clearly blood shot and seemed to be drooping below his forehead as if his cheek bones were no longer supporting them.

"Yes, Jamal, we have to go," I replied rather nervously.

"No, you can't go now," Jamal cried in a tone that sounded like a spoilt child who wants to get his own way.

Faisal then muttered something in his soft voice once again in Dari. The effect that Faisal had on these people each time he spoke to them in Dari was as if he were saying "Abracadabra", because each time he said something, people's reactions changed. However, the effect on Jamal was not as smooth as it was with Karim and Ahmed. Jamal slumped his arms by his side with a frustrated humph.

"No, please, stay. If you go now, it's the first and last time you ever come to this flat, you hear me?" he said rather exasperatingly.

Jamal's insistence was annoying and it caused me to hesitate. But Faisal went to the door and began putting on his shoes. I followed obediently.

"It's the first and last time you ever come to this flat, you hear me?" Jamal repeated.

Faisal and I left before giving Jamal any further opportunity to prevent us from going.

Once we got in the car, Faisal invited me back to his place and I obliged. I wasn't in a rush to go anywhere, only to get out of this crowd of people that, by the unfamiliarity, made me feel uncomfortable.

We arrived at Faisal's place and Faisal offered me tea. He appeared rather shifty and nervous, as if something were bothering him. When he returned with the tray of tea and nibblies, he sat on the floor opposite me. He asked if I wanted sugar and then remained rather quiet. After a slight pause, Faisal then asked, "Did you enjoy yourself tonight?"

I didn't know what to say at first. I was going to use the typical Anglo-Celtic diplomatic avoidance strategy of not saying what I felt by using some typical, ambiguous expression to hide my real feelings. However, I just felt that I could be honest with Faisal and so I told him frankly what I thought of the evening. I explained that I felt welcome but that it was too much for someone outside the culture to appreciate when I didn't really know anyone well at all. I explained that it wasn't the fault of the people there, it was simply my reaction to such unfamiliar surroundings that made me feel uncomfortable.

Faisal looked at his tea and then at me with his old, clinical expression that I remember from when I first met him. Faisal then went quiet and contemplated once again his cup of tea. I knew there was something bothering him that he did not want to talk about. With a sudden gesture, he stood up and excused himself.

"Just wait here a moment," he said and walked out the door.

I was left alone in the flat. Although Faisal seemed rather disturbed about something, I simply assumed that Faisal had left something in his car or needed to buy cigarettes or something as benign as this which explained his sudden need to go out.

I waited for a few minutes but Faisal did not return. The time moved on, five minutes, then 10 minutes, then 15 minutes, then 20 minutes. I began to get restless. Where did he go? What was he doing? Did he go outside and suddenly get attacked and killed? 30 minutes went by, then 40 minutes. Where had Faisal gone?

The alcohol and the tea finally had their effect on me and so I needed to dispense with some liquid from the body. I walked down the hall to the toilet. While there, I heard the front door of Faisal's flat open and the sound of a grown man crying. What was going on?

I quickly put everything back in its right place, left the toilet and walked up the hall. When I reached the loungeroom, there was Faisal standing stone faced with his hands behind his back, leaning against the wall and Jamal sitting on the floor, sobbing like a disciplined child.

It was both a tragic and amusing sight to behold. There was Faisal, this thin, frail stick-figure of a man standing boldly while this Jamal, a young, well-built Hercules sat penitently on the floor, tears streaming down his cheeks, over his beard and onto the floor.

I looked at Faisal and then at Jamal, not quite sure of what was going on until Faisal, like a stern father, said quietly a few syllables in this language I did not quite understand. Jamal looked at the floor, his body convulsing, spluttering out in sobs. He then looked up at me with wet, red eyes.

"I'm really sorry, Mr Michael, for what I said. I didn't mean what I said. You are welcome at any time at my flat."

It was both a pathetic and amusing sight! I had to bite the insides of my mouth to prevent myself from smiling. Jamal then repeated the same thing again and again. With that, I knelt down on the floor in front of him, took his hands in mine with a gesture to show that his apology was accepted, even though I knew it was totally unnecessary. Jamal then brought my hands to his lips and kissed them. I looked up at Faisal but the expression on Faisal's face had not changed. I then turned back to look at Jamal.

Jamal, this Herculean being, then lunged forward and wrapped his arms around my waist with such force that I thought I was going to topple over backwards. Jamal sobbed into my chest and I could feel the warm tears moistening my shirt. I stroked his back and his head, repeating that everything was okay.

Eventually, Jamal pulled himself together and sat back. I took a handkerchief from my pocket and wiped his eyes. They had become so red that I wasn't sure if it was from the alcohol or the crying. Jamal then got up. Faisal and Jamal exchanged a few words in Dari and they both then went outside.

Faisal returned alone. He was still grim-faced. I tried very hard to resist the temptation to laugh despite the seriousness of the situation. Eventually Faisal spoke.

"In our culture, no-one is allowed to speak like that to a teacher," Faisal said quietly.

"Faisal, I am not your teacher anymore," I replied. "I'm now your friend. And, in any case, what Jamal said didn't bother me. I realised he was drunk and he didn't mean what he said. It was just his way of saying that he wanted me to stay."

"I walked into that flat," Faisal continued, totally ignoring what I had just said, "and spoke very angrily with him, with Karim and Ahmed. I even swore at them. I don't usually swear but this was serious. I took my wallet out and told them I would pay for the meal if that's how they will treat their guests. I spoke angrily to Jamal and made him walk here to apologise."

He made Jamal walk here! That explained, then, the long absence. Karim's flat was a fair distance from Faisal's place. I tried to picture Faisal forcing Jamal out of the flat to come here. What did he say to Jamal? I was impressed by Faisal's command over

Jamal. I was sure that if Faisal and Jamal got into a fight, just by his bulk, Jamal was sure to win. Jamal just had to wrap his arms around Faisal and crush him to death. But Faisal had a commanding influence over Jamal that was spellbinding, so influential that Faisal had Jamal in tears.

I stayed with Faisal for a few hours after that. Faisal softened down and relaxed and we were able to pass the rest of the evening quite casually as if nothing had happened. At one stage, I apologised to Faisal for wanting to leave earlier and re-explained that I simply felt uncomfortable in this large gathering because I didn't know anyone well. I explained that in general I didn't like crowds.

Faisal smiled. "No, I don't like lots of people, too. I was happy to go because of Karim. And I went because of you. You wanted to go."

"Oh, Faisal," I replied. "I only went because of you. I don't know Karim. Personally, I prefer when there are only a few people. But I am glad you wanted to leave early yourself."

Faisal then offered me some more tea. While he poured, I thought of yet another question I wanted to ask him. I reflected about it and then asked.

"Faisal, how well do you know Ahmed?"

"I've known him for about a year. Why?"

"Is Ahmed Hazarah?"

"Yes, of course."

"And could you say he's your friend?"

"Yes," Faisal replied.

"And were there other Hazarahs at this party?"

"Yes. There were some Hazarahs. Why?" Faisal replied with a tone of suspicion.

"Nothing. I was just curious," I replied. I didn't mention anything about it after that. But I kept it in mind. Faisal was Pashtun and Ahmed was Hazarah, and they quite happily socialised with each other in Auburn. I thought to myself that if I ever saw Mohammed again, I would give him a piece of my mind.

Chapter 8

As Khatyn walked into the staff room the following Monday morning, she smiled at me and asked how I was.

"Good, thanks. How was your weekend?" I replied.

"Okay. Like every weekend. The usual cleaning, washing, looking after the kids. Did you do anything interesting on the weekend?"

"Yeah, I went to an Afghani party," I replied.

"An Afghani party? What was it like?" Khatyn asked and placed her bag on one of the desks and began taking books and folders out in preparation for her class.

"It was interesting to say the least."

Khatyn looked at me waiting for more information and then asked, "Did you go with that Afghani student of yours? What was his name again?"

"Faisal. Yes, I went with him. But it wasn't his party. It was the party of another Afghani who got his permanent visa."

Khatyn wanted to know all the details. So, I told her all about it, excluding the grand finale between Faisal and Jamal.

"You're really brave, Michael," Khatyn said with a smile. "I really admire your courage."

"They're not dangerous people, Khatyn."

Khatyn laughed. "I don't mean that! I mean that you went out of your way to be with people from a completely different culture. Not many Australians would do that, especially with Afghanis."

"They are, after all, just people like you and me," I replied a little bit angrily.

"Michael, don't get so defensive," Khatyn said with a sing-song in her voice to indicate to me that I did not understand what she meant. "You know what I mean. Everyone's scared of these refugees so everyone keeps away from them because of the way they are presented to us in the media. Like you, I know these people are people like everyone else. I have Afghanis in my classes, too, you know."

I realised that I was still sensitive and protective of Faisal and therefore of the Afghani refugees in general because of the atmosphere of suspicion that had been built up around them which contrasted with what I was beginning to learn about them.

"And how are you and Faisal," Khatyn continued with a hint of an innuendo in her tone of voice.

"Faisal and I are friends, nothing more than that."

"That guy loves you! I bet he'd do anything for you. I bet that he'd wrestle a bear if one were about to attack you!"

When Khatyn said this, I couldn't help smiling when I thought of the previous Saturday evening. If only Khatyn knew of what had transpired between Faisal and Jamal! But for some reason it was a story I thought too embarrassing to relate to her, especially after this last comment of hers.

But at the same time, her comment about Faisal's feelings towards me did not affect me as much as comments like these had in the past. Faisal's behaviour towards me had begun to lose its original intensity. And in any case, after seeing how Afghani men interacted with each other at Karim's permanent visa party, I was beginning to realise that Faisal's interaction with me needed to be interpreted within an Afghani cultural context. I had come to realise, and it would later be confirmed, that it was true that Faisal loved me, but it was a love that carried no sexual connotation. Faisal's love for me was extremely deep, a love between two men that is never expressed within the Australian culture but which comes freely and openly between men in Afghanistan.

Khatyn and I then began discussing this morning's class and we exchanged a few teaching ideas. While chatting, more teachers arrived and Khatyn ended the conversation abruptly.

"Just a minute, Michael, I have to do some photocopying before everyone else gets to the photocopier."

All my preparation was completed. All I had to do was walk into the room and start teaching. I was just savouring a cup of coffee, waiting for 9 o'clock so I could go to class.

Khatyn came back with her arms filled with reams of paper.

"Oh, Michael. I forgot to ask you. Do you need a heater or a lounge?"

"Why?"

"My neighbour wants to get rid of a heater and a lounge, if you're interested."

I thought about it for a moment.

"No, I don't need one. But maybe Faisal does. I'll ask him the next time I see him."

"You'd have to arrange for someone to pick it up. My neighbour doesn't have a truck."

"I'm sure we can organise something if need be."

"Oh, well. Just let us know," Khatyn concluded. She then looked at the clock on the wall. "Oh, look at the time! It's time to go. Enjoy your class. See you at the break."

With that, Khatyn scurried off. I collected my things and made my way to my classroom. But going to class was no longer the same. I still enjoyed teaching but Faisal's absence had taken some of the sweetness out the job. I couldn't believe I thought that! I could still remember when everything was very different.

At the break, I decided to ring Faisal and ask him if he needed the pieces of furniture Khatyn had mentioned to which he replied in the affirmative. He said it was better to wait till the weekend when both of us were free to go and collect everything.

Following this phone conversation, I told Khatyn that Faisal would take the furniture and we would organise to pick everything up on the weekend. Khatyn then decided to make a day of it and have the Afghanis stay for lunch.

"I suppose they won't mind," I replied. "But do remember that they are Muslims and so you can't serve them pork and they only eat halal meat."

Khatyn laughed. "Michael, you know I'm vegetarian so I'll cook vegetarian food for them. I'm sure that there will be no problems then."

I had quite forgotten. And when I thought about it, I realised the universal appeal of vegetarian food. In Australia, with our society so mixed, with different people having different dietary laws, it is always difficult to know exactly what type of meals to prepare when people visit. Knowing how to cook vegetarian meals is an ideal way of catering for such a mixed society.

When I got to Faisal's place the following Saturday, Sattar, Zaker and Parviz were also there. Zaker had borrowed a van from someone else in the Afghani community. Everyone wanted to come along to Khatyn's place. Poor Khatyn! I wondered how she was going to react to all these men landing on her doorstep to simply move one couch and one oil heater!

Khatyn was very welcoming and invited everyone in for lunch. I could tell that everyone except Faisal seemed rather uncomfortable in her presence and I wasn't sure if it was simply because Khatyn was of a different culture or because she was a woman.

Kylie and Brendan had gone to Katoomba to stay with Khatyn's mother for the weekend because it was snowing in the Blue Mountains and the children wanted to enjoy it while it lasted. It was a bit of a shame, really, because I wanted the two to meet these Afghanis for themselves and find out that they were just people like everyone else.

Khatyn was a wonderful hostess. She showed no signs of timidity or apprehension when the Afghanis came into her home. I was impressed how relaxed she was entertaining these foreigners in the same way she would welcome any other Australians. And I was impressed how well the Afghanis adapted to the new surroundings. Unlike in their culture, the Afghanis were seated at a table on chairs and they used forks to eat. But to me it looked no different to a gathering of Australians having a meal together of a Saturday afternoon. Further, no-one suspected that the food that Khatyn served up had absolutely no meat in it.

To top off lunch, Khatyn treated us to scones, jam and cream. They were nice, soft and fluffy. The guys just loved them! Sattar, in particular, couldn't help himself and gobbled down quite a few with cream stuck around his mouth like a contented five year old!

After such a hearty meal, I just wanted to go and lie down and have a nap but we were here to pick up furniture. The original story was simply a couch and an oil heater but in her eagerness to rid herself of unwanted furniture, the neighbour threw in a writing desk, a coffee table, a chest of drawers and a few other bits and pieces. Because we only had a small van, this meant that we needed to make a couple of trips back and forth between Faisal's and Khatyn's place.

I had never been in Faisal's bedroom before and so collecting all this new furniture which was destined for his room was an opportunity for me to discover what lay inside. The interior of his living room was bare enough but when I entered his bedroom, I was appalled by the lack of furniture. For a bed, Faisal simply had a mattress on the floor with a couple of blankets thrown over it. In another corner of a room was a tall cardboard carton where he kept his clothes. And that was it. Sattar's room was no different. It pleased me no end, then, when I was able to provide Faisal with a few extra pieces of creature comforts.

By the time we had finished moving back and forth, it began to get dark. We got back to Khatyn's place to pick up the last bit of furniture. Once everything was in the van, Faisal thanked Khatyn profusely.

"Would you like to come over for the evening?" Faisal asked.

Khatyn looked at me.

"Why not?" I asked. "I have to drive past your place to get home anyway so I can drop you off on the way home. Then you don't have to spend the evening on your own. You can also see that the furniture has been put to good use."

Khatyn hesitated a moment and then replied.

"Why not indeed! The kids are away and I don't have any plans. Just a minute, let me just get my coat. It's freezing cold out there."

Khatyn was made exceptionally welcome in this otherwise male-dominated environment. I was also amazed at how well Khatyn adapted to this situation without showing any signs of discomfort in the presence of people she did not know well and, moreso, because she was the only woman amongst this household full of men. She talked quite at length with Zaker even making him laugh. She spoke a bit with Parviz as well. Sattar, whose English left a lot to be desired, struggled to communicate in the few words that he knew. I snickered to myself, thinking that he would probably be enrolling in the next class at AELC!

Khatyn was a great guest. I remember when I first came to Faisal's place and saw only mattresses around the floor, the first thought that passed through my mind was, "my goodness, poor Faisal. He's so poor, he can't afford furniture." However, Khatyn took one look at the room and with a big smile said, "How cool! Is this where we're going to sit? On the mattresses?" and then sat down, bouncing up and down on the mattress to make herself comfortable.

As the evening progressed, more people began arriving. Three men, Saber, Qadus and Akram, walked through the door. Sattar welcomed them and then brought them into the living room. Everyone stood up to greet them and we were formally introduced.

Saber was a relatively young looking guy, a strapping big man with an unusually big head and body. His hairy arms and hairy chest growing up through the V in his shirt gave the impression that he was a grizzly bear. But he was a lively character who spoke broken English but with confident ease as if he didn't care if he didn't speak grammatically correct as long as he got his message across. Qadus was a much older looking man, rather plump, clean shaven, with rather fair skin that, if I hadn't known he was Afghani, I would have passed him off as an average Australian. Akram looked about the same age as Saber and reminded me very much of an uncle of mine.

When these three men came into the living room and saw Khatyn and me, they all became rather shy and timid as if we were two police officers. Saber and Qadus introduced themselves but the third, Akram, took one look at me, then at Khatyn, and then said rather abruptly, "Oh, is this your wife?"

I laughed. "No, she's just a friend of mine."

Akram held his grim composure and then said, "What's she doing here, then? She's a woman. Women don't socialise together with men. In our culture, women and men are separate. Women do their own thing and men do their own thing."

I was horrified by both Akram's rudeness and abruptness. I felt embarrassed and I felt embarrassed for Khatyn. This must have made Khatyn feel very unwelcome. There was a moment of silence. Faisal then came over to Akram with a look on his face so terrifying that I thought he was going to knock Akram out.

"We are in Australia, and in Australian culture, women and men socialise together," Faisal said sternly. "If this is the way you will greet my guests, you leave."

Akram looked at Faisal with a harsh expression on his face and there was a long moment of silence. Faisal then pointed to the door.

"Leave. You are not welcome here tonight."

Akram stared at Faisal for what seemed an eternity and I felt that Akram was resisting an impulse to punch. Faisal then said some Abracadabra in Dari and then, like a dog with its tail behind its legs, Akram turned around and left. Saber followed but then soon returned alone.

Faisal extended his arm towards the mattresses.

"Please, be comfortable."

Once seated, Faisal sat down next to Khatyn.

"I'm really sorry about Akram. I am very ashamed. Please accept my apologies for his rudeness."

I was amazed how Faisal had so much control over the entire situation. He dealt with Akram and put both Khatyn and me at ease after this rude intrusion.

And so, in the end, we had a pleasant evening. As the evening progressed, I discovered that none of the Afghanis actually liked Akram at all!

Khatyn, in her easy-going manner, was the star of the evening because of her ability to make these guys feel at ease despite the difference in culture and gender. I guessed, and Faisal confirmed this later, that this was the first time that these Afghani men had ever socialised with a woman in their presence.

As Khatyn and I were leaving, everyone insisted that she should once again come back and spend an evening with them. Whether or not they meant it, I'll never know. But I knew when Faisal said it, it was said in all sincerity.

That it was possible for men and women to socialise together quite freely must have been a real culture shock for these Afghanis. As they began to mix with the general Australian society, these Afghanis were slowly learning an entirely new way of communal living that in some ways came in abject contrast to what they were used to.

But there was still yet another cultural difference that these Afghanis were totally unaware of, which they would eventually have to come to terms with. If not the entire Afghani community, then at least it was something that I felt that Faisal, as my friend, had to know. I knew that, sooner or later, he would have to be confronted with a reality that defined a part of who I really was, something that Faisal may well not appreciate or accept. However, I could not go on forever hiding this part of me. One day I would have to tell him. I approached this day with great trepidation because this was something I knew that could completely break our friendship.

Chapter 9

Being in constant contact with people who have fled atrocities in their own countries and found refuge in Australia has made me realise all the more just how lucky I am to have been born here in the first place. But I have to say that I am forever grateful for having been born in Australia in this moment of eternity because of my freedom to live openly gay. There are many people in Australia today who are totally opposed to this sexual phenomenon but at least Australians in general have now come to accept that this is an integral part of the make-up of Australian society and, more generally, of humanity. An Australian may not like the fact that someone they know is gay but it no longer comes as a shock to discover that such people exist and form an acceptable part of our general society.

Because of the general acceptance of this sexual phenomenon, we are no longer burdened down with ridiculous constraints placed on us by belief systems which condemn such sexual expression when the belief systems themselves are internally inconsistent. That is to say, our sexual freedom has unshackled us from the absurd belief in a capricious Supreme Being who created us with a strong sexual urge for the same sex but who then condemns us for giving in to it.

As a result of our sexual freedom, despite whether we are gay or straight, we are under no compulsion to marry and it is not unusual to find many Australians living celibate lives. However, to an Afghani, this is completely strange. In Afghani society, men and women must be married by a certain age. This, mind you, is not unique to Afghanis but is a commonly held belief in many cultures. It was also a part of Australian culture during my parents' day. The freedom we have today in Australia to remain unmarried is quite a new phenomenon. So, it did not strike me too oddly when Faisal finally broached the subject.

While Faisal was still my student, I remember a time he spoke tenderly of his family and then asked about mine. When I told him I was not married, his reaction was very strong. Family, so he stressed, was the most important thing in life after the belief in God. It perplexed him that I did not have a wife and children trailing behind me.

His reasoning, however, was not purely religious. Marriage and family in Afghanistan are a matter of survival. Family, and by extension, clan and tribe, not only give the Afghanis their sense of identity, family also provides a blanket of security in times of crisis. Sons, so Faisal explained, are still much more preferable to daughters, not because daughters are unloved, but because sons are stronger and are the protectors of the family. The more sons a family has, the greater the protection for the family. This explains the importance of bearing progeny within Afghani culture and, in particular, male progeny.

Children are also of importance as security in old age. There is no such thing as superannuation or old age pension in Afghanistan, and so, the chances of single men or women being looked after in their old age are rather slim. Therefore, Afghanis don't have children simply out of the mere desire to see their genetic material replicated and passed on. Afghanis need children in order to have security and protection in the latter days of their lives.

Being a member of a family is also of great importance in Afghanistan for economic reasons. Faisal explained that, unlike in Australia, in Afghanistan it is difficult for everyone to get work. There are situations in which only one man in an entire extended family holds down a job and works not only for his own wife and children but for his brothers and their wives and children as well.

Marriage, therefore, is not simply a concept where a man and woman fall in love and decide that they want to spend their lives together, marriage is only a small piece of a larger overall communal network. Marriage is simply a means of strengthening the tribal fabric. This means that when a man and a woman marry, love between the two spouses is not a requirement but an optional extra, a bonus. Because marriage is the uniting of families and clans, it is important that not only do the couple get along together but that the families get on together as well. Thus marriage is more about tribal unification than it is about love, and therefore marriages are almost exclusively arranged by the parents.

Australian culture, by contrast, is so very different. It is the government, or the State, that provides for everything and thus makes the concept of family totally unnecessary. Family ties in Australia have simply been reduced to a tradition. In fact, family, in Australian culture, is almost optional. After all, there is a direct symbiotic relationship between the individual and the State. Australian citizens pay taxes to the State and in return, if Australians need protection, the State offers it, if Australians are unemployed, the State looks after them and, for some Australian retirees, the State also provides for them. In addition, the State provides for the economic situation which allows people to acquire enough wealth to sustain themselves in their old age so that it is accumulated wealth, and not offspring, which provides people in the last years of their lives the support and protection they need.

Such a society, therefore, allows for the liberty that we experience in Australia. If I lived in Afghanistan, I would have to go through the motions of getting married and siring children in order to complete my duty as a part of a collective and to ensure security in my old age, despite the fact that I find the idea of having sex with a woman totally repugnant. My individual desires and feelings would have to be put aside for the sake of family.

Further, in Australia, sex is not a duty but is available to each person fairly. It is, therefore, not only heterosexual men and women who have the luxury of enjoying sex, homosexual men and women are at liberty to enjoy it as well.

It was very admirable of Faisal never again to mention my marital status while I was his teacher. After our first discussion of marriage, Faisal never broached the subject. That was, however, until he met Khatyn.

I could almost taste how he was going to react when he observed my interaction with Khatyn. Khatyn and I get on very well. No doubt in Faisal's mind, this should easily have blended into a married relationship. After all, I am a man and Khatyn is a woman, and according to Faisal's world view, nature should have followed its predictable course. Nature had definitely taken its course, the problem was that Faisal was totally oblivious of nature's alternatives.

Telling a straight man that one is gay is probably one of the hardest things for a homosexual man to do – or should I simply personalise it and say it is one of the hardest things for me to do. I have had terrible experiences in the past telling heterosexual men that I'm gay. Some heterosexual men react so badly to this information and immediately terminate the friendship, believing that the only reason why I wanted the friendship in the first place was because I wanted to play smoochy-coochy with them naked in bed. Some heterosexual men just cannot come to terms with the idea that I can be friends with a heterosexual man with no ulterior motive apart from the simple desire to maintain a friendship because of the qualities in that person I admire.

Then there are other heterosexual men who take the entire situation well within their stride as if all I have told them was something mundane as my preference for coffee over tea.

Naturally, I can discuss this issue here because sexuality is openly discussed within Australian society. Australians, in general, are quite frank and blunt about sexual issues.

But Faisal came from a culture where sex was so concealed that even women were wrapped up to prevent men from having unnecessary erections. I was of the impression that sex was such a taboo topic that men did not even discuss it amongst themselves in an attempt to pretend or hope that sexual desires did not exist, or at least, although an integral part of our humanity, was a subject too ugly to talk about.

But I knew that one day I would have to tell Faisal the truth. I could not go on forever pretending I was something that I was not. Eventually he was going to find out. I also wanted him to hear about it from me, it would be much better coming from me than from someone else.

I was too frightened to tell Faisal. I now considered Faisal as a close friend and I did not want our friendship to end. But at the same time, I held to strong principles about friendship and one of them was honesty. I was now at an impasse. For me, there is no friendship without honesty and so, even though I hated the thought, I knew I would eventually have to tell him. But how, when and where?

Nature, or coincidence, or providence, or whatever it was that resulted in the following conversation that I had with Faisal provided an opening for me to discuss this issue. We were still in the depths of winter and fortunately this time I had made sure to wear snow socks to Faisal's place so that my feet didn't freeze from the biting cold. This was a day that Faisal was at home alone. This in itself was quite unusual because usually there were people constantly coming and going as if Faisal's home were the departure lounge of Kingsford Smith Airport. Faisal had done the usual offering of tea and nibblies and we had settled ourselves comfortably on the mattresses. Faisal now had a comfortable lounge but despite the fact that he offered me to sit there, I felt much more comfortable on the floor.

The subject of the furniture led to a conversation about Khatyn.

"Khatyn is a nice lady," Faisal commented. "Do you know her for a long time?"

"Have you known her for a long time," I corrected him. "For about two years," I continued. "She's been a colleague of mine now for a long time and I like her very much. She is a close friend of mine."

"How old is she?" Faisal then asked.

"About my age," I replied.

"Why don't you marry her? You like her and she likes you."

As soon as he said this, I had the impression that this entire conversation had been rehearsed. It was as if the answer I was supposed to give, the truth about who I really was, what Faisal had to know, the universe had directed this entire moment to this point. The answer was already there in my head, ready to slide down into my throat, to be whisked up through my mouth, bounce off my tongue and fly with ease into Faisal's ears for his mind to process. It was one of those strange moments beyond my comprehension where I felt like an outsider, watching and hearing myself do and say things that were outside my control.

"I like her," I heard myself say, "but I'm gay."

Faisal smiled and shook his head to convey the idea that he had not understood what I had said. This was not supposed to happen. But providence had taken care of that and Plan B was already in place to amend the situation. Once again, it was as if someone else and not me who said, "I mean, I'm a homosexual."

Faisal, for a second time, smiled and shook his head and said, "I'm sorry. I don't understand that word."

Providence was well prepared. Plan C was then thrown in to take over after the failure of Plan B.

"I like men, Faisal."

Faisal still had a bewildered look on his face. Suddenly I felt as if providence had left me and I was now alone with my own lucidity. I had to do the thinking and the talking. My mind went into action replay and I suddenly was fully conscious of what I had just been saying. But Faisal had not understood. I couldn't leave it like that. I was now forced to explain the entire situation. I had to find simpler language to explain what I was trying to say.

I paused for a moment, gathering my thoughts, thinking of a euphemistic way of explaining the situation. After some thought, I realised that subtlety was only reserved for those proficient in a language. Using eloquent phrases and imaginative allegories were no doubt more likely to confuse Faisal than elucidate him. I realised that I had no choice but to use direct and concrete language. So I said, "Faisal, you know when you see a naked woman and your dick…" and when I said "dick" I pointed at mine in a fashion that made it obvious which part of the body I was talking about, "…goes hard?" and at this point, I straightened out my right arm over across my groin and then, with a clenched fist, bent my arm at the elbow in the very obvious gesture of an erection.

"Well, mine goes flat," I said and at this point, I let my arm drop.

"And you know when you see a naked man and your dick goes flat," I continued, doing all the gesticulations in reverse, "well, mine goes hard."

Faisal just looked at me with a clinical expression. Time had slowed down and I wasn't sure what would happen next. I looked at Faisal and Faisal looked at me.

Faisal then said, "So, it's natural? You don't choose to be like that?"

"Faisal. Who in their right mind would consciously choose to be gay?"

"Oh, okay," Faisal said. There was a rather long moment of silence.

Faisal suddenly had a deadpan expression on his face. My hands began to feel clammy and my heart felt as if it had dropped to my feet. What on earth was going on in that man's head and what was going to be his reaction? Life then returned into Faisal's face and I could see he was about to speak. He looked at my empty cup and then asked, "More tea?"

I wanted to stand up and scream, "What? I have worked myself up into a frenzy because I thought I would lose you as a friend because of my sexuality because I *know* you come from a country which condemns it, and all you can say is 'more tea'?" I stared at him in disbelief until I was able to bring myself together and pass him my cup and reply, "Yes, please."

We became engaged in conversation about all sorts of other issues as if what I had told him was as mundane as saying I didn't like wearing red socks. And at the end of the day, when I went to my car, Faisal gave me a big bear hug as had become the tradition, filled with the same emotions as he always had.

As I drove home, I had mixed feelings. Had Faisal actually understood what I said and he sincerely didn't care or had he totally misunderstood which is why he reacted so nonchalantly?

The next time I saw Faisal, it was obvious that he had thought quite a bit about what I had said. I must have simply shocked him the first time that he just didn't know what to say.

As was customary, Faisal invited me in and asked if I wanted some tea. After the tea ceremony was over, Faisal bowled straight into the topic without flinching as if we were continuing from the last time I was there.

"So, you don't do sex with women?" he asked. "You don't like them?"

"To have sex with, no. I mean, I think women are nice people but I just have no physical attraction towards them."

"Not at all? Have you done sex with a woman before?"

"Had sex," I corrected him. "Yes, I had sex with a woman once."

"Didn't you like it?" Faisal asked, perplexed.

"No, Faisal, I didn't like it. It would be great if I did because it would make my life much simpler. However, there's nothing I can do about it, it's beyond my control. I know when you see a naked woman, when you see her breasts and sexual organs, something goes on inside your brain that says, 'Wow! Yum, yum! This is exciting! I have to touch and play with this'! However, inside me, something says, 'Ew! Yuck. I don't want to touch it or even look at it'. But it's the reverse with me. If you ever saw a naked guy, I'm sure you'd think, 'Yucky! I would never want to touch or even look at that', but inside me, I'm filled with excitement to touch and play with it. It's an impulse that occurs inside of me whether I like it or not."

I could see Faisal's mind ticking over. As soon as he had asked the question, I realised that in his mind he was trying to decide whether it was disrespectful or not to ask such personal questions to his teacher, someone he esteemed.

"So, what do you do when you have sex with a man?" he asked rather cautiously.

"I beg your pardon?" I asked, not really sure of the import of the question.

"I mean, like, do you do it, or does the other man do it to you?"

At this point, I couldn't help laughing and I then began to understand the reason for the question. Not only was I listening to someone who was unfamiliar with this sexual phenomenon or at least not familiar with a society which accepts it, I was listening to someone who came from a culture that distinguishes between passive and active homosexuality. From my encounters with gays from other parts of the world, I was aware that many cultures do not view male homosexuality as simply as two men who enjoy each other's naked bodies. Many cultures differentiate between the active partner and the passive partner, even having special words of differentiation.

"Faisal, does it make any difference to you what I do when I have sex?"

Faisal paused and looked at me.

"Well, I hope you're not...um...*koni*...I don't know how to say that in English."

I knew precisely what he meant.

"You mean 'passive'. Faisal, when I have sex with a man, what I do is personal between him and me. I mean, you asking me what I do when I have sex is like me asking you what you do when you have sex with your wife. It's a dreadfully personal question. How would you feel if I asked you that?"

Faisal blushed. It was the first time he had shown that he was capable of embarrassment.

"And what if I were *koni*?" I continued. "How would you know? And what difference would it make to you?"

Faisal paused for a moment and then answered.

"I prefer that you are…um…*bache bas*, the opposite of…what did you say is English for *koni*?"

"Passive. You prefer that I am active. What difference does it make which one I am? And how would you know? And what if I'm both?"

"Both?" Faisal asked, perplexed.

I explained to Faisal that one of the features of homosexuality is that both sexual partners are the same sex. This means that it is a much more equal form of sex, where neither one nor the other is necessarily dominant because both partners have the same physical makeup. When I reached this stage, I explained to Faisal that as much as he was my friend, it was too much inside my comfort zone to discuss what I did behind closed doors in the privacy of my bedroom.

Faisal went quiet for a moment. He then looked at me from head to foot.

"But you don't look…what is the word?"

"Gay," I replied. "I don't look gay? What does a gay man look like?"

"Well, not like you. You look normal. Those men look different."

I had to laugh! I knew once again what Faisal was trying to say. So, I explained to him that it was true that some gay men are effeminate but not all of them are. Some gay men like to prance around as if they were the leading stars of *Le Cage Aux Folles* while others are happy to live as blokes, drinking beer and playing football on the weekend. There is a wide variation in character amongst gay men, the common denominator is their programmed attraction to other men.

"So, it's natural then? You don't choose to be like that?"

"No, I have no choice. This is the way I am. Something inside my body makes me repulsed at the sight of a naked woman but excited to see a naked man irrespective of what I think about it. Religions may like to condemn it and governments make policies against it but it doesn't change the impulse. So, I have to live with it in a world where it is frowned on at best or is a severe crime at worst. At least I am gay here in Australia in the twenty-first century. I certainly would hate to be gay in a country like Afghanistan."

I said that rather pointedly, I know. It just came out. But Faisal reacted to this information quite well. I was amazed how well he accepted it. But it was also obvious that Faisal himself was not gay. Had he been, this would have been the opportunity to express his interest in men. But Faisal's questions were typical from a heterosexual perspective.

I could tell that Faisal was going through a cultural paradigm shift and he later confirmed that this was so. Although I no longer was his teacher, Faisal still viewed me with the same respect as if I were going to be his teacher forever. However, homosexuals were treated with contempt in Afghanistan to the extent that if they were caught indulging in this activity, they were put to death in a very horrible way. The possibility of a respectable teacher living openly a gay life and being a close friend of a heterosexual man defied all imagination and for Faisal was an entirely new concept.

But what Faisal did not realise was that his readiness to accept this phenomenon in me only concreted my belief that Faisal could in no way be a terrorist. As our friendship grew, Faisal did not shy away from giving me a traditional welcome and farewell hug whenever I visited. I could not imagine a terrorist, or at least a Muslim extremist, willing to accept within his circle of friends a person who experienced a lifestyle quite different from his own.

I was therefore very relieved and happy. I liked Faisal very much and wanted to keep our friendship, and my wish was granted. He had become the brother I never had. I didn't care that he was an Afghani refugee or a Muslim, just as long as he remained my friend, that's all I wanted.

And then I reflected back on those immortal words which will follow me for the rest of my life: "with a tie or without a tie, you're still Michael". I would never have imagined that this wonderful and succinct expression of tolerance, which was later expressed in actions, would ever have come from a man from the land of the Pashtuns.

Chapter 10

Winter, like an unwanted visitor, seemed to hang around tenaciously within the Sydney basin. Fortunately it doesn't snow in Sydney. I hear of people who rush to our snow fields in the south of New South Wales and north of Victoria to immerse themselves into this wondrous white wonderland during the winter months. I do not, however, share in this thrill but rather spend the winter months in a rather morose state of mind.

Faisal had changed all this. Because there was not much to do or no real place to go, I spent a lot of winter time visiting Faisal. It was also an opportunity for me to educate myself concerning this man and the entire central Asian region. Faisal was more than happy to spend hours answering any question I raised about his past and the past of his country. I wanted to learn more about Faisal and his people, about the Afghanis and Pashtuns, who they were and where they came from, and how the entire history of Afghanistan began and led up to the present day situation.

Faisal took me right back to the beginning by explaining to me that way back in the very distant past, the original name of the region in which we find Afghanistan today was *Ariana*. It is from this name Ariana that the modern nation of Iran derives its name. It is also from the name Ariana that the so-called race of the Aryans comes from which Hitler was many thousands of years later to use to refer to what he believed was the superior race of humanity. In fact, even today, the Germans hold a peculiarly close relationship with Iranians and Afghanis because of the belief that these people all descend from a common tribe.

Ariana was an independent entity until the Persians came. The Persians built an empire which, at the height of its glory, extended from present day India all the way to modern day Turkey. I was familiar with the Persian Empire from my studies of the Bible during my late teens and early adulthood when I was an avid Christian. The Biblical books of Ezra, Nehemiah and Esther are set within this period. The area in which Afghanistan occupies today was made into a state or *satrapy* of the Persian Empire and given the name Bakhtar or Bhakhtrish.

Faisal explained that the ancient name, Bakhtar, is still evident in this region of the world today. Located along the Afghani-Pakistani border near the city of Peshawar is an area known as the Tribal Lands. The Tribal Lands are inhabited predominantly, if not exclusively, by Pashtun clans. These Tribal Lands are divided up into provinces or counties, two of which are called Paktia and Paktika, remnants of the ancient name Bakhtar. Faisal further explained that it is from the name Bakhtar that we get the word Pakhtun, alternatively pronounced Pashtun, which illustrates an obvious link between this ancient state and Faisal's tribe.

Because modern day Afghanistan formed a part of ancient Persia, this explained, then, the relationship between Farsi and Dari. However, Faisal explained to me, and this has been confirmed by Iranian students of mine, that the language spoken during the Persian Empire was not Farsi but another language known as Pahlavi, which was the language in which the great prophet, Zoroaster, used to write the Zoroastrian Scriptures, the Zend Avesta. Pahlavi, for some reason, was later supplanted by Farsi. Both Afghanis and Iranians agree that Farsi was a language which originated from a region which encompasses modern day Afghanistan.

Today, the Iranians speak Farsi and the Afghanis speak Dari but the two languages are simply dialects of a common language. Iranians and Afghanis can speak their respective languages and understand each other very well. Iranians and Afghanis alike agree that Iranian Farsi is a more modern and a simpler version of the much more archaic Dari. For one reason or another, Farsi evolved and changed while Dari remained much the same as it was spoken many hundreds or possibly thousands of years ago. Iranians tell me that when they hear Afghanis speak, it sounds as if the Afghanis are speaking a literary form of language from a bygone era, probably equivalent to what an Australian would think of someone who spoke Shakespearian English today.

But why do the Iranians and Afghanis call the dialect of Farsi spoken in Afghanistan Dari? Faisal told me the origin of the name of this language but he was unsure whether this explanation was historically accurate or simply a myth. His explanation was that Dari comes from the word *dareh* which means "valley". When the Persians came to the heart of where Dari was spoken, they said that this was the language of a particular valley in the area, that is, a particular *dareh* and hence the name, Dari.

However, it was what I had learned at school about Alexander the Great which put ancient Afghanistan on the map, so to speak. Alexander the Great succeeded in making great conquests of the ancient Central Asian world, conquering land as far away as Bakhtrish, which the Greeks called Bactria. At the death of Alexander the Great, Bactria formed a part of the Seleucid Empire. However, eventually, years later, the people of the region once again obtained their independence and the Bactrian Kingdom once more became an independent nation.

With the advent of the prophet Mohammed, Islam spread east and west from the Arabian Peninsula. During the reign of Caliph Usman ibn Afhan, the third Caliph after the prophet Mohammed, the king of the ancient Bactrian nation became convinced of the veracity of the Muslim religion and hence he and all his subjects were peaceably converted to this faith.

Afghanistan fluctuated in its importance and greatness throughout its rich history but possibly reached its zenith during the time of Sultan Mahmud Ghaznavi. In the 11th century, the Sultan Ghaznavi successfully expanded his dominions, including conquering an immense part of India, and thus he became the ruler of an extremely large sultanate which encompassed an extensive area of land from the south of India to somewhere near the Caspian Sea.

However, this vast sultanate was not to last long. In the 13th century, the great empire builder, Genghis Khan, succeeded in taking over most of the known world of the Euro-Asian continent, to the extent that he reached treacherously close to the borders with both Europe on one side and China on the other. Genghis Khan and his people were Mongols and it is believed that this is where the race of the Hazarahs in present day Afghanistan came from. It is believed that when the Mongolian Empire collapsed, those Mongols living in the area of modern day Afghanistan simply stayed on in the region and adopted the Afghani religion and customs, and assimilated with the local Afghani people. This explained why the Hazarahs developed the features they have today, a combination of Asian and Middle Eastern. Little did I realise when Mohammed was my student that I had within my classroom a living remnant of a great stage in history.

From this time on, the area in which we find Afghanistan appeared to be simply a region populated by different, autonomous tribes who governed their own affairs on an admixture of Islamic principles and old traditional customs. This might have continued to be so if it weren't for European interests in this part of the world.

Because of commercial interests, Europeans began sailing the high seas to establish their dominance and authority in lands that they had only heard of in the past. One of the last nations of Europe to sail the world for distant lands and to have the greatest impact on much of them was Great Britain. The British had the notorious knack of successfully conquering lands and taking over them, and soon Britain had total control of one of Afghanistan's neighbours, India. At the same time, Russia was beginning to expand its territories to the east and it wasn't long before Afghanistan became tightly squeezed between these two superpowers.

It was at this time that Afghanistan, in its present geographical location and political entity, was about to take form. With the superpowers of the time beginning to encroach on the territory that the tribes in this region had inhabited from time immemorial, all was needed was a significant figure to bring the tribes of the land together to form some sort of confederacy. In the late 1700s, a man by the name of Ahmad Shah united the tribes of the region and Afghanistan as a nation was finally born. The name *Afghanistan* means *Land of the Afghans*. And from this comes the enigmatic question: what is an Afghan?

Faisal explained, and this has been confirmed from talking with other Afghanis and reading literature about Afghanistan, that the name *Afghan* refers to the Pashtuns. That is to say, originally, *Afghan* and *Pashtun* were synonymous. The tribes that Ahmad Shah was attempting to unite were the different Pashtun clans. However, other tribes in the area, Uzbeks, Tajiks, Hazarahs and any other tribe that lived within these borders eventually came to consider themselves as Afghans as well.

Afghanistan, in this epoch, encompassed a much larger area of land than it does today, particularly a large section of what is now Pakistan. Despite the military might and the technological advances of both the British and the Russians, the Pashtuns made a name for themselves as ferocious warriors who could hold their ground. Britain, which held India, tried to advance into Afghani territory but was defeated in what is known as the first Anglo-Afghani war.

However, both Russia and Britain were eager to gain control of this region of the world and hence in 1878 the second Anglo-Afghani war began. Despite the Afghani resistance, this time Afghanistan was led into a compromise with Britain to bring the war to an end. In order to end the conflict, in 1893, Afghanistan accepted to cede a considerable amount of territory to British India under what was known as The Durand Agreement. However, it was not land that was forever lost to Britain. Rather, as it was with British Hong Kong, land originally belonging to Afghanistan would be returned to Afghanistan at the end of a 99 year lease. With the simple signing of documents between a handful of men, the nationality of thousands upon thousands of Pashtuns changed from Afghani to Indian without these Pashtuns moving a single sand grain distance from their homes.

Thousands of Pashtuns who were citizens of an Afghani state now became, in one fell swoop, the inhabitants of the British Commonwealth. The original border between Afghanistan and India, which later became known as the Durand Line, was moved thousands of kilometres west to the point where it appears in modern maps today. Faisal explained to me that at this present time, the Pashtun tribes are located straddled along both sides of the current Afghani-Pakistani border as a result.

The condition of the Durand Agreement was that land leased to British India should have been returned to Afghanistan in 1992. But unbeknown to Britain or Afghanistan, India would not belong to Britain for the duration of the lease. In 1947, India won independence from Britain and, as a result of the Muslim-Hindu conflict, British India became two countries: India and Pakistan. As a separate country, Pakistan had an opportunity to develop as an independent nation. But the problem for Pakistan was simply this - most of Pakistani territory occupies land that was leased by Afghanistan to British India which should have been returned to Afghanistan before the close of the twentieth century. But if Pakistan were to give back Afghani land, there would not be much land left for the Pakistani nation to occupy. Pakistan would be reduced to a small strip of land squeezed in on all sides by great nations.

Pakistan also claims that the Indian state of Kashmir belongs to Pakistan. With the knowledge that Pakistan could one day lose a large swab of territory that is claimed to belong to Afghanistan, incorporating the state of Kashmir into Pakistan is not simply a desired objective but a question of Pakistani survival. If Pakistan were to be reduced in size, it could no longer contend with India and may once and for all be yet again reluctantly absorbed into this sub-continent nation, which is not what the Pakistanis want.

Faisal explained that as a result, civil strife and unrest within Afghanistan work in favour of Pakistan because it takes the mind of the Afghanis off their claim to parts of Pakistan. Whenever there is fighting within Afghanistan's borders, the Afghanis are too occupied with local troubles to worry about claiming back neighbouring land. Faisal further explained that Pakistan was one of the very few nations which recognised the Taliban as the authorised governing body in Afghanistan when the Taliban came to power.

Faisal went on to explain that this was not the only reason for the current problems in Afghanistan. The greatest problem that Afghanistan faces is its geography. Afghanistan is located conveniently in the centre of Central Asia with nations all around trying to extend their territory. Russia in the north is still trying to grab Afghanistan for itself in order to gain access to the Indian Ocean which is what resulted in the Russo-Afghani war that Faisal himself and many of the Afghanis living in Australia today were eye-witnesses to.

Afghanistan also has to contend with its western neighbour, Iran, which is attempting, in this modern era, to regain the power and dominance that it once boasted of in the past. And now, other nations are present in this region of the world. This, to the Afghanis, is just the continuous repetition of a frustrating history of the nations of the world looking on lustfully at Afghani territory.

"But why can't they leave us in peace?" I remember Faisal saying on several occasions with an air of hopeless desperation. "Pashtuns are a quiet and peaceful people. We are quite happy keeping our customs. We are happy to live our lives the way we have for the past thousands of years. After all, it's our land. America, Iran, India, Britain and Russia have enough land of their own. Why do they need ours?"

Faisal's comment of the tranquillity of the Pashtun tribespeople was so very different from the comments I had heard and read about them. Mohammed had said they were mere thugs. Whenever I looked up articles on the Internet about Pashtuns, these articles always portrayed the Pashtuns as violent and barbaric. But Faisal was such a peaceful man and matched up more with his own evaluation of his tribe than what outsiders said. No doubt there are Pashtuns who are violent and barbaric. However every educated person the world over knows that negative characteristics as well as positive characteristics find their cognates in all the races of the world. Neither good nor bad characteristics are nor ever have been a unique entity of any one particular race or tribe.

Because of the current problems in Afghanistan, a new page in Afghani history had been turned, the start of a mass exodus, an Afghani Diaspora, where Afghanis had begun to be scattered abroad to every country of the world.

However, the Afghani presence in Australia is not a completely new phenomenon. Afghanis had already entered a page in Australian history well over a hundred years ago. During the mid-nineteenth century, Afghanis were brought out to Australia to help construct the Adelaide to Darwin telegraph system. Because of Australia's dry interior and its similarity to the desert areas of Central Asia, many Afghanis and their camels were brought to Australia. This historic legacy is still evident in Broken Hill where there is a mosque still standing which was built by the Afghans, and a walk through the Broken Hill cemetery reveals many tombstones written in Arabic script. Even the name of the famous Adelaide to Darwin railway locomotive, the Ghan, is simply a shortened form of "the Afghan" in memory of these past desert wanderers.

But my biggest question was, who were the Pashtuns? Where did they come from? When I began embarking on my quest in search of the origins of the Pashtuns, I did not realise that I was about to enter a subject matter which still remains enigmatic today as it was when the Pashtuns were first enquired about.

There have been many modern visionaries who have attempted to establish a worldwide language. In real terms, nations the world over have tried to standardise one language over all the other languages and dialects present within their borders. Australia is a good example of this linguistic unification. Where there were over 200-odd Pama-Nyungan languages spoken over most of the Australian continent for millennia, the arrival of the

English in 1788 has resulted in the extinction of many of these languages. Many of the remaining languages are dying out in favour of the accepted universal language, English, which certainly brings far greater economic success. However, whereas having one common language has its obvious advantages, there are also many advantages for preserving other languages as well. Of the many advantages of linguistic diversity, there is one thing that different languages and dialects can tell us that no other piece of evidence ever will – it can tell us something about our history.

The fact that Dari and Farsi are similar, for example, illustrates quite clearly that the peoples of Iran and Afghanistan were no doubt once the speakers of the same language. The differences indicate that somewhere in the history of Afghanistan and Iran the two peoples were separated which resulted in the two languages developing separately. The fact that a Dari speaker and a Farsi speaker can comfortably communicate with each other means that the separation of the two peoples occurred relatively recently.

The language of the Pashtuns, Pashto, however, is quite a different language altogether. Pashto differs considerably from Dari to the west but also from Urdu and Hindi to the east. The enigma of the Pashto language is that it suddenly appears in this part of the world, in an area where no other language seems quite like it. This indicates that the Pashtuns are a people who came to this area of the world from somewhere else. But from where?

A recurring theme that I heard among the Afghanis themselves, either with a sense of contempt, usually by Hazarahs, Uzbeks and Tajiks, or with a feeling of pride, often by the Pashtuns, was the belief that the Pashtuns are the descendants of one of the Lost Ten Tribes of Israel. From the way it was talked and laughed about, I developed the impression that it was simply a means of amusement between the different Afghani tribes but was not something to be taken seriously.

But to Faisal, this was not something mundane to laugh away as a trivial piece of information. Faisal was convinced that the Pashtuns are truly one of the descendants of the Lost Tribes of Israel. Faisal explained that there are a lot of similarities between Pashto and Hebrew which substantiated this claim and many similarities between Pashtun customs and Jewish Old Testament laws.

But the strongest piece of evidence was the origin of the name *Afghan* itself. Faisal explained that the name *Afghan* clearly proved the Pashtun connection with the Lost Tribes of Israel. According to Faisal, the name *Afghan* comes from the Pashto *Afram-ghwunde*. The prefix, *Af*, in *Afram* is simply the shortened form of the name *Afraham* or *Avraham*, the Hebrew version of the English *Abraham* which is then shortened to *Afr* and then simply to *Af*. The suffix, *ghwunde*, which has been shortened to *ghan* makes a noun into an adjective in Pashto. This means that the word *Afram-ghwunde* describes a person who is like Abraham, or perhaps "made of the same material as

Abraham", that is, genetically a descendant of Abraham.

How very ironic if all this were true. The Jews, the descendants of Abraham through Abraham's great-grandson Judah, have a well-known history of persecution simply because of their heritage. And now the Pashtuns have been faced with the same dilemma as the descendants of one of Judah's brothers. This gave meaning as to why the Pashtuns were written and spoken about so pejoratively.

Within the same vein of thought, I was intrigued to discover that it was not only the name *Pashtun* that had become debased during this modern Central Asian phenomenon. Even the name *Taliban* also had quite benign beginnings. The sad thing about the name *Taliban*, so Faisal explained, was that it did not originally carry the negative connotation that it does today. Originally, the Taliban was a religious vocation. The name, *Taliban*, comes from the Arabic, *talib*, meaning *student*, and by extension within the religion, a student of Islam. Prior to its popularity in the western world, someone who became a *taliban* was simply someone who had become a pious follower of the Islamic faith in much more peaceable terms. Originally, in Islam, a Taliban was something akin to a Christian monk, someone whose life was dedicated to the study of the religion.

However, under the guise of an extremist Islamic movement, the Taliban that is familiar to the West was a strong political party which was injected into Afghanistan and subsequently took over the country. Faisal, like many Pashtuns and Afghanis of all the other tribes who were known to be openly against the Taliban, fled to neighbouring countries, to Iran, Uzbekistan, Tajikistan, or, as in the case of Faisal, to Pakistan. The intention of the refugees was to wait for the Taliban to collapse or for the refugees to be instrumental in its demise, in order to return safely to their own country.

Faisal explained that although he was officially across the border from Afghanistan in Peshawar, this border was not safely guarded and it was easy for anyone to slip over from one country into the other. Peshawar is located near the Afghani-Pakistani border, close to an area known as the Tribal Lands. These Tribal Lands are autonomous regions that straddle the Afghani-Pakistani border and neither Pakistan nor Afghanistan has any control over these areas despite the clearly marked lines in our Atlases which show border areas between these two nations. The reason for this lack of control is simply because of the difficulty, or as Faisal explained to me, the outright impossibility of controlling these areas. The Tribal Lands are located in mountainous areas and despite all the attempts by foreign powers throughout history, the Tribal Lands have succeeded in remaining autonomous. Mighty nations like Russia and Britain could not penetrate this part of the world, and today, even the Superpower, the United States of America, is unable to enter this area of the world despite all its attempts. It is within the Tribal Lands that Osama bin Laden is supposedly hiding away from the rest of the world but still commanding a strong control over it.

Faisal was for a time under the protection of Pakistan against the Taliban in Afghanistan. However, as it had now become clear to me, the border between Afghanistan and Pakistan is much more nebulous than the clear demarcation as indicated on present day maps. As Faisal had explained once before when he was my student, and I was later to discover when I read United Nations reports about the situation, it was quite clear that the Taliban phenomenon spilled over into Pakistani territory, in particular, around Quetta and Peshawar. Stories of kidnappings and killings in these areas by the Taliban began to surface which illustrated that Faisal fell in a dangerous predicament against his life. Just because he was over the border from Afghanistan, the Taliban could at any time slip across the border into Pakistan, kidnap Faisal, take him back to Afghanistan and simply execute him.

What amazed me about Faisal was his outright willingness to answer any question I asked him. The other Afghanis that I had met through Faisal were reluctant to divulge their story and conveniently were unable to understand my questions whenever my questions became too probing. By contrast, Faisal not only could answer my questions, he was always able to show me concrete evidence to support various aspects of his story, the newspaper article from Pakistani *The Nation* newspaper, UNHCR reports and other bits and pieces of paper and documentation which supported his claim.

Faisal, therefore, definitely had a strong case that supported his refugee status. Surely if it was convincing enough for me, the Immigration Department would definitely have no problem in granting Faisal permanent residence.

Chapter 11

The August Winds is a rather tumultuous time of year in Sydney where weather is concerned. The name itself says it all. August is a windy month, a terribly windy month, with day after day of wind blowing in different directions, as if the Sydney Basin were at the bottom of a spin drier. The atmospheric struggle is so fierce that it is as if the monster of winter, who has sat with its extensive lazy rump over the area, is reluctant to cede its place to the light-footed springtime being, who begins magically to bring everything back to life. And so a bitter struggle ensues in which, in the end, graceful spring springs forth triumphantly. August is therefore not a predominantly cold or hot month but rather a mixture of extremes from one day to the next, as each ethereal being wins its successive small battles but with spring the final victor.

This particular August was not merely another bumpy transformation from winter to spring but was the beginning of the great struggle that was about to confront both Faisal and me – of course, much more Faisal than I. On one particular Saturday, Faisal sent me an sms and asked me to meet him at a café called Karar down the main street of Auburn.

The word "auburn" once conjured up the image of a certain seductive colour of hair that men found alluring in women. But the suburb, Auburn, has become erroneously synonymous with Mafia ghettos found in many of the great cities of the world. I was terrified of Auburn based on the accounts people made of the place as a suburb so out of character with the rest of the Anglo-Celtic nature of Sydney. Auburn was portrayed as if there were hash-hish assassins in front of every shop, holding a knife ready to attack and kill any unsuspecting westerners who happened to pass uninvited down the main street.

This day was the first time I had ever been to the town centre of Auburn. Although Faisal lived in Auburn, I never had to go near the main street to get to his place. Now he was asking me to meet him there and so I was terrified. Why was Faisal risking my safety by asking me to meet him in this most dangerous of Sydney suburbs?

I decided to park my car at Faisal's place and then walk to the main street which was a good two to three kilometres away. After all, I reasoned that if I parked my car closer to the centre of town, there was all the likelihood that my car would not be there when I got back or only skeletal remnants of it.

However, as I began walking along the main street of Auburn, my reaction to the place gradually changed with each step. Both sides of the main street were neatly paved with modern paving stones and there were a number of outdoor cafés generously sprawled across the pavement for people to enjoy a cup of tea or coffee outdoors. Fortunately these cafés were partly closed in by tarpaulins at this time of year to protect customers from the elements.

The description of the main street of Auburn as a slice of Cairo or Istanbul did have an honest ring about it but not in the morbid, negative exaggeration that had been portrayed of the suburb. Just in my short stroll to Karar I saw many different nationalities, mainly from central Asia, such as Arabs, Turks and Afghanis, gathered together or strolling by. But I also saw many Africans and Chinese which broke up this otherwise concentrated Middle Eastern tributary. Intermingled among them were Anglo-Australians. What was unusual, and I must admit, rather daunting at first sight, was that each nationality dressed in their own traditional garb which only highlighted that these people came from a completely different culture and set of customs that I was used to as an Anglo-Australian. Later, when I had become accustomed to this phenomenon, I came to the decision that this is what gave Auburn its unique character. I now think this is what makes Auburn a great place to visit.

When I reached Karar, it took me some time to recognise Faisal amongst the crowd. This was because he had changed in a week since I had last seen him – he had grown a beard! If he looked like a terrorist when he was clean shaven, you can imagine how much the beard accentuated this perception! However, I felt that the beard suited him much better and gave his entire features a much more balanced and handsome look.

Faisal was accompanied by a well-dressed man wearing a business suit, with an impeccably clean briefcase at his side and official papers sprawled over one of the café tables. I could hear that they were speaking in Dari as I approached the table.

As soon as Faisal saw me, his face beamed with a smile. He stood up and gave me his usual big bear-hug squeezes. I commented on his beard and rubbed it with the back of my hand to reinforce my appreciation. His beard really enhanced his facial features remarkably well.

The man accompanying Faisal also stood up to greet me but with a much less emotive reception. Faisal introduced me to this man who, he explained, was his lawyer, Farqad Salaahid. Once the greetings were over, Farqad pointed to the closest chair and invited me to sit with these men for a cup of tea.

"So, *you're* Michael," Farqad said.

"Well, yes," I replied rather bewildered by the familiarity when we had only just met.

"Faisal talks a lot about you as if you were his brother. I had to finally meet this Michael that I had heard so much about."

I could feel a flush in my face and a touch of warmth in my heart.

"So, I guess you already know that Faisal has his interview in a couple of days," Farqad continued.

"Yes, I am aware," I replied. "What are his chances of getting his permanent visa?"

Farqad laughed.

"Oh, he's got nothing to worry about. His case is good. He only has some paperwork he needs to finalise. He just needs to relax when he goes in for the interview and answer all their questions."

I looked at Faisal. His face suddenly went sullen. I could understand why. The result of this interview determined his destiny. Now the results of his interview affected more people than himself.

"If you'll excuse me," Farqad continued, "I just need to explain to Faisal some final details and then I must be going."

Farqad and Faisal then continued conversing in Dari, little of which I understood, while I stared around Karar café. It had a Middle Eastern style to it. I could tell from both what the waiters were wearing and the décor of the place that the owners were Turkish. However, at various tables were certain groups of people. At one table were two what seemed like Australian women dressed how Australian women dress for winter, happily enjoying a cappuccino. At other tables there were people of other nationalities, congregating and enjoying the afternoon at a local café.

Even the people walking past along the pavement were a complete mixture of nations. There were men and women dressed in the traditional Middle Eastern clothes and I remember seeing a number of women completely covered with only their eyes exposed to the greater world. But there were also people from non-Middle Eastern countries, all walking around along the one street. It was as if the nations of the world had come to the one place to do a bit of shopping.

I instantly developed a new perception of the place. This Auburn was a great place after all. Within the one suburb there were Iraqis, Iranians, Afghanis,

Sudanese, Sierra Leoneans, Turks, Chinese and Anglo-Australians all living together harmoniously in the one place. Auburn, it appeared to me, was symbolic of the Australian aspiration towards multiculturalism.

However, the longer I observed around me, the more I realised the stark reality of what type of multiculturalism was really developing in our country. It was true that different nationalities lived side by side in this one suburb but I questioned if they were really harmonious. For although there were Iraqis, Iranians, Afghanis, Sudanese, Turks and Chinese all living together in one small area, I noticed that the Iraqis sat in groups made up only of Iraqis, the Iranians with Iranians, the Afghanis with Afghanis, Africans with Africans and Chinese with Chinese, the Anglo-Australians with Anglo-Australians. There appeared to be about as much unity between these different nationalities as there is between oil and water. To create greater unity, there has to be more intermingling and relationship building between the different cultural groups.

Suddenly Farqad began to collect all his papers and put them in his briefcase, which was the signal to leave. While in the process, Faisal disappeared into the café to pay the bill. I used his absence to ask the truth of the matter.

"Farqad, what *really* are Faisal's chances of getting his PV?" I asked almost pleading.

Farqad stopped for a moment and took a deep sigh.

"His chances aren't too bad. The problem with Faisal, however, is that he is too honest. He wants to tell the whole story as it was which will play against him."

Faisal returned and while we got ready to go, what Farqad said to me about Faisal began to haunt me. Faisal is too honest. Too honest? What did he mean?

The three of us went to Faisal's car which was parked not far from the café. Faisal told me that he needed to drive Farqad to Ryde and once he had dropped Farqad off, Faisal was then free for the rest of the day. On our trip to Ryde, two conversations ensued, one in English, between Farqad and me, and one in Dari, between Farqad and Faisal. During the trip, I discovered that Farqad had left Afghanistan twenty years previous and had settled in Australia. He now had no family in Afghanistan as his family had all left at the time of the Russo-Afghani war, some settling in Australia, some in the UK and some in the United States. Farqad had been aware of the problems that had been developing in Afghanistan but as the years rolled by, they became less and less significant to him as he became more and more settled in Australia. It was only now as Afghani refugees came pouring into Australia that his country once again meant something to him.

The conversation terminated with our arrival at Ryde. Faisal then suggested that we return to his house where he had some food prepared. On the way back to Faisal's place I commented on his beard. I told him that he looked much more handsome and that the beard enhanced his features. Faisal then explained to me that he had had a beard since he was 18. He had shaved it off when he arrived in Indonesia because a beard made it too obvious that he was not Indonesian. It was also a commonly held belief that Middle Eastern men who wore beards were suspected as terrorists and so, once in Australia, many men from this part of the world simply remained clean shaven as a result. Faisal had gone along with this advice. However, he recently had a change of heart, preferring to regrow his beard despite what people thought. And I agreed with him. There were many Anglo-Australian men who grew beards simply for appearance and no-one suspected them of being terrorists.

At Faisal's place, I used the opportunity to practise some Dari. I had reached a stage now where I could actually string sentences together. So, Faisal decided to do some dictation for me.

Dari uses Arabic script. This meant that I had to become accustomed to writing with this unusual alphabet that looped and flowed from right to left with a myriad of dots above or below letters to distinguish one from another. This was one feature of the Arabic alphabet that I found extremely difficult to master. The Roman alphabet has two letters which require dots, i and j, but without the dots, these letters are still distinguishable, they just look incomplete. By contrast, the dots are extremely significant in Arabic script where both the number and position of the dots around a letter changes its sound. For example, one dot above one letter makes it 'n' but below the same letter makes it 'b', two dots above the same letter makes it 't' whereas two dots below the same letter makes it 'y' and so on. So significant are the dots in Arabic script that you can change the meaning of an entire word by erasing or adding a dot. Faisal once told me that in Dari the word for "elephant" and the word for "lift" differ only by a dot, so much so that there is a saying in Dari that "one dot can lift an elephant".

But although written using Arabic script, Dari is an Indo-Iranian language which means that it belongs to the same family of languages as European languages. This is evident when we examine the grammar of the language. The tenses we use in English find a cognate in Dari. Even certain words in English indicate an ancient but solid link between the two languages. The words for nuclear family relationships, that is, "mother", "father", "brother" and "daughter" which in Dari are "maader", "pedar", "berader" and "dokhter" respectively, are similar in both languages. Even one of the most simple and common words in English, "is", shows a common link with Dari. In Dari, "is" is "hast", which in Classical Greek is "est", in German "ist" and finally in English, "is".

Another feature of Dari I thought was rather curious was the word order. The verb, in Dari, comes at the end of the sentence in very much the same way as it does in German which indicates a closer link between these two rather seemingly disparate languages.

However, there are certain sounds in Dari which show an Arabic influence, in particular, the guttural sounds of the letters qaf and ayin. Qaf in Arabic sounds like a k stuck in the back of the throat which has been modified in Dari to sound like someone trying to gargle air. Ayin, however, is such a difficult sound to master for an English speaker because there is absolutely nothing like it in the English language. When Faisal pronounced it for me for the first time, I thought he was suddenly in pain or in the process of vomiting. Had I never tried to learn Faisal's language, I would have gone through life not realising that the sound we make when we stub our toe or about to throw up is a consonant in someone else's language.

But all the while that Faisal and I spent the afternoon together, what Farqad had told me of Faisal being too honest troubled me greatly. What on earth did he mean? I wanted to ask Faisal but I had no idea how to frame the question.

Eventually, I had enough trying to struggle through this difficult language. Faisal made another pot of tea and then we both lit up.

"So, when's your interview?" I asked.

Faisal blew out a puff of smoke as an exclamation mark.

"Next Tuesday at 3 o'clock."

"Are you nervous?" I asked. I wasn't sure if this was the right question to ask but I asked it anyway.

Faisal looked rather reflectively into empty space.

"I have nothing to be nervous about," was his reply. "I have been honest with the Australian government. I have nothing to hide. I won't do what my lawyer has told me to do and tell lies."

This comment hit me quite off balance.

"I'm sorry? What did you say?"

Faisal took another drag on his cigarette and then smiled at me.

"Michael, do you believe that *all* the Afghanis that fled Afghanistan to come to Australia were in danger of the Taliban?"

I looked at Faisal rather bewildered.

"Well, yes. Well, no," I corrected myself. "I thought that some of them might be terrorists."

Faisal laughed.

"Terrorists? Do you think terrorists would come by boat to Australia? It's too risky," and Faisal laughed again. "Who told you that?"

"No-one," I lied. I had often heard the comment that we should not allow refugees into the country because perhaps some of these refugees were simply terrorists pretending to be victims of the troubles that they themselves were causing.

"There are two Afghanis who are seeing my lawyer who don't tell all the truth," Faisal commented. "It is true that we Afghanis fled persecution. But they no longer have anything to worry about in Afghanistan. The situation in Afghanistan has changed enough for them to go back but they know that they have a chance of a better life here in Australia. So, they lie about the problems they had, well, not lie, they just don't tell all the truth. They just make their cases look more serious than what they really are."

I sat and stared at Faisal dumbfounded. I don't know if he was aware of the significance of what he was telling me. I wasn't sure what to say to that. But Faisal continued.

"You know Sattar?" he asked. "You know how he said he is half Pashtun and half Uzbek?"

"Yes," I replied.

"Well, he's not. He's fully Pashtun. Because he was afraid of being rejected, he said that his mother was Uzbek and his father was Pashtun and this explained why he could speak Pashto. He escaped Afghanistan because he was afraid that, because he was Pashtun, he would be forced to join the Taliban. I mean, he was scared about his life as well. But he now knows that if he goes back to Afghanistan, the Taliban won't do anything to him because he was not a member of any political party against the Taliban. He did nothing against the Taliban. But he's seen how good life is here and he wants to stay."

I sat there for a moment stunned. Faisal was telling me information that maybe I should not be listening to. But now he had created a lot of curiosity in me.

"But what about you?"

Faisal looked at me with a stern expression on his face.

"No, I didn't lie. I told the truth. I said that I was fully Pashtun. And my life is still threatened even if I go back now because of my past political involvement. Even so, I know I was nearly rejected. But I argued my case very strongly. But also you can easily check everything I say. It's written somewhere. I suppose my interviewer at the Woomera Detention Centre could verify everything that I said which is why I finally got my TPV."

"But what about Sattar? If he lied, why did he still get his TPV? Can't the authorities just check out his story?"

"How?" Faisal asked. "What documents?"

"Birth certificates, marriage certificates, anything."

"We don't have these in Afghanistan," Faisal replied.

"So, how do you know when your birthday is?"

"We don't. We don't celebrate birthdays, it's not in our culture. I'll show you something."

Faisal reached into his pocket, pulled out his wallet and then showed me his driver's licence.

"Look at the date of birth on my licence."

It said 1st of January.

"You see? The first of January is not my birthday. I mean, I don't really know exactly when my birthday is. When I arrived in Australia, the authorities gave this to me as my date of birth. But I have no real way of knowing.

"And your wife? How do you prove you are married?"

"I know who my wife is!" Faisal said with a snort of laughter. "How do you know your parents are married?"

He had a point there. We think about the marriage certificate as being conclusive evidence that two people are married but when you think about, how many people's marriage certificates have we really seen? When a man introduces a woman as his wife, we just accept it. No-one questions it or asks to see evidence of this. A marriage certificate only becomes significant when one of the married couples dies or if the couple immigrate.

This was also something I was going to discover between the two cultures. In Australia, we just love paper. For just about everything, we have to fill in a form. It's as if, as soon as we leave the womb, we need to fill in a form to prove that we have been born in order to provide evidence of our existence. We then continue to fill in reams and reams of forms throughout our lives until the day we are about to put our foot in the grave when we have to fill in a form to say that we are leaving this life. We need a piece of paper to prove and justify every step of our existence. Without a piece of paper, we have no evidence of anything and it's as if it's impossible that we exist. This incessant need for documentation to prove and justify every aspect of our lives is so embedded in our thinking that we don't realise that there are places in the world where this is quite a foreign, and for some, an absurd concept.

I then brought the conversation back to Sattar.

"So, how did Sattar prove that his mother was Uzbek and his father Pashtun?"

Faisal sighed.

"How are the Australian authorities going to prove him wrong? They don't know Afghanistan. They don't know the situation there. So, they have to accept that Sattar is telling the truth. They can't do otherwise."

I must have looked at Faisal with a perturbed look on my face because Faisal laughed.

"Don't worry," Faisal said through his smile. "It's only a small detail. It's not like he told a big lie that is dangerous."

But then Faisal's face turned rather serious.

"You know, he's not alone. Another of the Afghanis seeing my lawyer is in very much the same situation as Sattar. Like all of us, he was terrified of what the Taliban could do and so he fled the country. He was not directly affected by the Taliban but he saw what happened. But our lawyer decided to use what he witnessed to build up a case. This same guy told his case officer about a girl in his village who had been killed by the Taliban. This guy said the girl was his cousin and then he burst into tears. He was so convincing that the case officer handed him a packet of tissues. It was true that he had seen the execution but he was in no way related to the girl at all."

I must have had a disturbed look on my face because Faisal then laughed.

"Don't worry, Michael! It's not dangerous people who our lawyer is doing this for. And, anyway, Afghanis are really quiet people. They mean no harm here. Those who lied did not come here to kill people. It was just an opportunity for a better life and they just don't want to go back and remember all this, even if they can live safely back there. They won't cause any problems here."

It was disturbing to know that these two Afghanis had inflated their cases in order to gain entrance into Australia. However, although I didn't approve of the method, I could understand why they did it. There was obviously not much of a life to go back to in their home country. If these Afghanis, then, were able to get their visas and their cases weren't that strong, then I felt confident that Faisal would definitely get his because his case was very well supported.

However, not all interviews had a dark side to them. There were some interviews which showed the lighter side of all that was going on with these refugees. Faisal told me about Ahmed and his adventures at the interview. Ahmed, the spindly, chimpanzee-looking Hazarah I had met at the party the night of the fiasco between Faisal and Jamal was called up for an interview one afternoon at about 3 o'clock. Ahmed arrived an hour early at the building where the interview was held and decided to go to the local pub to have a drink. "Have a drink" would be an understatement. From the way Faisal described it, and Ahmed later confirmed, as he, himself, was quite happy to relate the story, Ahmed tucked the beers away. In a rather insouciant manner, Ahmed struck up a conversation with a guy at the bar and they chatted together like two long lost friends. At one point, this guy at the bar pointed at one of the barmen who had a goatee and commented, "See that guy over there? His goatee is so ugly, he should stand on his hands and use his arse as a face!" This amused Ahmed no end.

At one point, this guy at the bar asked Ahmed what Ahmed was doing in this pub which made Ahmed remember why he was there in the city. He looked at the clock and saw it was 4 o'clock! By this stage, Ahmed was quite drunk but managed to arrive at the building where the interview was to take place.

Despite his tardiness, Ahmed was called in for the interview. Ahmed did not go in with any representation, no lawyer, nothing. The only support he had was the aid of an interpreter. As soon as Ahmed walked into the interview room, his case officer, who had a goatee, greeted him. This was too reminiscent of the comment made by the man in the bar. As a result, Ahmed got into a laughing fit. While the case officer asked questions about Ahmed's past history in Afghanistan and his escape to Australia, Ahmed could not help laughing. Eventually, the case officer reprimanded Ahmed and told him that this interview was a serious matter and that he should calm himself down. But Ahmed couldn't.

Eventually, the case officer, through the interpreter, demanded to know what was so amusing. Ahmed, through splutters of laughter, told the interpreter what was the source of his laughing fit. After explaining the situation to the interpreter, the interpreter looked horrified at Ahmed and said, "I can't say that to the case officer!"

Ahmed, still in his drunken state which made him feel ten metres tall and bullet proof retorted to the interpreter, "You're the interpreter! Your job is to interpret what I say, not *tell* me what to say!"

At this stage, the interpreter must have coughed and cleared his throat before he was able to bring himself to tell the case officer, "Ahmed said, 'You, too. Your goatee is so ugly, you should stand on your hands and use your arse as a face'."

In another of Ahmed's interviews, Ahmed's case officer was an Indian woman. When she asked Ahmed why he had left Afghanistan to come to Australia, Ahmed answered not just with his lips but with his whole body in colourful gesticulation, "What a stupid question. Why do you ask? I mean, why did *you* come to Australia? You came because there was no food in India! I came to escape guns in Afghanistan!"

In times of crisis, there are moments of humour. As far as I know, however, Ahmed is still waiting for his permanent visa!

Chapter 12

I remember the day that Faisal went for his interview. The interview was held somewhere in the city but I was told that I was not allowed to come. So, I spent the afternoon walking around Auburn Park waiting for what seemed like days until Faisal finally sent me an sms to say that he had returned home. I jumped in my car and shot around to his place before my car had a chance to warm up.

When I arrived at his place, there were people everywhere. It was as if Faisal were a leading media personality who had just attended a grand court case where he was being tried for a crime he had not committed and now he was surrounded by a crowd of paparazzi and journalists. It was as if the entire Afghani community had come out of the woodwork and descended on Faisal's place. Farqad was there as well, dressed impeccably in a suit and tie with a strong smell of some potent aftershave which overpowered us more than his attempt at authority ever would.

I could see that there was no way to gain Faisal's attention and so I stood on the periphery of the crowd and listened to Faisal speak to those there as if he were delivering the Dari version of the Sermon on the Mount. I knew I would have to wait for a private audience before I could get the details in English.

Eventually the crowd began to disband. With the decrease in the number of people, Faisal was able to distinguish me from the rest of the crowd and immediately signalled me to approach him. This made me feel very special, that of all the people who formed a part of Faisal's entourage, I was the person who he singled out.

Faisal brought me inside his flat. There were a few others who came as well, including Farqad and Sattar and a few other Afghanis I had never met before. It was Sattar who conducted the tea ceremony so Faisal was able to give me his full attention and explain how everything had turned out.

Faisal explained to me what had happened. He had been asked many questions and he had answered them all as honestly as only Faisal could. Farqad confirmed that Faisal had done a great job in answering all the questions appropriately and that Faisal had a ninety-nine percent chance of obtaining that long sought after permanent visa. Many Afghanis before him had received theirs and usually it took only about a month after the interview before they received it.

Both Faisal's and Farqad's appraisal of the interview indicated that everything had turned out well. Pretty soon, Faisal would be given a permanent visa, be able to begin the process of bringing his family out to Australia and then finally be reunited with his family once again. The most difficult part of the entire process had finally come to an end.

Now that the interview was over, there was nothing left to do but wait. The waiting was such a painful process because there was absolutely nothing we could do except wait. It didn't matter whether we spent the day walking around the house, wringing our hands and giving out exasperated sighs every five minutes or going out and living life as if the world would end tomorrow. Until someone in the Department of Immigration finally made the decision, we were stuck in the same place in the process, watching the sun rise and set, rise and set, rise and set, and how we dealt with the waiting was entirely up to us.

What made it more torturous for Faisal was the separation from his family. Even if everything had gone well during the interview, he was still unable to have any physical contact with his wife and children. His only contact with his family was still only over the phone.

Being a single man put Faisal into another predicament. Faisal had gone from being a husband and a father with responsibilities that come with this role, to a single man with only himself to look after. He was in a totally foreign country with different customs and expectations. Faisal had once explained to me that learning to wash, iron, cook and generally keep the house clean was very difficult for him and for all male Afghanis who came here alone. This was because in Afghani society these chores fell to the wife and mother just as it was in Australian society before the 1960s. But what I admired about Faisal was how well he had adapted to his new conditions and accepted it all in his stride. This Faisal was really made of tough stuff.

Because Faisal did not have a family of his own for the moment, I used this as an opportunity to introduce him to mine. Unfortunately, my family was not as prolific as Faisal's and by two accidents of nature our family lineage had finally come to an end: I was gay so the chances of me having children were highly unlikely, and my sister and her husband could not have children in the natural way.

This, in itself, created an interesting situation and probably was instrumental in making my sister's husband, Peter, finally accept me for who I was. I get on quite well with Peter. However, when my family discovered I was gay, he was at first very critical of my sexual orientation. Like many heterosexual men, Peter used the worn out traditional arguments against this sexual phenomenon as an excuse to condemn me for gaining physical pleasure the way my body was programmed to enjoy it.

I remember Peter first arguing that homosexuality is wrong because it is unnatural, to which I replied that acrylic socks, cars, mobile phones, cappuccinos, Internet and pretty much everything that forms a part of our twenty-first century existence is also unnatural but this has never led anyone to see any wrongness in any of these facets of our lives.

Another time, Peter said that homosexuality was immoral, to which I replied that to a Muslim, eating pork, drinking alcohol and singing in church are immoral, to a Hindu, eating a meat pie is immoral, and to a Jew, wearing a T-shirt made of a blend of cotton and polyester is immoral, which illustrated that morality is not as fixed and concrete as he would like it to be.

His greatest argument was that sex is purely for procreation. This argument against homosexuality seemed to be the most convincing. The meaning of this argument, of course, is that anyone who has sex for any other purpose than for wanting children is doing something very wrong. The implication, however, is that we can count the number of times a married couple has had sex by the number of children they have. My parents had two children, Karen and me, but I can hardly imagine that throughout their entire married lives, my parents only ever had sex twice.

What followed some time after Peter had made this point was poetic justice. After a few years of marriage, Peter and Karen remained childless for reasons beyond their control. After a medical examination, it was discovered that Peter had a low sperm count and the doctors told him that he would never be able to father children. When I found out, instead of being sympathetic, I couldn't resist using Peter's argument against him by saying that he should now abstain from sex because sex was merely for procreation. Because Peter was unable to have children through the sexual act, there was no longer any need for Peter to indulge in any sexual activity and further, according to his own argument, it would have been sinful for him to do so. Peter was totally speechless at my brazen attack and from that moment on, the subject of sexuality has never been raised.

However, I completely admired the way Karen and Peter approached their inability to have their own children. Karen and Peter made the decision to devote their time to fostering children and were rewarded with a large family of surrogate sons and daughters even if these children belonged to them only for a short period of time.

My relationship with my mother, however, was a lot more tenuous. There was a lot of baggage that I carried around as resentment because, the day my parents found out I was gay, I was unceremoniously shown the door of the house with no prospects of ever returning. With the death of my father thirteen years later, my mother had a change of heart and wanted to re-establish a mother-to-son relationship all over again. Karen explained that our father's death brought it home to Mum that life on earth, after all, is not eternal, and eventually she and all of us will die. As I had not changed over the years, it was quite clear that I never would, and so my mother had to re-evaluate the way she acted towards me. As a result, we re-established contact with each other and there has been some sort of relationship ever since.

It was not much of a family to introduce Faisal to. We certainly weren't the Twelve Tribes of Israel. But it was my family and I wanted Faisal to become a part of it.

I told my mother, Karen and Peter about Faisal and they were all intrigued and wanted to meet him. After all, as it was for me at the beginning, Afghani refugees were just people you saw on the news, they weren't really flesh and blood. This was a novelty for them to finally meet one of these people they had heard so much about.

Before we travelled out to my mother's place, I explained to both my mother and my sister in a concerned tone that Faisal was Muslim and therefore had certain dietary restrictions, in particular, that he only ate halal meat and he could not eat any meat that came from pigs. My sister's reply to my panic situation was that although she lived in the outer western suburbs of Sydney, this didn't mean that she was a complete ignoramus, ready to dish up to Faisal pork chops or bacon rashes and that she had already located a halal butcher.

My mother lived in Emu Plains and my sister in North Penrith, both suburbs at the western end of Sydney, about 60 km from the central business district. Although the metropolitan area of Sydney is fast becoming a patchwork quilt of different nationalities where each suburb is characterised by a particular nationality, the inhabitants of Penrith and Emu Plains are still predominantly, if not exclusively, Anglo-Australian, and it is such a change from the multicultural suburbs closer to the city.

I was greatly amazed how well Faisal fit in with the rest of the family. At first, he was very quiet because my family and I naturally began with conversations that were particularly relevant to us.

Karen had brought along her current foster daughter, a four year old by the name of Tabitha. It was the first time I saw how paternal Faisal was. He took to Tabitha like a benevolent uncle, picking her up and carrying her around, and listening to her unending nonsense stories. As any normal four year old does, Tabitha asked Faisal a million questions about everything around her and Faisal answered them all in the best way he could in his accented English.

When we sat down to lunch, my mother and Peter began asking Faisal questions, not really sure what they could ask. Eventually they realised that all topics were open season and this led to asking about his escape to Australia. In the same way as I reacted to Faisal's stories, jaws dropped and questions were asked as Faisal related once again the story of how and why he had left Afghanistan and then Pakistan to come to Australia. I heard the story from start to finish once again but it was a story I never got tired of. My family asked questions about his family, about life in Pakistan, how he liked Australia and so on.

My mother has a huge dining table so long that you have the impression that she often conducts a meeting with a board of directors. When lunch was served, there were bowls and bottles scattered over the centre of the table. All this clutter worked in Faisal's favour because it hid Faisal's hands. From where I was sitting, I was the only one who could see how Faisal was attempting to attack the food. This was something I had never thought about before – Faisal didn't know how to use a knife and fork!

It's absolutely amazing how much we take so many simple things for granted, like our ability to use eating utensils. As soon as I saw Faisal struggling with these implements, I immediately became embarrassed at my own insensitivity. Why had I assumed that Faisal knew how to use these utensils? After all, at his place we always ate with our hands. I wanted to reach over and show Faisal how to operate these eating tools but then decided that this was not really the appropriate moment to do so. No-one except me could see that he was struggling to cut up the food. He did eventually successfully get the food into his mouth. In any case, it wasn't the method but the result that was important.

After lunch, we settled in the loungeroom for coffee. Tabitha had taken such a liking to Faisal's attention that she ended up around his feet or sitting on his lap. She brought dolls to him and asked him to look at them. She then brought books out for him to read to her. It was quite a picture to behold. It was a wonderful image.

But there were moments while he was nursing Tabitha that made me picture him back in Pakistan, dressed in Afghani clothes, nursing his own children. The most saddening thought was that Tabitha was about the same age as Faisal's youngest daughter, Ziba, whom he had still not yet seen, and I wondered if this had already gone through his mind.

When we left, Faisal thanked my mother and family for the invitation for lunch. Karen made a special mention on how well he and Tabitha got on together and Karen suggested, tongue in cheek of course, that Faisal could borrow Tabitha for a couple of days if Faisal so desired. On the way home, Faisal commented on how welcome he had felt at my mother's place. I was pleased that he had felt relaxed and that he fit it.

Since then, Faisal has accompanied me many times to visit my mother and family and, as a result, he has become a part of the family. My mother told him that he was welcome at any time and, when his family finally arrived in Australia, they were all welcome. With Faisal's wife and six children in this one house, and the members of our family, it would certainly make one small party! At least Mum's dining room table was of a sufficient size to cater for us all.

After a visit to my family, Faisal's interview results once again became the central focus of his case. Ever since Faisal's interview, whenever I rang him or visited, after the introductory greetings, the first question always was, "Do you have any news?" Usually it was followed with a frustratingly negative reply.

But on one particular day, Faisal told me that the case officer had asked for further information to support his case. During his interview, Faisal had mentioned that he had married his wife in Pakistan which led the case officer to assume that Faisal's wife was Pakistani. If this were the case, Faisal could claim citizenship in Pakistan which meant that he could safely live somewhere over there and this would take the responsibility of his protection away from Australia. However, Faisal explained that, although he had married in Pakistan, his wife was from Afghanistan as much as he was. The case officer wanted evidence of this.

"This means that my wife has to get a passport. How can I get a passport for my wife? It's not the same as in Australia where you just walk into a local chemist, get some passport photos taken, then go to the local post office, fill in the right forms and then within a couple of days the passport is ready. It will take time."

"How much time?" I asked.

"I don't know. Now I'm in a difficult situation. I have to get my cousin to travel from Kabul to Peshawar to help my wife because my wife does not know how to do all these things."

Just the thought of it made me tired and I was a mere spectator. But, unfortunately, if this is what the Australian government wanted, this is what Faisal had to do. There was simply no room for negotiation.

Of all the difficulties that face refugees when they arrive here, one of the greatest is the constant waiting. For each step along the process, there is no prescribed waiting period. For example, Faisal had been fortunate enough to spend only two months in the Woomera detention centre but I would later meet other Afghanis and other refugees in general who had remained behind bars for as long as four years.

Once leaving the detention centre, the next part was waiting for the end of the TPV period, which was in effect three years, and was then followed by an interview which determined the ultimate fate of the refugee, either to be sent back to their country of origin or win the treasured permanent visa. But even though this was supposedly the standard procedure, I would later meet refugees who were granted a three year TPV but somehow had these three years extended for unknown reasons.

After the interview, once again there was the waiting. And once again, there was no set waiting time. Some refugees obtained a result of their interview within a month while for others the time they received an answer seemed just to drag on. And this was the case with Faisal. Every time I visited him, which was probably every second day, as a part of the general formulaic greetings was the usual question, "Do you have any news?" This was always replied in the negative.

What made this waiting so frustrating was that it robbed Faisal's ability to plan. Faisal could not make decisions about his future, whether or not he should continue his studies at TAFE studying English and then go on to do another course to improve his working life. Further, he couldn't make any plans for his family, to have them prepared to leave Pakistan and live in Australia. It was as if he had been suddenly caught in a time warp, unable to move forward or backward, always in the same position as he was yesterday, the day before and the day before that.

Faisal told me on many occasions that his wife often asked him why he had not yet obtained his permanent visa but Faisal was unable to explain what the hold up was all about. What also made it difficult was trying to explain the delay to his family back in Pakistan. Faisal told me that he rang his family at least once a week and always had the same news to tell them, that he did not know his situation.

What made it complicated was his inability to explain why he didn't know. What were those in the immigration department doing? After all, the immigration department had already examined his file when he was an occupant of the detention centre. Since then, he had been living in Australia and had no criminal record.

There was something, however, that Faisal had, or at least, something I thought was a trump card in his favour, and that was that he had a friend who was an Australian citizen. Unlike many of the refugees who had established themselves in Australia, and many of them who had already obtained their permanent visas, Faisal had taken the step to socialise and make a connection with the Australian community and to learn the language. I met a few Afghanis, and later, refugees from other countries, who lived in cultural clusters, totally ignorant of the general Australian community at large. I often asked myself how on earth these people got their permanent visas so readily while Faisal even went so far as to tolerate a gay, non-religious man as a friend who regularly visited and whose extended family he had sat down with to a meal, despite the fact that he himself still ate halal food, prayed regularly and observed, so I would guess, all other Muslim practices. To me, Faisal was a representative of the type of people we wanted in Australia, people who, despite the fact that they continued to follow the traditions they grew up with, were just as comfortable with those who followed a completely different set of customs. Neither of us felt uncomfortable with the other's way of life. Quite the contrary. Because of Faisal, I had mellowed in my view of Muslims and realised, as it was with Christians, that Muslims fall within a spectrum from the very tolerant to the ultra-intolerant.

Because of Faisal's acceptance of me, I was ready to stand up and defend him as if I were his bodyguard. Even with all this in mind, I was ill-prepared for the storm that was brewing.

Ramadan was approaching. Because I regularly visited Faisal, I was fully aware of the coming of Ramadan in very much the same way as we are fully conscious of the coming of Christmas in the months that lead up to it. There is a lot of anticipation and readiness as the days approach the first day of this fasting month.

Before I met Faisal, I didn't know terribly much about Ramadan. What I did understand of Ramadan was that it was a name of a month and that Muslims were not allowed to eat during the daylight hours of this month. But that was all, so there were a lot of questions to be answered regarding this entire affair.

First of all, why did they fast during the month of Ramadan? It was explained to me that the reasoning behind fasting in Ramadan was that it was during the month of Ramadan that the Koran was revealed to Mohammed, the prophet and founder of the religion. As a result, the month of Ramadan is holy. However, I could not quite grasp the connection behind the abstinence of eating, drinking, smoking and sex, and the timing of the revelation of the Koran. In what way does engaging in these common basic necessities of life during the daylight hours of each day of the month in which the Koran was revealed affect the Koran in any way? Not to mention, the abstinence of food and drink only occurs during the day but then is resumed in the evening hours, so people still eat, drink and smoke during this month in any case. To add to the difficulty in understanding all this, because we live on a spinning globe, at any time within the twenty four hours of every day of Ramadan, Muslims somewhere on the globe are eating, drinking and smoking anyway.

As we approached Ramadan, other Afghanis, and other Muslims in my classes, attempted to explain the significance and importance of Ramadan. One student proudly explained that it was a good opportunity for everyone to experience what it was like to be poor and have no money to buy food and drink. But even this did not satisfy my enquiring mind. If this is the case, why do it only one month a year, and why on the month of Ramadan? Not only so, the poor not only do without food during daylight hours, they're lucky if they eat anything at all, day or night.

But if Ramadan is all about understanding the plight of the poor, it follows that there should be other months dedicated to understanding the plight of other downtrodden groups of people. Why not, I reasoned, have a month where everyone takes on the role of a woman to find out the struggles women go through especially in these male dominated societies? Or why not spend a month being African, or Jewish, or gay?

Another difficulty I had with Ramadan was the timing. Did this mean that Muslims could not eat during any form of sunlight, which meant that as soon as the first rays of the sun broke the night Muslims had to stop eating, or was it when the sun began to climb up into the sky from behind the horizon?

Then there was a question of the length of the day. The daylight hours are different in different locations. Sydney, for example, is about 33° south of the equator and so the daylight hours vary between 7.30 am and 4.30 pm in midwinter to about 5.30 am to 9.30 pm in midsummer. Hobart, by contrast, is about 42.5° south which means that there is a much greater variation in daylight hours between summer and winter. What would happen if I lived in Ushuaia in Argentina, at 55° south of the equator? Or, to really make matters complicated, what if I were a Muslim living on Mount Kirkpatrick in Antarctica, well within the Antarctic Circle, where there were six months of daylight followed by six months of night?

I respected Faisal too much to be antagonistic and test his knowledge in this area so I never braced the subject with him. However, this was an aspect that played against my understanding of Islam as universal because, to be a world religion, it had to display a knowledge of the world. The possibility of a part of the world having six months of daylight followed by six months of darkness just wasn't common knowledge until quite recently.

The exact time when eating, drinking and smoking had to stop and when it could all resume again at the end of the day was clearly set out on a poster that Faisal proudly displayed on the wall. Faisal explained to me that Ramadan moves back 10 days each solar year, that is, Ramadan begins each year 10 days earlier than it did the year previous. At least this illustrated some fairness because within a 37 year cycle, all Muslims in the world have a chance to benefit from the short winter days in their own locality.

However, even though I questioned the validity of all this, I respected the fact that Faisal believed in it with all sincerity. After all, it didn't affect me. The problem was, however, that I did not feel comfortable visiting Faisal during the daylight hours because I knew I would want to eat, drink and smoke while Faisal would not be able to do so. In particular, I did not want to visit Faisal on the first day of Ramadan which was a Saturday this particular year. However, despite what I wanted, a visit was imminent.

I can't rightly remember exactly what I was doing that Saturday morning which was the first day of Ramadan. However, whatever it was, it surely was not important in comparison to the tone in Faisal's wording when he sent me an sms message. The message was strange and sent a chill down my spine. Something was wrong and I rang Faisal immediately.

"Is everything all right?" I asked.

I knew Faisal would say that everything was fine even if the sky were falling in. However, his voice betrayed something ominous.

"Would you like me to come over?" I asked nervously.

"Are you busy?" Faisal asked. I could hear in his voice a combination of respect in that he did not want to disturb me of a Saturday and a desire for me to visit in order to offload a major disaster. These three words were said in a reserved tone I had never heard Faisal use before and it caused a knot immediately to form in my stomach.

"No," I replied once I was able to compose myself. "I'll be right over. I'll be there in 30 minutes."

If we had unlimited speed limits on Australian roads like the German autobahns, I'm sure I would have pressed my car to travel at its maximum speed. Respecting the road rules was not an easy task while my heart raced and my hands sweated causing my grip to slip over the steering wheel.

I think I parked in Faisal's carport space at 60 km/h and if I could have, I would have driven the car itself up the stairwell and into his living room. I must have flown up the stairs in my haste I was so fretful. When I knocked on the door, Faisal opened, looked at me and behind me as if to check I had not brought an accomplice with me or the Muslim thought police to make sure he respected Ramadan entirely. As soon as he was satisfied that it was only me at the door, he brought his left hand around to his mouth and at the end of it was a lit cigarette. Faisal was smoking and it was the first day of Ramadan. I knew Faisal enough to know that something had to be disastrously wrong if Faisal broke this Muslim tradition.

Faisal invited me inside and offered me tea as was customary. Once we were on the floor, Faisal poured me tea but he also poured himself a cup. Again, a second sign that Faisal was breaking Ramadan. Despite the fact that I knew something was terribly troubling the man, Faisal remained remarkably self composed. I wanted to say something, to ask him why he was not observing Ramadan but just felt it was none of my business. Once the tea ceremony was completed, Faisal sat down on the floor.

"Are you all right? Would you like a cigarette?" he asked.

His request was more urgent than polite and I dutifully pulled out my packet.

"Yes, I have one here," I said and began lighting it. I knew there was a problem and I was busting to ask what it was but at the same time I just couldn't bring myself to ask him. When he was ready, I knew that he would finally drop the bundle.

"Are you comfortable there? Would you like a cushion?" he asked.

"No, no, I'm fine, thank you. How about you? Are you okay?"

This was the only way I could brace the subject and it was the right thing to say.

"My lawyer rang me yesterday. I've got my result," Faisal said without a hint to betray which way the information was leading. This was making it all the more suspenseful.

"Well?" I asked, fearing the worse.

"I've been rejected." It was said with all the mechanism and lack of emotion that was so characteristic of the man when I had first met him. It was as if a robot or a mannequin or some sort of automaton said it, not a human being. He had been rejected.

I have absolutely no words to describe precisely the sunken feeling that this news brought. The only way I could compare it was to imagine Faisal being condemned to death and that feeling of remorse and helplessness that follows as you watch an innocent person you love dearly fall within the hands of an organisation which has the power of life and death beyond your control.

"What do you mean, rejected?" I asked as if it were possible for Faisal to have used the word incorrectly. Faisal presented me with two sheets of paper which were a photocopy of the letter sent from the Department of Immigration and Multicultural and Indigenous Affairs, otherwise known in its acronymatic form, DIMIA, to his lawyer which explained his outcome. The letter began with an introductory blurb about Faisal's application for protection in Australia. The letter then explained that Faisal's application was rejected because of a new point of law relevant to refugees, known as the Seven Day Rule. The Seven Day Rule simply states that if a refugee fled a country where he or she had a well-founded fear of persecution, and resided in a second country before arriving in Australia, if this refugee resided for more than seven days in the second country and did not apply for refugee protection in this second country, or did not apply for protection in Australia through any of the UNHCR offices in this second country, this refugee could be refused permanent protection in Australia.

What this meant in Faisal's case was this: Faisal had fled Afghanistan and resided in Pakistan for more than seven days – in fact, Faisal stayed in Pakistan for about four years. Because he did not apply for a visa to come to Australia during these four years, he was not entitled to a permanent visa in Australia.

However, there was a footnote to the Seven Day Rule. The Minister could waive the Seven Day Rule and grant the refugee a permanent visa if the Minister believed that it was in the public interest to do so.

At the end of the letter, it was explained that this did not necessarily mean that Faisal would be rejected outrightly but it meant that the best he could now hope for from the Australian government was another three year TPV. This meant that Faisal could reside under the protection of Australia for a further three years and then have his case reassessed. But because it was only a temporary visa, this further implied that he would have to remain separated from his family for another three years where he would not be able to return to Pakistan nor would his family be allowed to come to Australia during this long period.

In all fairness, I could understand the reasoning behind the Seven Day Rule. The Seven Day Rule was put in place to prevent refugees who had fled their countries and who had resided quite happily in other countries, such as Indonesia and Malaysia, for many months, even years, and who had heard that they could earn a much better living in Australia, and so gathered themselves together once again and made for Australia.

But I understood Faisal's entire story. It is true that Faisal sought protection from Pakistan and did gain some protection for the four years he lived there. But Pakistan gave him protection in Peshawar, close to the Afghani-Pakistani border which, as I now understood, is a rather nebulous border between these two countries.

I just looked aghast at the letter and then at Faisal. I really didn't know what to say at first. I just sat and looked from the letter to Faisal back to the letter, shocked at the news and numbed by the powerlessness of the situation.

"So, what happens now?" I asked.

"I have to go back to Pakistan."

"But it doesn't necessarily say that," I replied. "You can still get a TPV for another three years and then reapply."

"And what do I do with my family in the meantime? I am a husband and a father. I have a responsibility. Doesn't the Australian government believe in keeping families together?"

Faisal took another deep puff from his cigarette.

"I can't wait another three years. And why me? I know other Afghanis who have also lived more than seven days in another country before coming to Australia but they got their permanent visas. Why didn't I get mine? Why does the Seven Day Rule apply to me and not them?"

I could not answer Faisal's question and, what was worse, I later discovered that what Faisal had said was true. There appeared to be no rhyme nor reason as to which refugees fell under the Seven Day Rule or which didn't. It appeared to be left up to the clemency of the case officer looking into the case which meant that some refugees were simply luckier than others.

I looked once again at the letter and then noticed some information I had overlooked. According to the letter, the Seven Day Rule did not apply to anyone who applied for a permanent visa before the 27th September, 2001, and I mentioned this to Faisal.

Faisal puffed out a cloud of smoke.

"I don't understand that. You know, I got my TPV on the 11th September, 2001. When the authorities gave me my TPV at the Woomera detention centre, they told me that I had thirteen months to apply for a permanent visa. Now they say that if I applied for my PV before the 27th September, 2001, the Seven Day Rule would not apply to me?"

Faisal's comments were like needles being stabbed into my body.

"I mean," Faisal continued, "we all wanted a permanent visa. Because we had thirteen months to apply, we worried about more important things – we had to find somewhere to live, we had to find a job, we had to learn English. Now, three years later, DIMIA is telling me that I had fifteen days to apply for a permanent visa?"

The powerlessness of the situation. I wanted to get up and scream and yell out of frustration because there was just nothing else I could do. Here was my closest friend, Faisal, sitting with me having tea together, but it was not within our power to be together. Powers and authorities much higher and stronger than the two of us together could make the ultimate decision as to the fate of our friendship, and there was nothing we could do about it.

Faisal rescued the situation of the moment and suggested that we go out for the day and have a picnic, far away from Auburn, far away from the Muslim community. I decided that we should go way out west, to Penrith, and sit on the banks of the Nepean River and try to forget everything. I told Faisal that I would not let my family know we were out there, it would just be a private picnic between the two of us.

It was the first day of Ramadan and Faisal was supposed to be abstaining from food during the daylight hours. However, he not only stocked up on enough take-away food to feed a battalion, he bought quite a few bottles of assorted alcoholic beverages from beer to hard spirits as if he were about to cater for a major party. I was quite stunned at what I was seeing. Through my eyes and from what I knew of Faisal, this was extremely unusual behaviour and it appeared to be a way for Faisal to take out his frustrations on the very God he worshipped, the very being who was supposedly in control of the universe. Yet, despite his devotion to his God, it appeared that God was greatly letting him down and now Faisal was showing God his disapproval. Whether that was really Faisal's intent, I'll never know, but it certainly had every appearance of it.

The banks of the Nepean River are certainly a wonderful place to sit and relax and enjoy an afternoon with friends and family. Both banks on the Penrith and Emu Plains sides are accessible to the public and have been wonderfully built and prepared for picnics. There are undulating hills which run perpendicular to the river and, close to the water, there are pathways to allow people to enjoy a walk beside the tranquil waters that this slow moving river can provide for its visitors. So, it was the appropriate place to sit and forget that the rest of Sydney, the rest of Australia, and the rest of the world actually existed.

We lay out the blanket on the grass and then placed the food in the centre. I tell you, there was enough food to feed the entire Emu Plains population. Faisal began to tuck into the food with what appeared to be someone with a very hearty appetite. He had completely changed in composure from a man in desperation to someone who lived a life of luxury and was simply enjoying the fruits of his labour.

His heartiness to the food was matched by his consumption of alcohol. He drank at a relatively good speed, fortunately not too fast to knock him out all at once. He seemed quite in control of the situation.

It appeared to be a tranquil afternoon with just the two of us. We ate, drank and smoked as if it were just a normal afternoon, as if nothing had happened earlier in the day. Faisal commented a lot about the river and the surrounding land and compared it to the mountainous regions of Afghanistan where he lived as a child. He talked about the clarity of the water in the rivers of Afghanistan and the purity of the water, so pure that the taste left a tingling sensation in the mouth. He talked about once bathing in the water at a waterfall and how the water was cold but crystal clear and magic to the touch.

Faisal had to get up at one stage and dispense with some of the liquid which had accumulated in his body and so he decided to walk down to the side of the river away from view of the general public. However, on his way down the slope, I could tell that he was quite inebriated as he could not walk in a straight line but weaved all over the place as if the earth were moving beneath his feet.

When he returned, he slumped on the ground with the appearance of satisfaction of a job well accomplished. Faisal then began to breathe deeply as if his journey to take a leak and return required a great amount of physical exertion.

It began as a mere trickle, like the subtle sound of the first few drops of rain so gentle and harmless without you realising that it is the first sign that the heavens are about to burst open. Faisal began to sob. It happened without warning. I wasn't sure what to do. Many people seem to know precisely what to do if someone begins to cry but it freaks me out so much that I like to ignore it and hope it goes away or the person signals that everything, after all, is okay. But in this situation, it wasn't. Faisal's sobs began to get heavier and heavier until it was obvious that the water in the deep well of his emotions was surfacing with a torrent.

I knew I couldn't just sit there and ignore it by looking at the river or distracting him with some mundane conversation. It was too late, the bitter weeping had begun. With the only thought of what to do, I slid over to where he was lying and gently touched his forehead. With that, the weeping was verbalised.

"Why? Why me? Why is my case officer doing this to me? I have told the truth from the first day I arrived here. Everything I said has a document to prove that I'm not lying. I have a family to protect. Why is my case officer doing this to me?"

I was now sitting on my heels and in the position I was in, Faisal was able to stretch his arm across my legs and ram his teary head into my thigh.

"I decided to drink to forget. But I can't. Why is my case officer doing this? I don't understand it."

Faisal's weeping had a contagious effect. I could feel his body throbbing as he held my legs. This all had an overwhelming effect on me, Faisal weeping and the helplessness of the situation. I couldn't help it and so I just wept with Faisal. I just couldn't hold it in.

But there was also a sense of guilt resting on my shoulders, as if I, an Australian citizen, were in some way indirectly responsible for the decision, for it was, after all, a decision made by my government. But it wasn't a decision I could agree with. It was a sad and pathetic situation, two grown men in a park on a picnic blanket weeping together.

But Faisal wept bitterly as if the deep caverns of his heart were expulsing the last great coldness of despair that could be brought forth in all its fury. I wept with him because it was the only thing left that I had that could be of help in this otherwise helpless situation.

It took some time for Faisal to finally overcome his weeping fit. Once he had resumed his self-composure, we gathered everything together, put it all in the car and began to drive home. There were no words shared between us. Faisal looked out of the passenger window and I just looked straight ahead at the road before me leading us back towards the city. I put the radio on a little louder than usual to break the silence in the car.

Things seemed to have reached a calm serenity until Faisal began energetically signalling me to stop the car. We were on the M4 Motorway so it wasn't really a thoroughfare where we could just stop the car at leisure. But Faisal's insistence and earnestness to stop increased so I pulled over to the Motorway shoulder. With that, Faisal jumped out of the car in such a quick action that I thought he was pushing himself through the metal that made the car door. As soon as he was outside, I watched him double over and allow the contents of his stomach freely cascade onto the bitumen. Despite the fact that it made my stomach turn, I got out of the car and stroked Faisal's back to comfort him.

"It's okay," Faisal groaned and then heaved again. Again, I was in a powerless situation, wanting to help but really having nothing to offer in this respect. If someone is going to be sick, all you can do is wait until the person has completed the task.

Faisal finally settled down and slumped on the roadside railing which indicated to me that the convulsions were over. I brought over a bottle of water for him and he rinsed his mouth and took a good slug for his stomach. But what was the most disturbing was how the colour had completely gone out of Faisal's face. He looked deathly white, whiter than I had ever seen him before, as if what he had evacuated from his body was not just the contents of his stomach but his very soul.

Faisal finally mustered up enough strength to get back in the car. Once in motion, Faisal began to nod off and soon he was sound asleep. Every once in a while I reached across and stroked his head, probably just as much as a sign of consolation as an opportunity to assure myself that the man was still alive.

When I arrived at his place, it was dusk. Fortunately, nobody was home. I woke Faisal and walked him to his flat, up the stairs and finally into his bedroom. I asked if he wanted some tea to settle his stomach but he replied that he just wanted to sleep. Faisal followed me to his flat door and I knew, as was his custom, that he wanted to follow me out to the car and wish me farewell out of politeness but I told him that it was not necessary, especially under the circumstances. Faisal then apologised for what had happened. But he then said something that gave the abuse of alcohol its true perspective.

"You know? I drank because I wanted to forget. But it just made me remember more." This was just another way of stating the familiar saying: 'alcohol doesn't drown your sorrows, it irrigates them.' Faisal had learnt this lesson in one afternoon in one powerful, personal experience.

But this was only the first part of the unforgettable experience that he and I were about to endure.

Chapter 13

Although language is a wonderful tool for conveying a thought from one person's mind to the mind of another, this means of communication is not perfect. Words are like vessels which carry meaning, but these vessels do not have a fixed form but are rather variable and changeable, like a cup made of rubber.

Take what appears to be a simple word, like the word "mountain". For me, my first experience of mountains were the Blue Mountains which begin their ascent about 60 kilometres west of Sydney and form a part of what is generally known as the Great Dividing Range, a mountain ridge which extends almost parallel to the entire east coast of Australia. The Great Dividing Range is the highest elevation of land on an otherwise very flat continent and for the average Australian, these mountains are pretty high up indeed. But for anyone who comes from any of the other continents, as soon as they see the Blue Mountains, the general comment is, "These aren't mountains. They're just hills." In fact, the original name the English gave the Blue Mountains was *The Carmarthen Hills*.

But Australia has nothing to compare with the European Alps, the North American Rockies, the South American Andes or the Central Asian Himalayas. The dividing line, therefore, between a hill and a mountain is not accurately defined and really depends on a person's experience of these geographical features.

Even the word "blue" does not have a fixed meaning. When people first hear of the Blue Mountains, they imagine mountains of a similar colour to the sky. From a distance, the Blue Mountains do look, in fact, blue, but it is rather a dark greenish-blue colour than the colour of the heavens in daylight or the colour of certain people's eyes.

I could take other simple, every day words, such as "hot", "cold", "good", "home", "triangle" and so on and so on and it is easily seen that no two people on the planet will have an identical understanding or appreciation of a word. How, then, we successfully communicate ideas has a lot to do with how well we know the people we are speaking to and the context within which these words are used. Anyone who knows me, for example, will know that when I say "it's a cold day, today", the temperature is below 20°C. However, anyone who doesn't know me will interpret "it's a cold day, today" within his or her own personal experience. A Laplander, for example, will interpret "it's a cold day, today" to one where the mercury has dropped to something like -40°C which to me is so cold, it's almost evil.

A system of law, then, that relies completely on the interpretation of words is open to misunderstandings, and is certainly not the most efficient way to distribute justice and equity among the human species. But then, we have nothing better to replace it and so we are stuck with it.

This was the difficulty that we had with understanding the exact meaning of "it is in the public interest to do so". That is, the Minister can waive the Seven Day Rule "if it is in the public interest to do so". What is the public interest? Who is the public? Is it the entire Australian population? Does this mean that, in order for the Seven Day Rule to be waived in the case of Faisal, we have to prove that each and every Australian would benefit from Faisal's presence in our country? Or does it mean only a certain number of Australian citizens? And how many?

And what do we mean by "public"? For example, we use the word "public" in the expression "public utility". The water collected at Warragamba Dam is an example of a public utility which provides the Sydney basin with potable water. "Public" in this sense is obviously limited to the number of people who make up the Sydney metropolitan area which at present is about four million people. But what of the water supply to Cocklebiddy in Western Australia, a small town consisting of a service station, a motel and a pub? If the water supplied to this little place is called a public utility, and it provides only for a hundred-odd people, can we interpret "public" as this small number of people?

To help Faisal, then, gain a waiver by the Minister required us to understand what is meant by "the public interest" but we were not sure exactly what "public" and even further, "public interest" really meant. I knew it was in my *personal* interest that Faisal gained his permanent visa so that he could be my friend forever. But did I constitute enough people to be the public? And was my "interest" in our friendship good enough, or strong enough, for the Minister to consider a waiver? Or did it have to be much stronger? How interesting did this "public interest" have to be?

But what was an example of "public interest"? That Faisal was so strong that if there were a fire, he could pull two people out of a burning house at a time? That Faisal was such a fantastic lover that he satisfied the entire female population of Australia? That Faisal had superb, healthy organs that were self replicating and which could be transplanted as required? That Faisal held within his head the secret cure to AIDS, cancer and the common cold? What "public interest" did Faisal need to satisfy that would be enough to grant him a Seven Day Rule waiver?

Faisal's lawyer, Farqad, was unable to enlighten us much more than what we had already surmised. He believed that we needed to prove that Faisal was, in some ways, so necessary to the Australian community that it would be to the detriment of the Australian community if the Seven Day Rule were not waived.

Writing a letter to the Minister of Immigration and Multicultural and Indigenous Affairs seemed to be the only thing I could do. It was important to word the letter correctly in such a way that it was not too strong but at the same time forceful enough to make an impact. I wrote the letter several times until I was satisfied that I had made the situation clear. The contents of the letter were broken down to an introduction, to explain who I was and what I did for a living, stressing the fact that I was an Australian citizen, in order to show that Faisal had local back up. I then mentioned how that, in my job, I meet refugees from many different countries but Faisal was the only one who I ever wanted to befriend. I then explained that Faisal had become a part of my own personal community, that is to say, he knew my family and friends. This was the only way I could bring out that the Seven Day Rule waiver was applicable because of "the public interest".

I explained in the letter that the decision by DIMIA had had a negative impact on Faisal's health as well as mine. I then went on to explain how I could not understand the decision to reject Faisal based on the premises of the Seven Day Rule because it had been clearly explained, and it was well documented, that Faisal had resided in Pakistan for more than seven days because he was simply waiting for the Taliban regime to collapse and therefore allow him to safely return to Afghanistan. Unfortunately, the Taliban came into Pakistan, at least in the border areas where Faisal was living, and this is what prompted Faisal to leave Pakistan and come to Australia.

I ended the letter in as strong enough terms possible, mentioning that I was aware that Faisal had a profound fear for his life if he went back to Pakistan but also that it would be outright torture if he were separated from his family for yet another three years with no assurance of making his stay here permanent and safe.

Faisal received even stronger backup because, on speaking to my mother about the entire situation, my mother herself volunteered to write a letter to the Minister. It was a simple letter but it backed up mine, particularly as I had said that Faisal had become a part of my family. My mother, a staunch born-again Bible Christian wanting to write a letter in favour of a Sunni Muslim was short of miraculous.

Faisal fortunately received yet further backing from the Afghani community, from a Hazarah who I had never met, who stressed how much Faisal had been key in helping Afghanis settle in Australia. That it was a Hazarah who wrote such a fine letter further helped to show that Hazarahs and Pashtuns were not forever staunch enemies. I was already aware of Faisal's assistance of other Afghanis because Afghanis of all shapes and religious persuasions came to visit Faisal to have letters translated, to write forms, to ring public utilities and so on. I tried to imagine how these Afghanis would survive in Australia without Faisal. How would they operate within our society?

There was also something else which made the relationship between Faisal and me important which I included in my letter. Faisal and I had become a bridge over the waters of fear between the Afghani community and the general Australian population. It was through Faisal that I had become friends with other Afghanis and discovered what they were really like as people. On the same token, it was through Faisal that these Afghanis met members of the Australian community. This, surely, was in the public interest. After all, the Australian government had made our country a safe haven for those escaping atrocities from other countries. Not only did Australia want to provide a solace for refugees, this country no doubt wanted newcomers to the country to integrate within the framework of Australia's multicultural society.

Faisal held an extremely important position among the Afghani community and he was influential in changing the mindset of other Afghanis. Faisal was a central figure, someone everyone looked up to. Because I had been Faisal's teacher, and teachers are much more highly respected in Afghani society than they are in Australia, the Afghanis therefore respected me as well.

When the Afghanis found out that I was gay, this was a challenge to their thinking. Homosexuality is a criminal offence in Afghanistan and death is the punishment if two people are caught in the act. This, then, was a challenge to the Afghani way of thinking, to allow homosexuals to be an acceptable part of the general society. I remember Saber saying to me on several occasions, "I can't understand how a good man like you, who is a teacher, can be gay." This simple statement succinctly illustrated the mindset within Afghani society, and the mindset of people in most societies and cultures now and in the past, that homosexuality can never be associated with goodness when it has been shown in countries where homosexuality has become legalised that it is simply a form of sexuality, nothing more nothing less.

Fortunately, a few Afghanis got used to the idea and it no longer bothered them. Many, however, didn't like it at all. I could feel it in the way they communicated with me. There was a lot of confusion as to how to approach me. Outwardly, they treated me with courteous respect but I could tell from their body language that they could not come to terms with what I did in my private life. It was doubly complicated for them because, not only was "gay" and "teacher" incongruent in their thinking, Faisal, someone whom they respected within their own community, treated me with respect and as an equal despite my inclinations.

As a result, many of these Afghanis no longer associated with me. But what made me even angrier was that many Afghanis simply assumed that if Faisal and I were such good friends, then it simply followed that Faisal and I were having an affair. I was so cut up with anger by this attitude. For one thing, it simply wasn't true and, in any case, I couldn't understand why it was generally assumed that a close relationship between a gay man and a straight man had to have a sexual component to the relationship. More importantly though, it worried me that Faisal might be affected by what these people thought and decide to avoid having anything to do with me. But I was even more surprised at how Faisal dismissed these rumours with a disposition that he did not give a damn what these people thought.

Faisal had also been key in his acceptance of women as equals, even if they did not wear the veil.

When Khatyn came for dinner, it was Faisal who made the point of allowing women into the same assembly with the men, which is totally disallowed in Afghani culture. Faisal had also accepted to sit at the table with my mother and sister who not only do not wear a head covering of any sort but belong to an entirely different religion. Therefore, because Faisal, who was highly respected within the Afghani community, was able to accept this difference between the cultures, it forced the other Afghanis to at least see another way in which a community lives and operates.

My association with Faisal was also a challenge to my entire way of thinking. I had always thought that there could be something called a multicultural society where people with different cultural opinions could live harmoniously together. My relationship with Faisal and my observation of Auburn taught me that when people of completely different cultures come together, there are certain aspects of each person's culture which can co-exist because they do not affect other people around them. For example, because Faisal is Muslim, he prays regularly whereas I don't pray at all, he eats only halal meat and avoids pork whereas I eat anything, and he celebrates Ramadan whereas I celebrate Christmas.

However, after much reflection, I began to realise that there are certain aspects that make a multicultural society an impossibility. Although people of different cultures can live together while they each adhere to their own cultures, there are certain cultural differences that cannot co-exist and therefore a choice has to be made as to which cultural aspect should prevail.

The situation of women is a point at hand. In Australian culture, women and men gather together freely in social gatherings but in Afghani culture, men and women socialise separately. Every Afghani party I ever went to was an all-male affair, there was not one woman there unless I brought Khatyn along. This then raised certain issues which I have never been able to resolve. For instance, if I were to have a party at my place and I invited Afghanis and Australians, should the Afghanis bring their wives and daughters like Australians do or should the men come alone? Or, if I walk down the main street of Auburn and see an ex-female Afghani student of mine walking with her husband, should I stop and have a conversation with her or simply ignore her to protect her from a reaction from her husband?

Further, what if I were a woman in my profession as a teacher? How would a male, Afghani student appreciate that? In fact, I discovered through Khatyn that it was very difficult for female teachers to teach Middle Eastern and African men for this very reason. The general attitude is that women should not teach men, a mentality that women in many western countries fought against during the 1960s which resulted in our modern society based on equality. How, therefore, can you have a multicultural society when two cultures have not only different but contrary opinions of women within that society?

And so it is with other aspects. How can there be a unified society where different cultures have contrary views of sex and sexuality, of the attitude towards people outside the cultural or religious group, of the importance of marriage, of marrying someone of a different cultural or religious background, of the number of spouses one can have, of dress codes, dietary laws, the importance of keeping one's word, the need to be punctual and so on?

My thoughts were further challenged when I tried to think of culture as a permanent, static entity. But by trying to come to a clear understanding of what a culture is, I realised that culture is not like a solid, unchanging rock but is more like water which moves and changes with the times. For example, what we call Australian culture today did not arrive with the First Fleet but has developed from a willingness to question customs and values, and adjust them accordingly. Already Anglo-Australian culture completely supplanted the culture of people who had already been living here thousands of years before the English had arrived. And then, even in the history of Anglo-Australia, much of what the Afghanis, and pretty much every culture around the world, believed about society was at one time very similar. About a hundred years ago, women in Australia had to clad up to the hilt, women stayed at home and looked after the children, and sex outside of wedlock, not to mention between two men or two women, was frowned on if not outrightly criminal. It was only during the last thirty-odd years that the Australian culture that we enjoy today came to be.

Australians, in general, feel that they enjoy a culture and a society which provides a considerable amount of freedom which is only dreamed about in other countries. But also, it is a freedom which our parents and grandparents in this same country never experienced. Culture, therefore, is not a static entity but an ever evolving reality.

The conflict between cultures concerning their core cultural values, and the fact that culture is fluid and changeable and not static and permanent, made me question why so much support is given to the preservation of culture above all other things. Is it possible that the focus on the preservation of cultures comes at the cost of human rights - and even human lives? If within a culture women are viewed as subhuman and therefore expendable as men see fit, or homosexuality is treated as a criminal act simply because of some people's distaste for it, or those outside a particular cultural, tribal or religious group, including native born Australians, are looked on as unacceptable partners for one's children, or cannibalism is viewed as an acceptable form of cuisine, should we still do our best to preserve the culture? If there were people in Australia today whose cultural values were identical to those current in Germany in the late 1930s and early 1940s, would we want to preserve that culture? Is it possible that our determination to preserve culture above all else is misguided and that, rather, before preserving a culture, we should first preserve human rights, and then make the culture readjust and fit in accordingly?

This enigma was only more brought out when I listened to my students. What intrigues me about those who escape atrocities in other countries and then settle in Australia is how they all say they love Australia because they feel free here. Whenever I ask my students why they like living in Australia, the answer is universally the ungrammatical but yet quaint statement that Australia is "a freedom country". But these same people then condemn, even to the point of social persecution, members of the general Australian society who live free lives, and further, condemn members of their own communities who either become somewhat relaxed about or completely abandon the traditions and customs of the countries they left behind.

Although I have never told my students I am gay, there have been times I have had to broach the topic of different relationships acceptable in Australia. One of the things I teach my students is how to fill in forms. Because many forms mention *de facto* relationships, I have to explain what a *de facto* relationship is, and that it not only means a relationship between a man and a woman but also a relationship between two men or two women. My students' condemnatory laughter or hateful outbursts are extremely painful moments for me. Little do they realise that this fills me with so much indignation that, if it were in my power, I would pack them all on a boat and send them back to where they come from, even if this placed them back under horrific circumstances. Suppressing my anger, I have to explain to them in the best politically correct language possible that same sex relationships are a part of the freedom that my students admire about this country. But a lot of my students do not appreciate this expression of freedom. They just don't seem to get it. They just don't seem to understand that the freedom they appreciate from others is the same freedom they are also expected to give.

By contrast, Faisal, himself a refugee, had adopted a completely different mentality and this was something I admired very much in him. Faisal had strong beliefs of his own but respected the beliefs of others. He appreciated that this country provided him the freedom to follow his version of Islam but at the same time he respected my freedom to conduct my life the way I wanted as long as it did not infringe on him or anyone else. He even went so far as to admit to me that, as much as he would hate it to happen, if any of his children changed their religion or turned out to be gay like I was, he would still love them because his only wish was that they grew up to be good people.

But despite these admirable qualities, Faisal's application for a permanent visa had been knocked back. Unfortunately, the Department of Immigration did not see these qualities in him nor was I able to succinctly describe them in a short letter. To really appreciate the type of person Faisal was, one had to know him personally on a day to day basis.

After our day on the Nepean River, Faisal resumed his adherence to Ramadan. I had no particular problem with that but I decided during this time to limit my visits to the evening when he could freely eat and smoke. But although Faisal was hospitable, I could see that all was not well. When the time came to break the fast, I noticed all the other Afghanis tuck into the food. By contrast, Faisal just picked at the food as if food had lost its charm. His lack of appetite was only compensated by his increased need to smoke. It was obvious that the letter from the government had a profoundly negative effect on him. I could also see through the change in the texture of the skin in his face how much the entire situation was getting him down.

Faisal also admitted that he had difficulty sleeping and had been prescribed sleeping pills to assist him. But Faisal was not alone with his disrupted sleeping patterns. His problems had begun to invade my psyche to the point that not only did I have problems sleeping, I began to have terrible nightmares about Faisal being sent back to Afghanistan, and he and his family being brutally slaughtered.

Faisal had another problem to contend with and that was his employment. He had initially told me that he was a carpenter but he was, in fact, simply a labourer. This did not mean that he had lied to me. Rather, in his current job as a labourer, he carried out carpentry work. Because of his lack of English but, moreso, his lack of qualifications, it was difficult for him to find a job of any substance. As a result, labouring work was all he was able to do.

This was yet another issue with Faisal. I had got to know the man very well and one thing I realised was that he was more suited to completing some sort of university qualifications. Faisal had told me that he had completed one year of study at university in Afghanistan doing architecture. But, because of the war, he had to abandon his studies and take up arms and fight. I remember Faisal explaining this in very picturesque words, saying that "they took our books out of our hands and put bombs and guns in them instead". His whole grievance was that, because of external politics, because so many different countries wanted to put their hands in and interfere with Afghanistan and its people, Afghanis, like Faisal, could not carry on a "normal" life, that is, a life similar to what we enjoy in Australia.

I can still hear that helpless pleading in his voice whenever we discussed this issue: "Why can't they leave us alone? We, Pashtuns, we are a quiet and gentle people. All we want to do is live in our land and live our lives. Why can't the other countries just leave us alone? Don't they have enough land in their own countries?" For whatever political, commercial or dominating reason, other nations, both past and present, have tried to get their hands on this small piece of terrain.

This is the eternal story of humanity, the need to dominate and control. What is in human nature that possesses us to do that?

Faisal's plight made me think back into history and at humankind's grotesque need to dominate. For example, I remember learning about the Roman Empire at school. The Romans went all over Europe, North Africa and the Near East in order to take control over this area of the world. The way this piece of history was presented to us was as if the

Romans were the saviours of the universe, bringing civilisation to otherwise barbarous nations.

However, I could never really appreciate why the Romans had to do it. Because I was brought up in a Christian home, I was presented with an alternate view of the Romans, one viewed through Jewish eyes. The Jews had an ancient tradition, documented in what Christians call the Old Testament, a tradition which attached them to their land and to the city of Jerusalem. Then the Romans came. If the Romans really were concerned about how archaic and backward looking the Jewish traditions were, the Romans could have simply pointed this out to the Jews and allowed the Jews to reflect and make appropriate changes. But the Romans didn't do that. With a might of iron, they completely took over the Jewish homeland and made it a state of their vast empire.

To really make the poignant point that they were set on domination and control, the Romans had laws which differentiated between Roman and non-Roman citizens, where non-Roman citizens were treated as lower class. When a Jew was born in the land of his or her ancestors that had now been absorbed into the Roman Empire, that Jew was born a second class citizen.

On every continent and in every phase of recorded history, we repeatedly hear this eternal story of domination and control, of oppression and tyranny. For the "little" people like Faisal and me, who have absolutely no influence on world affairs, all we can do is hope for the best to try and make our lives a little happier and better as we are tossed around here and there like tiny corks on a vast ocean.

What amazed me about Faisal, however, was that, despite his abilities and qualities, he did not look down on any job he took on. No occupation was beneath him, fruit picking in Victoria, labouring in Sydney, now working as a carpenter. Work for him was simply a means of gaining money, and more importantly, enough to provide for him and his family the basic necessities of life, and with a little extra work, a few small luxuries.

During Ramadan, Faisal's lawyer, Farqad, advised Faisal to see a psychiatrist and get a report which showed that Faisal was in no psychological state to return to Pakistan, let alone live another three years in separation from his wife and family. I read a copy of the report and was absolutely amazed at how succinctly the psychiatrist had documented what I had precisely observed in Faisal's current behaviour.

Once all the documentation was put together, it was submitted to the case officer. All we had to do was wait. Fortunately, this time, we did not have to wait long. As we approached the end of Ramadan, Farqad rang Faisal to tell him that his application had been rejected. As a result, his choice was either to leave the country or take his case to the Refugee Review Tribunal, or the RRT.

For Faisal, there was no choice. If the case officer had directed Faisal to the RRT, it was to the RRT we would go.

Chapter 14

Faisal's hearing at the RRT was scheduled for the following February. This meant that we had a three month wait before his case could be heard. I asked Faisal if I could attend the Tribunal and to my amazement discovered that not only could I attend, I could stand as a character witness.

The RRT is a special court of law dedicated to hearing cases directly related to refugees. In a country where the population of refugees is now significant, it made sense to have a special legal facility aimed at listening to the cases of refugees. For Faisal and me, this was a comforting thought seeing neither of us really believed that Faisal's case had been properly heard.

Yet again, more waiting. This was probably the most strenuous and frustrating part about Faisal's flight from Pakistan, the constant waiting. However, I suggested that there was no point sitting at home moping life away and so decided to take the opportunity and make Sydney a holiday destination where we would go out and do things.

Sydney is a wonderful city to live in with so much to do. However, when you have grown up here, there is always a danger of taking everything for granted. This then breeds complacency and indifference which sets in boredom and leads to simply overlooking what this city has to offer. I have travelled to many countries of the world but in the end I am thankful that I live in this wonderful city.

I took the opportunity to show Faisal, and many from the Afghani community, some of the places worth seeing. One day we went to Manly and spent the day there. I enjoy Manly Beach very much because it is one of the few beaches near the city that has a stretch of terrain behind the beach with lots of trees for shade. Some of the other beaches have just sand and sea with nothing to protect you from the sun's harmful rays, which means that if you want to get out of the sun, you have to bring a beach umbrella or you have to leave the beach.

Manly is not just a place to swim. There are volleyball nets on the beach waiting to be used if people come with a volley ball and enough players to make up two teams. The Afghanis, so I discovered, were very good volleyball players and it wasn't long before I was totally out of breath trying to keep up with them in this active sport.

When we had had enough of volleyball and it had become too hot, we all hurtled into the surf with such exuberance as if we were the introduction to a sunscreen commercial. We really enjoyed our time in the water, although it became obvious that because these Afghanis come from a landlocked country bodysurfing and swimming are certainly not one of their strong points.

On another occasion, we took a trip to Wiseman's Ferry, a town in the north of Sydney on the banks of the Hawkesbury River. Here there is a wonderful picnic area with large tracts of grassland on one side of the river and a backdrop of sheer cliffs on the other. There was plenty of space to play volleyball but the Afghanis wanted to play soccer. Running around after the ball eventually got us all hot and sweaty, and so we got into our cossies and jumped into the river. After getting all wet, we went and had lunch and watched a group of people playing cricket. I commented on how boring a sport cricket was (a comment which in Australia borders on blasphemy!) but it wasn't long before Saber, daunted by nothing, went over to the group, asked how to play and soon we were all involved in possibly the first Australia versus Afghanistan cricket match.

Another time, we went to the Blue Mountains to see the Three Sisters and to walk down the Giant Staircase. There was a suggestion to walk out to the Ruined Castle but because it really was a full day's walk out there, we declined the idea.

One night, we went out into the city. Strangely enough, the guys wanted to see what happened in a gay bar and so we went and had a look. We watched one of the drag shows but after that, the boys felt a little uncomfortable and so we went to King's Cross, the heterosexual sex centre. Here, all the boys disappeared for some time in some place of ill repute while I stood outside waiting, holding their coats like St Paul at the stoning of St Stephen.

We went to the harbour to watch the fireworks for New Year's Day, a display which illuminated the Harbour Bridge in a majestic display of lights. We went to the Powerhouse Museum, we walked around the bay at Five Dock, we took the ferry from Parramatta to the city, we really spent time in Sydney as tourists. It was a wonderful time. This had a particularly positive effect on Faisal because I noticed that this brought life back into him, his appetite returned and his countenance took on a nicer shine. This didn't mean that Faisal was forever happy all through summer. There were moments when he would become very quiet and reflective, and it was during these times that I left him alone because I knew these were moments that he really needed to be left undisturbed.

Eventually February came around once again. It was time for Faisal to attend the hearing at the RRT. Because I was so determined to participate, I had taken a day off work to attend.

Faisal asked me to be at his place at 8 o'clock. I didn't get much sleep the night before and so I was rather tired when I got to Faisal's place. When I arrived, Faisal and Qadus were already dressed and ready to go. Qadus, so Faisal explained, was going to be a character witness also. Qadus was going to verify that everything Faisal had said about his trip from Peshawar to Australia was true because Qadus had accompanied him part of the way.

Qadus' role as a character witness, therefore, was much more important than mine. I could only testify to the type of person Faisal was since he had resided in Sydney or, more correctly, during the short period that I had known him here. I was simply banking on the hope that because Faisal had an Australian citizen as a character witness, this would play in his favour, illustrating that he was a bona fide refugee with no terrorist leanings.

When I arrived at Faisal's place, to my great delight, Faisal offered me a cup of coffee! All the time that I had known him I had never seen him or any Afghani drink coffee. I had always been of the opinion that Afghanistan was a nation purely of tea drinkers.

I wore a tie to this hearing because in all courthouse movies, the male witnesses always wear a tie. I was therefore expecting Faisal and Qadus to do the same. However, contrary to my expectations, Faisal and Qadus were dressed rather casually. Obviously, Farqad in his usual incompetence had not briefed these men for the occasion. Because we were restricted for time, I thought it wise to say nothing. It was too late for them to change, and I thought it may have made Faisal more unsettled than he needed to be.

We left Faisal's house and walked to the main street of Auburn to Faisal's lawyer's office. When we arrived, the office was locked.

"What time were you supposed to meet Farqad here?" I asked Faisal.

"Eight thirty. And it's eight thirty now. He should be here. I'll just ring him."

Faisal punched the numbers on his mobile phone, pressed the phone to his ear and then waited. He waited and waited but there was no answer. I heard him say something in Dari and then he hung up.

"Where is he?" I asked.

"I don't know. I just left a message. We'll just wait."

We waited another ten minutes. I was becoming more and more tense. Faisal rang again and this time he got through to Farqad. After their dialogue in Dari, Faisal explained to me that Farqad had woken up late and would be on his way soon. Faisal said this with his traditional clinical expression but I was beginning to panic. How could the lawyer be late? This hearing was so crucial in deciding Faisal's fate.

Waiting for Farqad only increased the anxiety of the moment. If Faisal was nervous, he certainly did not show an ounce of his feelings.

Finally we saw Farqad waddling slowly down the main street towards his office carrying a suitcase in one hand and a wad of papers in the other, his face somewhat red and sweaty from extenuating himself. Farqad was not my lawyer so I didn't feel it was my place to begin ripping strips off him for being so late. I left that to Faisal who abracadabrad in his usual way but the reaction he got from Farqad was a glance at his watch and an arrogant snort with some comment which I guess meant that we were not late at all and had plenty of time.

Farqad had to go into his office first before we made the trip on the train. I don't know what extra material he needed for the trial. With all the documentation he was already carrying, it seemed as if every supporting document that backed up the life and times of Faisal were sufficiently present on his person. However, when he returned from the office, Faisal himself was laden down with more papers.

The appearance of all this made me muse that we were trying to get a drug smuggler through a serious court case.

From here we wandered slowly to Auburn Station to catch the next train into the city. The train we caught was rather crowded inside which meant that all four of us had to find separate seats on the train. I managed to get an aisle seat near the back of the carriage while the other Afghanis were scattered about throughout the carriage in front of me. I looked around the carriage, at Faisal, Farqad and Qadus, and then at everyone else on the train. The majority of the commuters were dressed meticulously in their business clothes ready for another bland, routine day at the office. I wondered how many of these people really knew the situation of the refugees in Australia. How many of them really understood what was really happening in the daily lives of these people who had escaped the atrocities of their own country and were now fighting for their lives to find a safe haven in a country so far away from strife? I wondered how many of them realised that someone in this very present situation was sitting in the same carriage with them.

Our destination was Town Hall Station where we followed the crowd, like a guided flock of sheep, up the escalators, through the turnstiles and then onto the busy streets above the underground. From here we walked to Elizabeth Street where we arrived at the building that housed the current RRT. I had walked past this building a thousand times in my life but was totally unaware that this was where refugee trials were heard. It was a tall, white, modern imposing building that shot up into the sky like an extremely large refrigerator.

We entered the building. I glanced at my watch and could see that it was already 9.30. That was the time that Faisal had told me the hearing would begin. I was totally nervous as if I were personally the one undergoing the trial. My hands felt sweaty and clammy, and I was constantly wiping them down the sides of my trousers. We went up a set of escalators which led from ground level to the first floor and from here we entered a set of lifts that shot us up to our level with breathtaking speed. While in the elevator, I turned to Faisal and asked him if he was nervous. His answer was amazing.

"No, I'm not nervous. Everything I'm telling in the Tribunal is the truth. Why should I be nervous?"

I wanted to hug him there and then! I wished he had said that earlier. It had the greatest therapeutic effect on me and amazingly calmed me down.

We arrived at our level and then walked into the modern foyer, partitioned off with an immaculately transparent set of glass doors with Refugee Review Tribunal emblazoned in gold letters as if the RRT were a private corporation. We were led into a waiting room as if we were in a hospital and there seated were obviously other refugees waiting for their trials to be heard. Farqad was about to go to the reception desk when he turned to Faisal and said in Dari, "You don't need an interpreter, do you?"

Fortunately I understood what Farqad had said. While Faisal squinted his eyes thoughtfully, I answered in his place.

"Faisal, you speak good English. But in this situation, if you can have an interpreter, get one. You want to focus on the details of the trial, not the niceties of expressing your ideas correctly. If you get nervous, it will be really difficult to express yourself well, particularly in a language which is not your own."

I was speaking from personal experience. I was familiar with what it was like speaking a language which I was not well acquainted with, particularly to the depth Faisal needed for the trial. When I was trying to learn German, I remember that a flurry of nervousness was like pressing a button in my brain and all my German would then flush out of my head and out into the ether.

Faisal took up my advice. With that, Farqad waddled over to the reception desk and I could see him flashing documents at the receptionist and pointing in our direction, and then he returned.

"We have to wait till 10 o'clock," he said.

"Why?" I blurted.

"Because the interpreter won't be here until 10 o'clock. So they have moved the hearing till 10 o'clock. Let's go downstairs and have a cup of coffee."

We were back in the elevator and went right down to the basement of the building where there was a café. Faisal ordered cappuccinos and raisin toast for all of us. This was just so unique! I had never seen Faisal sit down at a café drinking a cappuccino before. To me it meant that he had finally been initiated into Australian city culture. I wanted to take a photo, take it with me to the tribunal and then, showing the photo to all present, exclaim, "See? This man is trying to integrate into our society. He MUST be a refugee, he can't be a terrorist! Can you imagine Osama bin Ladin sitting in a café drinking a cappuccino and eating raisin toast?" and then watching the judge and all those in authority inspecting the photo through black rimmed spectacles and hearing the judge comment, "Yes, this is very convincing evidence. Yes, I'm ready to make my judgement now."

At one moment, Faisal left to go to the toilet. During his absence I used this opportunity to speak privately to Farqad.

"What are his chances?" I asked almost in complete desperation.

Farqad chuckled condescendingly.

"Oh, Michael, he has a ninety-nine percent chance of success. He's fine, he has nothing to worry about. Everything will turn out fine. His entire case is very strong. I've done this for other Afghani refugees who have had weaker cases and they have managed to get their PVs. There's nothing at all to worry about."

Despite his confidence, there was something false and insincere about the way he talked, as if he were a salesperson trying to sell me something I really didn't want or need. And after all, I had heard this same comment before when he went for his first interview and the outcome was totally unfavourable.

When Faisal came back, there was a lively conversation between Faisal, Farqad and Qadus in Dari. I understood bits and pieces of their conversation, that they were discussing certain details about the hearing. At times, Farqad would pull out papers and show them to Faisal and Faisal would point and make a statement. But I really wasn't very interested. The only thing on my mind was getting into the Tribunal.

It's a terrible thing when you've watched over the years court cases in movies and you see one of the key witnesses, who can testify the innocence of someone on trial, grilled by the lawyer of the opposition to the extent that the witness's testimony ends up sounding at best like a bunch of lies or at worst the testimony of a person whose memory is as good as someone in the latter stages of senility. My greatest worry was that somehow the lawyer of the opposition would be skilful enough to cast doubt on every piece of evidence that I had to support what I knew of Faisal.

What made it worse for me was that the only evidence I had that Faisal was telling the truth about his flight from Afghanistan and then Pakistan was his insistence on truth the whole time I had known him. It may have been true that many of the things he had told me he had documentation to back his statements or I had found information independently on the Internet or from other Afghanis which substantiated his claims. But the only primary evidence I had was the fact that Faisal had no difficulty becoming a friend of a non-Muslim gay man despite his Muslim beliefs. I was counting on this as my supporting evidence of the plausibility that Faisal held views too liberal for the Taliban to tolerate which led to the Taliban wanting to dispose of him.

When it was five minutes to ten, Farqad gathered everything together and we once again went up the elevator to the RRT level. We were ceremoniously greeted by the interpreter. I was quite shocked at his appearance, dressed in jeans and an open-necked khaki shirt as if he had just arrived from the Red Centre of the Northern Territory off the back of a camel.

We were then led down corridors to the court room. I remember as we approached the doors that led into this room expecting, on entering, to see on the left hand side a jury of twelve members, at the other end of the room a judge wearing a woollen wig and holding the gable, the lawyer of the opposition and then long bench seats where there would be crowds of onlookers ready to silently watch this suspenseful trial unfold.

However, as soon as the doors were opened, all I saw inside was a small room about three metres by four metres, with a long bench which extended from one end of the room to the other in such a way that it formed a barrier between us and those on the other side. Along the walls on our side of the room were a series of chairs. Qadus and I were asked to be seated here.

At the bench were three wooden chairs clearly ready for Faisal, Farqad and the interpreter to be seated. There was a woman sitting on the opposite side of the bench. She smiled and welcomed us, and then she moved to the left side of the room where there was a microphone into which she spoke.

The woman asked Faisal's identity, his address and origin of birth. She then asked about the identity of the rest of the party that came with Faisal: his lawyer, Qadus and me. Her body language showed that she had met this interpreter before but she went through the standard formality with him to prove he was an interpreter and that he was under oath to never disclose anything about the trial outside the Tribunal.

The woman then asked if Qadus and I were merely there as spectators or as a part of the trial. Through the translator, Faisal explained that we were there as witnesses. As this trial was to substantiate whether or not Faisal was really a refugee, I was expecting the woman to make some statement to the effect that I should not be present as I could hardly provide any proof regarding Faisal's movements in Afghanistan and Pakistan as I had never known him there. However, the woman just smiled and continued with the formalities.

The next thing was what book to swear on. This made me laugh inside. One hundred-odd years ago, and probably even quite recently, there was only one book, the Holy Bible, on which a person in Australia would swear in a court of law. Now with people of different religions, Australian courts of law probably have an entire library of books to swear on for each individual taste. Naturally, Faisal and Qadus swore on the Koran. But even non-religious people like me were catered for – I was to swear on the Affirmation.

"Okay, now that we have sworn you all in, please wait a moment for the Tribunal Member to enter," the woman continued. Throughout the entire process, I had thought *she* was the presiding Tribunal Member! This woman then explained the entire ceremony we had to go through when the Tribunal Member entered, how to stand up, say this, the Tribunal Member say that, the Tribunal Member sitting down and then inviting us to sit down.

We waited for about five minutes. Soon the door on the opposite side of the room opened and the Tribunal Member, who would preside over the hearing, entered. He was a rather tall, well-built, bearded man, with ginger hair, blue eyes and freckled face, and the overall appearance of a regular surfer, which gave me the impression that he had been particularly chosen for the job because of his all Australian look. We went through the formalities and then were invited to sit down.

You assume a lot in someone's voice when you meet for the first time. Although young and dynamic, the Tribunal Member had a tone of voice which seemed to express indifference towards non-Anglo-Celts. Throughout the introductory ceremony, the Tribunal Member came across as abrupt and non-sympathetic, but in hindsight I guess that it was the nature of his job to do so. However, this rather brash approach already made me feel a foreboding about the outcome of this hearing.

The introductory process required that the Tribunal Member confirm the identity of each person in the room, the lawyer, the interpreter, Faisal, Qadus and me. Once we got past all these formalities, the Tribunal Member's tone changed abruptly from brutal indifference to rather paternal.

"Okay," the Tribunal Member said, addressing Farqad, "my apologies for arriving late. One of the reasons I'm late is that I was actually looking at the submission that you sent last night. I mean, it's a matter for you, when you send your submissions, in terms of starting on time, it is a little easier if you send them slightly earlier."

Farqad apologised for his tardiness but I looked on in horror. What? Farqad sent a submission last night? Damn the man, I thought. He's supposed to be a lawyer. He has known for three months that Faisal was having this hearing today. How could he have left something for the last minute which delayed the court?

The Tribunal Member then addressed Faisal through the interpreter. He stated Faisal's full name and then verified that he had correctly pronounced it. Faisal, through the interpreter, replied in the affirmative and the Tribunal Member continued. Throughout this part of the trial, each time the Tribunal Member spoke, he paused to allow the interpreter to speak to Faisal and for Faisal to reply.

"Okay," the Tribunal Member continued. "As you probably are aware, I do not work for the Department of Immigration. I work for a separate organisation called the Refugee Review Tribunal.

Now, my primary function will be to assess whether or not I think you have a well-founded fear for one of the reasons provided for by the Refugees Convention. What is meant by this is a well-founded fear of persecution for reasons of race, religion, nationality, membership of a particular social group or political opinion."

All this verbiage was translated into Dari. At this point, I really regretted not knowing enough Dari in order to be able to listen to how well the interpreter translated all these technical terms. I was curious to know if there were exact equivalents in Dari for all this technical jargon.

The Tribunal Member then continued, "Mr Faisal, do you know the interpreter?"

Faisal through the interpreter replied in the negative.

"Do you have any problems if we keep using this interpreter at this hearing?" the Tribunal Member then asked, to which Faisal replied that he had no problems with this interpreter. The thought did cross my mind, though: what if Faisal, for some reason, didn't like the interpreter? What happens in a situation like that? I mean, what if Faisal said something like, "No, I think this interpreter is an outright arsehole and does not look like he can competently do his job. I think he will mistranslate everything I say so that everything sounds crooked, distorted or outright lies." What would the Tribunal Member do then? Should the Tribunal Member believe the interpreter if the interpreter said this?

"Okay," the Tribunal Member continued. "You probably know this but I'll mention it. Both the interpreter and myself have confidentiality obligations which means that neither he nor I can reveal anything that you tell us at today's hearing. One important exception, however, is that I will write down what you tell me today on a decision record and that will be sent to the Department of Immigration for them to act upon. However nobody in your country of origin or any other place will be given this information. I've had an opportunity to read your claims and, am I right in suggesting that your primary claim is that you have a well-founded fear of persecution as a Pashtun in and around Kabul city? Is that correct?"

Faisal replied in the affirmative.

"Okay," the Tribunal Member continued. "Now I understand that you come from a village which is in the order of ten kilometres from the centre of Kabul?"

"Yes," the interpreter replied after explaining all this to Faisal.

"Now, I understand that you were born in Afghanistan and you left to live in Pakistan in 1996, is that correct?"

"Yes"

"And your wife is currently living in Peshawar, in Pakistan, is this correct?"

"Yes."

"Okay, before 1996 you lived in Afghanistan."

"Yes."

"You were living in your village which is near Kabul city at that time?"

"Yes."

"Okay. And where were you born in Afghanistan?"

"I was born in Kabul."

"Okay." The Tribunal Member then looked back at his papers and appeared to be leafing through documents before he continued.

"Now, your migration agent, Mr Farqad Salaahid, presented a submission last night and because of this I needed to look up a few things. This means that you're appealing on two matters at today's hearing, one is whether or not you have a well-founded fear of persecution for a convention reason, and the second one is whether or not you qualify for a permanent protection visa or a temporary protection visa. Is that correct?"

"Yes."

The Tribunal Member then put his papers down and leant on the back of his fingers. There was a momentary pause before the Tribunal Member finally spoke.

"Now, my preliminary view is that you have a strong case. In that regard, I mean a strong case with respect to a well-founded fear of persecution for a convention reason. Your claims have been consistent throughout your application and, based on the alleged anxiety that you have, I would be more than a little reluctant to find anything against you on credibility grounds. What I want to talk about today is the second aspect of your claim."

The Tribunal Member then turned his attention from Faisal to Farqad. "Er, Mr Farqad, this is going to be more up your street than it is your client's."

The Tribunal Member then re-addressed Faisal through the interpreter. "Would you mind if I directed some questions to your migration agent?"

Once again, the interpreter garbled on in a language I did not fully grasp, although on occasion I understood a word here and a phrase there. However, I would have loved to have known what all this information sounded like in Dari.

The Tribunal Member then began a monologue regarding certain points of law, making reference to this Act and that Subclass of an Act and so on. I heard mention of something called the Migration Act and then a series of different numbers which apparently related to different types of temporary protection visas each assigned with particular numbers. I had initially thought that there was one temporary protection visa. But from what the Tribunal Member said, and from what I discovered later, there are many different classes of temporary visas, each assigned with a specific number.

At the end of this introductory prelude, the Tribunal Member moved from the temporary protection visas themselves to what Farqad submitted the night previous – the submission regarding the Seven Day Rule.

"Now," the Tribunal Member continued, "I just want to mention a couple of things. My first concern is that I'm not sure that I have jurisdiction to hear this aspect of your claim. The reason I think that is because, if you are refused a permanent visa, but you are granted a temporary visa, I'm not sure that this equates to the refusal to grant a protection visa which would give me power to actually hear the matter. I haven't made a final decision. I have a power to refuse or grant a protection visa. Now whether or not that means that I also have the power to determine whether or not the protection visa should be permanent or temporary is something I'm not sure of.

Now, let's just say, for example, that I *have* jurisdiction. We then have a problem. Was your client in a position to seek protection from the UNHCR in Pakistan during the four years he was there? Now, from what I have read of this case, I think your client definitely has a well-founded fear of persecution in Afghanistan and I am further persuaded to believe your client also has a well-founded fear in Pakistan. The evidence suggests to me that, in his case, Pakistan is not a country of effective protection. This is based on what I can see is rock solid consistency throughout his claim. So, if I have jurisdiction to consider the Seven Day Rule, then I envisage a potential problem for your client."

The Tribunal Member then looked down at his papers and then back up at Farqad and continued.

"Now, I'm quite happy to give you a reasonable amount of time to make further submissions that may help your client. Even so, this aspect of your claim has a really negative impact on your client and I'm not sure how we can get around this."

Because this was the first time in my entire life that I had ever attended anything that could be considered a court of law, it was the first time that I was exposed to the Australian legal system in a direct way. This meant that the legal jargon used that I had not seen in any of Faisal's documentation was totally meaningless to me, which meant that significant information flew right over my head. But Farqad was a lawyer, or, as in the words of the Tribunal Member, Farqad was at least a migration agent. Whatever his title, Farqad should have recognised immediately the significance of the Tribunal Member's comment that the Seven Day Rule probably did not fall under his jurisdiction. Rather, Farqad just ummed as if he had understood all this information about as much as I had. Finally he was able to say something with meaning.

"But when I presented this entire case to DIMIA, DIMIA accepted his case," Farqad replied. "The problem was that Mr Faisal's case was delayed. The case officer was of the opinion that Mr Faisal's wife was a Pakistani national because Mr Faisal and his wife were married in Pakistan. So, we had to prove that Mr Faisal's wife is not Pakistani but that she is Afghani as much as Mr Faisal is. So by the time we proved that she was an Afghani national, the Seven Day Rule was put into effect. And this affected his case.

Mr Faisal has explained on several occasions that the reason why he stayed so long in Pakistan was that he thought that eventually he would be safe to return to Afghanistan. The problem was that his situation in Pakistan became life-threatening. While he was in Pakistan, he became an active member in certain activities."

"But that goes to his claims and I'm pretty satisfied with this," the Tribunal Member replied.

Farqad paused in reflection and then continued.

"Well, prior to this time, his life was not targeted. That's why he did not feel that he needed to apply for protection through the UNHCR. However, in the latter end of his stay, he had to escape for his life."

"But," the Tribunal Member said, "that was only in the last stages of the applicant's residence in Pakistan. And that's the concern. I mean, I read that in your submission yesterday and I'm just not sure what I can do with it."

"Well," Farqad continued, "the other aspect is that if you can take it into consideration that it's not easy to access the UNHCR in Pakistan...."

"...where a mandate of refugees are," the Tribunal Member contradicted gruffly. "No, I've got a map of all the UNHCR offices. Their assistance is quite extensive."

Farqad paused for a moment, taking care to word his following statements a little more thoughtfully.

"Well, it's not that easy to get there," Farqad replied. "If refugees try to get to any of the UNHCR offices in Pakistan, there is always a high chance that refugees will be attacked or forced to pay if they want to put through an application."

"So, you want me to base my decision on hearsay?" the Tribunal Member said as he straightened himself back on his chair. "And that's all it is. The evidence I have, all objective evidence at my disposal, indicates that refugees are provided with ample assistance. You might like to say that this is not the case from what you know. But all evidence in my possession tells me that refugees are quite able to apply for assistance. I'll be persuaded by objective evidence in writing. If I get a range of evidence which says that assistance is provided in Pakistan, especially from an organised body such as the UNHCR, then I find this persuasive evidence and will include this when I write my decision record."

The Tribunal Member then paused, looked at the papers on the bench before him and then back at Farqad.

"Look, I realise this is a difficult situation for you, that is, your client. I really don't know what we can do. Considering the circumstances and because I am not sure of my jurisdiction to hear this aspect of your claim, I'm going to give you the opportunity to provide further submissions. This will also give me the opportunity to check up on a few things. One of the things that I want to know is whether or not your client is, in fact, caught by this, but I'm just not sure."

"From my experience," Farqad replied, squirming in his chair in such a way as if each movement released the necessary words from different parts of his body, "most people who were caught by this seven day ruling had their application waived by the Minister."

"I also noticed you put this application through to the Minister who declined to waive it," the Tribunal Member replied. "It might be true that the Minister can waive it, but I don't have that same power to waive it. On the contrary, I have to consider it."

"But isn't it within the power of the RRT to make a decision about a refugee's status, whether he is accepted as a refugee or not?" Farqad asked. "Can't the RRT simply make the claim that my client should be granted protection? Then the matter could go back to DIMIA and then they can decide what to do regarding the seven day ruling."

"But because you've made a submission on the Seven Day Rule, I have to deal with it," the Tribunal Member explained. "Further, you not only make a submission surrounding the Seven Day Rule, you also brought to my attention which subclass will be granted. So I have to deal with it. If I don't, this will constitute a jurisdictional error."

Farqad looked down at his papers, then at Faisal, then back at the Tribunal Member.

"DIMIA," Farqad continued, "when DIMIA refused my client's application, they refused his application merely on the seven day ruling. They have accepted everything about what he claims about persecution and fear he has experienced in Afghanistan and Pakistan. It's just the seven day ruling that caused them to refuse his claim."

"No, no, no," the Tribunal Member stated emphatically and stressed the point with vigorous shaking of his head. "They refused to grant Mr Faisal any form of protection. They decided that Mr Faisal was not someone whom Australia has protection obligations under the refugee convention. This basically means that they decided that he did not have a well-founded fear of persecution in Afghanistan. Now, I don't agree with that. I intend to set this aspect of his claim aside. Of course, in their decision, they've also included the aspect of the seven day issue, and that's what will have the greatest impact on his case."

"But," Farqad implored, "in the earlier part of his time in Pakistan, his life was not in danger. He didn't apply to the UNHCR because in Pakistan he was safe."

"Yeah," the Tribunal Member replied, "I understand your point. However, it's not a matter of whether you need to apply for protection in a third country. Your client escaped his country of origin because he believed he had a well-founded fear of persecution and so he sought refuge in Pakistan. He resided there for four years. He subsequently found his way to Australia. The problem is that it doesn't matter whether or not he had a well-founded fear of persecution in the second country. This ruling looks at whether your client applied for effective protection there. He didn't. Now, when he thought he had a well-founded fear of persecution in Pakistan, he left, which is totally understandable, and travelled to Australia. But the problem is that he was in Pakistan, a second country, for more than seven days."

The Tribunal Member paused to take a breath.

"Now, I'm not saying that this is my final decision and this is the way it is," he continued. "I'm only telling you what I think and the way I view this ruling. But if you want to dispute that, that's not a problem. Now, when I consider your client's case, I can tell you that unless something completely unusual happens, I think he has a well-founded fear of persecution. And on that basis I am satisfied to put aside that aspect of his claim. But it's the seven day issue that I cannot put aside. So if you want to make further submissions on that, I would be more than happy. In the meantime, I will make my own enquiries because that's the concern."

"All right. I can do that. Yeah," Farqad replied in a rather defeatist tone.

"Ah, but as I say, it's a matter entirely for you," the Tribunal Member replied. "I mean, you're the best judge of this because you're privy to the applicant's claims."

The Tribunal Member's end comments appeared to be inviting Farqad to continue to take up the fight in order for the proceedings to turn out much more favourably for Faisal. But Farqad said nothing more. He just shuffled papers around on his desk in such a way that it appeared that he was getting ready to leave.

The Tribunal Member then turned to the interpreter.

"Now, I do apologise for speaking all this time without having this interpreted. There are issues which we were discussing which your migration agent is probably in a better position to explain to you in your first language. I am of the preliminary view that you have a well-founded fear of persecution for a convention reason and hence am therefore prepared to set aside that part of the departmental decision. The second part I may not be prepared to set aside, that is, whether or not you qualify for a permanent or temporary protection visa. I've explained to your migration agent this morning my reasons for my concern. It's my intention to provide him with two weeks to put forward further submissions."

The Tribunal Member once again turned to Farqad.

"Okay. Do you want to say anything else?"

"No," Farqad said in a defeatist tone. "I will provide you with further submissions. Can I ask you on the seven day ruling what kind of information you need?"

"You see," the Tribunal Member then continued with a hint of urgency in his voice, "the main problem I have is that you're saying that your client didn't need to seek protection in Pakistan because he wasn't at risk there – granted that he was not safe only in the later stage of his residence in Pakistan. But in the earlier stages, he could have applied for protection. But then you say that he was always at risk in Pakistan. So there seems to be a contradiction in what you say. On one side, he's unlawful and therefore can't continue to live there, but on the other side, he was able to live there and therefore did not need any protection, or at least any help. Now if he was able to live in Pakistan, he had the possibility to seek protection in order to get refugee status in Pakistan."

"Yes," Farqad said in defence, "you know that in Peshawar, Afghanis are restricted in movement. They cannot move around freely in Pakistan because Afghanis are given an ID card which restricts their movement to only certain areas of Pakistan."

"Where did you say your client lived?" the Tribunal Member asked. "Was it Peshawar?"

"Yes, Peshawar."

The Tribunal Member then held up a map of an area of Central Asia like a kindergarten child giving a presentation for show-and-tell. "See, this is a map with the UNHCR offices and UNHCR presences. It's pretty extensive. You know, I could give you this map if you want."

"I know the UNHCR has an office…"

"Not just an office," the Tribunal Member interrupted. "They have offices all over the country. And they have UNHCR presence all over the country."

"But an ordinary Afghani is not able to go to the UNHCR asking for protection. The officers there would just block him from gaining access. The police or the guards would not allow that person to apply."

"Have you got information to back this up?"

"Yes. I have witnesses."

"But, then," the Tribunal Member continued, "what you have to realise is this. Even if you get me a handful of people who say that they weren't allowed to go to an office, you have to convince me that your client was in a similar position. But this is also in light of the hundreds of thousands of refugees in

Pakistan who do apply and have applied. Hundreds of thousands of other refugees were able to go into one of the UNHCR offices or approach one of the UNHCR personnel during four years of residing in Pakistan. I mean, I'm playing devil's advocate but I want you to know how I might think about things. Do you understand?"

"Um, yes, I quite agree with you," Farqad said unconvincingly, "but also there is also the evidence of corruption, what's going on over there. UNHCR local staff."

"I worked for the UNHCR in Pakistan," the Tribunal Member replied as if he were the brunt of an intentional insult. "I'm aware of allegations of corruption in many of these offices. But I don't think that this would assist the application because it does not appear that your client has sought the protection of the UNHCR in Pakistan throughout the four years that he was there. Now if he was worried about living there illegally, why didn't he seek migration status while he was there? In fact, what you are saying is that he didn't need to seek assistance because he didn't have a well-founded fear up until his latter stages of residence in Pakistan."

"No, he had a well-founded fear in Pakistan," Farqad said.

"Then why didn't he seek protection?"

This last question was met with sheer silence from Farqad. Farqad's lips quivered and it looked as if he were going to make a reply, but no reply was given. The Tribunal Member then sat back in his chair, looked down at his desk and then back up at Farqad.

"Look," the Tribunal Member continued, "I do apologise. I do not intend to come across as sounding belligerent. I'm really trying to be as clear as possible and to give you an idea of the things I'll be thinking about when I put forward my final decision. So this will give you an idea of the types of things you can address in your submission."

There was a moment of silence. Everyone was expecting Farqad to say something but Farqad sat there speechless, his face blank and his lips pursed like a naughty child who is pouting after being told off.

"Listen," the Tribunal Member concluded, "is two weeks all right? I know that a decision will be better than no decision. In any case, I want to try and get this out as soon as possible. Just hang on a second. I have a calendar here."

The Tribunal Member then set a date for the next hearing and then turned to Faisal.

"Okay, Mr Faisal, is there anything you wish to tell me today?" the Tribunal Member said, directing the question back to the person who was really in the hot seat.

"He just wants you to give him an overview of your talk with the representative," the interpreter replied.

"I have one problem and that's the Seven Day Rule. That's my problem," the Tribunal Member said.

"Well," the interpreter replied after babbling in Dari to Faisal. "I have many reasons why I did not apply in Pakistan that I can't put them all on paper."

"So, you've got too many reasons to put them on paper?" the Tribunal Member asked with a rather perplexed expression on his face.

"No," the interpreter replied. "I can't condense it all on one page..."

"No problem," the Tribunal Member replied without allowing the interpreter to finish the sentence. "Would you like to give them to me orally now? We've still got a fair bit of time."

"When I was in Pakistan," the interpreter began, "I had some problems, some difficulties, but still I lived in Pakistan. I fled to Pakistan because Pakistan offered some protection. At that time my life was in danger."

"So, why didn't you apply?"

"The problems I had weren't life-threatening. I mean, I did not see a need to seek refugee status or seek protection from the UNHCR at the outset. It was in the year 2000 that things changed and my life was threatened in Pakistan which caused me to make the decision to leave Pakistan. It was at that time I knew my life was in danger, not before then."

"Okay," the Tribunal Member replied paternalistically, "the problem is that this ruling only allows for the fact that if someone with a well-founded fear of persecution for a convention reason resides for seven or more days in a second country and during that time he or she does not seek assistance through the UNHCR, then based on my understanding of the regulation, it doesn't matter whether or not your life became threatened in the second country. The power I am granted on this matter is not wide, it is very limited. Irrespective of what I think is right or wrong, I must obey the law. This is what I've been explaining to your migration agent, Mr Farqad."

"Thank you so much for clearly explaining this to me," the interpreter said on Faisal's behalf.

There was a momentary pause and I thought we had come to the end of the proceedings. But then suddenly Farqad's voice was heard once again.

"Can I say just one thing?" Farqad said, suddenly coming back to life. His face sparkled as if he had just come up with a brilliant idea. "I thought the Tribunal's power was simply to reject or accept refugee cases, not to decide on the type of visa that can be granted."

"Yes," the Tribunal Member replied, "that was my understanding as well. I am of the view that I have no power or jurisdiction to consider the Seven Day Rule. But because you raised it the submission you sent yesterday, I have to take it into account."

"I raised it...I thought, that, er, it was what I had to consider in this hearing. But originally I was more of the understanding that the RRT only made the decision either to refuse or grant protection. I never had any..." Farqad sputtered, concluding his sentence incomprehensibly as if his final words turned into glue as they left his mouth.

"Am I right in understanding that you are intending to withdraw the submission you made yesterday?" the Tribunal Member said in much earnest.

"Yes, yes!" Farqad replied hurriedly in confirmation. "I want to withdraw my submission in relation to the Seven Day Rule."

"Okay. I have no problems. Could you just put this on record? Then I can make a decision this afternoon."

"I wish to withdraw my submission in relation to the Seven Day Rule because I am of the understanding that the function of the Refugee Review Tribunal is simply to consider whether or not to refuse or grant a visa."

"So you don't think we have power to make a decision on the Seven Day Rule."

"No."

"No, well I don't either. So, if you now wish to withdraw this second aspect of your claim, then I will record it in my decision record and say that it was initially brought to the attention of the Tribunal but subsequently withdrawn. The Tribunal is therefore only concerning itself with the well-founded fear aspect of the claim."

"Yes. I withdraw my submission in relation to the Seven Day Rule," Farqad said once more for good measure.

"Mr Farqad, thank you very much. Can I ask you to put that to the applicant because this is Mr Faisal's case. If he wants me to consider it, I'll consider it. But you need to get Mr Faisal to agree. Of course, if he doesn't, that's not a problem. Can you just confirm that your client is also satisfied with this situation?"

"Yes."

Farqad then muttered to Faisal in Dari for some moments. When he had finished, he explained to the Tribunal Member that there was nothing more to be said on the matter for his client.

The Tribunal Member then addressed Faisal through the interpreter.

"So, for the record, that issue has been withdrawn. I can just look at this case now as a well-founded fear case and I can tell you now that unless something completely unforeseen happens, I am satisfied you have a well-founded fear for a convention reason. And I will not consider the Seven Day Rule issue. Okay?"

"Thank you so much," the interpreter replied.

"Gentleman, thank you for your attendance. Ah, just sit around for a minute. We have a certain protocol. I'll just get someone in to close it off."

Both the Tribunal Member and Farqad began packing up documentation and closing folders, and Qadus and I just looked at each other. Neither of us was necessary and the case seemed to have come to a close but I could not tell what the verdict was.

When we were finally outside of the room, Farqad began cheering and raising his hands in the air with great delight.

"What? What?" I asked in anticipation.

"Faisal has got his permanent visa. He got his PV!" Farqad said jubilantly.

"What? How do you know?" I asked bewildered.

"Didn't you hear what the Tribunal Member said at the end of the case? He doesn't need to worry about the Seven Day Rule. He is clear!"

"Why? Why doesn't he have to worry about the Seven Day Rule?" I asked perplexed, unable to share in Farqad's joy. Farqad said something but he didn't seem to make any sense. He was using a lot of lawyer jargon to bewilder us all which meant that we could not share in the excitement. Rather, we watched, well, I watched Farqad outwardly express his joy while I thought that the only reason he had so much for Faisal's case because he was paid to do the job.

On the way home on the train, I tried once again to get Farqad to explain to me the significance of the hearing and why the Seven Day Rule was put aside so readily. Farqad glocked and gleeked in lawyer jargon once again. He may as well have explained everything in Pashto as far as my understanding was concerned. Faisal appeared just as bewildered as I was. I felt so sorry for Faisal. He didn't know whether or not this meant that it was the end of his struggle or not. I couldn't allow him to continue in a cloud of ignorance and so decided to consult my family lawyer and see if he was able to enlighten me.

The family lawyer, David Murray, I sought advice from was really my mother's solicitor whom my parents had consulted throughout their lives for mundane issues such as buying and selling houses and writing wills. I didn't know if he knew anything about immigration law but at least I knew he would know something about lawyer jargon.

David Murray had been my parents' solicitor almost as long as my parents had been married. He was now an elderly gentleman, with a thick crown of grey hair atop a very red face as if he had just come in from a long jog or suffered from permanent sunburn. An odour of bath soap surrounded him and this, coupled with the feeling of his smooth, cold hands when I greeted him gave me the impression that, like Pontius Pilate, he literally washed himself from everyone's affairs each time he concluded a case.

Mr Murray worked in an office in the centre of Penrith. The building in which he worked must have been from a bygone era as indicated by the creaking staircase as I climbed up to the first floor, and the old, dark wooden furnishings that made the building. Mr Murray had managed, however, to blend the antiquity of the building with technological modernity in an aesthetically pleasing and balanced way.

I entered his office at his request and was offered a seat in an old wooden chair that appeared to have been there as long as the building had been but lovingly looked after to preserve its original appearance.

Mr Murray welcomed me into his office and then entered into an introductory conversation about my family, particularly asking questions about my mother since my father had died. This was followed by a discussion about my welfare, a comment about how much I had grown since the last time he had seen me, and what my future plans were.

Finally the conversation arrived at the topic that I really wanted to discuss. I began by explaining who Faisal was and then gave a basic overview of the tribunal proceedings. I explained that I had heard the word "jurisdiction" mentioned on occasion and how that in the end the Seven Day Rule was miraculously removed from the entire case. When I mentioned this, Mr Murray laughed.

Although not an immigration lawyer, Mr Murray was familiar with the proceedings required for refugees and therefore was able to explain to me in simple, layman's language what had transpired. When a refugee first comes to Australia, he or she must apply for protection through DIMIA. It is the responsibility of DIMIA to examine the case and then decide whether or not the applicant is a refugee. If DIMIA decides that the applicant is not a refugee, this doesn't mean that the applicant is automatically rejected. The applicant has a further opportunity to appeal the case by taking the application to the RRT.

The function of the RRT, so Mr Murray explained, is to listen to cases that are rejected by DIMIA in a similar way to a court of appeal. If the RRT agrees with DIMIA's decision to reject the applicant's claim, the person has no other alternative but to return to his or her country of origin, or at least leave Australia. However, if the RRT disagrees with the findings from DIMIA but accepts that the applicant is a refugee, the RRT returns the findings back to DIMIA and DIMIA must then grant the applicant a protection visa.

The key issue that I was not clear about but that Mr Murray was able to explain was this. The Seven Day Rule was legislation that DIMIA had to consider. However, the Seven Day Rule was non-existent as far as the RRT was concerned. The role of the RRT was to determine whether or not an applicant was truly a refugee, and that was all. When the Tribunal Member said that the Seven Day Rule was not in his jurisdiction, he meant that it was not his business to worry about it. His only concern was to decide whether or not he agreed with the decision by DIMIA regarding an applicant's claim to being a refugee.

However, by law, the RRT must consider any claim raised by the claimant. Farqad had included the issue of the Seven Day Rule in his submission which forced the Tribunal Member to have to decide upon it. It was a stroke of good fortune, therefore, that Farqad finally recognised this and decided on withdrawing the submission of the Seven Day Rule at the last moment, which meant that the Tribunal Member no longer had to consider it.

Mr Murray concluded that he was convinced that Faisal had won his permanent visa. All we needed now was to wait for the handing down of the report. A report would be written by the RRT and then two copies made, one submitted to DIMIA and the other given to Faisal. Faisal had the choice of returning to the RRT building two weeks later to collect the report or simply waiting for it to come in the mail which would probably take yet another two weeks to receive. I was happy that he opted for the first option, to go and physically collect it.

When Faisal received the report two weeks later, I couldn't wait to get to his place to read it. My first question was, "Well? What was the result?"

Faisal just handed me the entire report. It was a thick document of about twenty A4 size pages. The covering letter that accompanied the report was addressed to Faisal. The letter began with an introductory blurb to explain that there was some consideration before coming to a conclusion. Near the end of the letter were those immortal words: the Tribunal has decided that you are a refugee. This means that you are a person to whom Australia has protection obligations.

"Yes, yes, yes!" I screamed and hugged Faisal so hard I thought all his internal organs would ooze out like toothpaste from a toothpaste tube.

"I have permanent visa?" he asked.

"You mean, you didn't know?"

"Well," Faisal said. "Farqad said that I had it but I never believe him. I don't understand all the words in the letter."

"My goodness, Faisal," I replied. "Let me explain it to you in simple terms."

I read through each sentence of the front page and then explained the meaning in much simpler English than was contained in the letter. The covering letter simply stated that Faisal had proved that he was a bona fide refugee. I explained that the attached twenty page report just supported how the Tribunal Member came to this decision.

I took the report home and later read through it carefully and slowly, page by page. It was thorough and it addressed each issue of Faisal's claim, finally making it extremely clear that Faisal was a refugee. The Tribunal Member not only used documentation that Faisal himself had provided, the Tribunal Member had also relied on other points of law not mentioned in the hearing, and reports from the UNHCR in Pakistan concerning the situation in Pakistan and Afghanistan against those of a similar background to Faisal, namely, members of opposing parties to the Taliban, Sunni Muslims and Pashtuns, three aspects about Faisal that had placed his life in danger. What pleased me was to read how the Tribunal Member stated that not only was Afghanistan no longer safe for Faisal to live in, neighbouring Pakistan was not a safe place for him either, something he mentioned in the hearing, which only strengthened the reason that the Seven Day Rule should be waived in Faisal's case.

I was so happy. Faisal told me that other people who had been through the RRT and were accepted only had to wait about a month before they finally received their permanent visa. Once Faisal had that visa in his hand, he could return to Pakistan and see his family once more and finally bring them back to Australia so that they would all be reunited at last.

It was now only a matter of time. I was filled with a combination of joy and satisfaction that Faisal would finally obtain his permanent visa and be reunited with his family.

Chapter 15

The Cornelia Rau and Vivian Alvarez Solon cases could not have come at a more propitious time. When these two women made headlines, the damage to the lives of many refugees was already irreparable. However, it allowed those yet to be adversely affected by the immigration department finally something to lean on. The immigration department was now under the microscope of the Australian media and the Australian public in general. Refugee cases now had to be resolved within a three month period.

Faisal received his report from the RRT in February and the results had been passed back to the department of immigration. All there was left to do was wait yet again. But what was making it all the more frustrating for Faisal was the fact that one after the other, many of his other Afghani friends were all suddenly beginning to get their permanent visas. Permanent visas were being issued like junk mail flyers and we were being invited to one permanent visa party after another. Many of these Afghani refugees had applied, like Faisal, to the Minister and had had the Seven Day Rule waived.

The noble thing about Faisal was that he put on a good face each time we attended an Afghani permanent visa party. He clapped and sang along with the music, watched the dancing and the festivities continue as if all was peaceful in the universe, but I knew that deep down he was saying to himself that this was not fair. The beauty of Faisal was that he was angry at the system, not at the person. He was happy for each person who received their permanent visa because he knew their struggle had ended and they could now begin a new life in a safer environment.

Another difficulty for Faisal was that many of the Afghanis who received their permanent visas soon after flew back to Pakistan. During their time in Pakistan, these permanent visa holders visited not only their own immediate family but also the families of those who were still in Australia, including Faisal's wife and children. Although Faisal was happy to be able to pass on messages and presents through these Afghanis on his behalf, it was frustrating that contact with his family was still by a third person. The problem with this was that it made his family raise questions about Faisal's real intentions. Faisal complained to me that his family held the belief that Faisal no longer cared for his family anymore and just wanted to live the good life in Australia and had thus abandoned his family. I could understand his predicament. How could he possibly explain all the intricacies of Australian law and the problems associated with it in a simple telephone conversation? Even I, an Australian citizen, was having difficulty trying to understand everything that was going on.

The months rolled on and finally, after three months of waiting, Faisal received a letter from his case officer. Faisal had a copy which he allowed me to read in order for me to explain the contents.

The letter began by referring to a telephone conversation between Farqad and the case officer and then went on to state that the case officer understood that Faisal had not provided additional submissions for the Seven Day Rule waiver request. But then the letter took on a peculiar course. The letter continued by stating something to the effect that, before all his paperwork could be finalised, Faisal needed to provide evidence from a health professional to confirm that he required ongoing medical treatment beyond a three year term and that such treatment was not available in Afghanistan. This would then prove to the case officer that a further three year TPV is no longer an option and Faisal could be issued with a permanent visa.

I looked at Faisal.

"Do you understand the contents of this letter?"

"I'm not sure, but I think my case officer wants me to prove that I'm sick."

"That's precisely the point," I snorted. "Your case officer is asking you to provide evidence that you are so sick and that you have to stay here. If you go back to Afghanistan, there is no doctor or hospital there that can help you so you should stay here for more than three years."

Faisal looked at me, then at the letter, then back at me.

"But I didn't come to Australia because I was sick. I came to Australia because they were going to kill me."

"I know," I continued. "Not only so, even if they had all the best hospitals and the most advanced medical treatment in Afghanistan, it has been clearly established in the report from the RRT that you cannot go back to Afghanistan. You cannot avail yourself of any help from Afghanistan. What the hell is your case officer on about?"

"I don't know," Faisal said frustratingly. "I don't understand what this case officer wants. Every time she asks for something, I give it to her but it is never enough. She wants something else. In the end, she put me under the Seven Day Rule law. But not every Afghani refugee has had the same problem. I know lots of Afghanis who spent more than seven days in another country but their case officers didn't seem to see this as a problem and they were issued with permanent visas. My case was rejected, it was taken to the RRT to prove that I am a refugee and this report was given back to the case officer and she still has to find something else that I have to provide to stop me from getting my visa."

I read the letter once again. I could not understand either what this case officer wanted. All I could guess was this case officer was doing everything possible to prevent Faisal from gaining a visa, thinking that Faisal was simply an opportunist who caught the refugee wave out to Australia. It was as though she thought that if she frustrated him enough, Faisal would get sick of all these procedures and would simply return back to his domestic, routine life in Afghanistan. But Faisal did not have a life in Afghanistan, nor in Pakistan for that matter. If neither Afghanistan nor Pakistan were countries where Faisal could safely live, it simply stood to reason that the country in which he was pleading asylum, Australia, was the only country he had left to live in, so granting him a permanent visa should have been automatic.

Neither Faisal nor I could fully understand what was going through the case officer's mind but it appeared that she simply did not want Faisal to stay in Australia for personal reasons that she alone was privy to. I remember a few days after explaining to him the contents of the letter, Faisal said to me, "You know, sometimes I want to go to a park and see my case officer walking around and simply watch what type of life she leads. I would like to go up to her and just ask her, 'Why are you doing this to me? Don't you like me?' I want to see if she has her own family, a husband and children and I want to ask her, 'How would you like to be completely separated from your family?'"

I was desperate to find a solution as much as Faisal was. But I didn't know enough about Australian law to know exactly what to do. This was just as new to me as it was for Faisal and for all the other Afghanis and refugees in general.

I decided to pay another visit to my mother's family lawyer. During the visit, I asked Mr Murray what we could do. I even told him I was willing to pay for his advice. This must have signalled to him the seriousness of the matter and how much it meant to me. He asked for a copy of the documentation I had in my possession concerning Faisal's case and I passed the lot on to him. About a week later, he called me.

"Michael, I just need one piece of information from you. When Faisal left the detention centre in Woomera, what was the date that he left?"

"The 11th September, 2001."

Mr Murray laughed through the receiver.

"My goodness! That's an auspicious date! If that doesn't prove it, nothing else can prove that he is not a terrorist! Or at least he was not involved in that particular event! However, it is also a memorable date. It's a date that even the case officer could not forget, don't you think?"

"Of course," I replied bewildered, not understanding the importance of the comment.

"I have some paperwork that might be of interest to you. When would you like to come to my office and pick it up?"

"Immediately!" I yelled through the receiver and almost dropped the phone in a rush to get to my car and to Mr Murray's office. If it were possible, I would have squeezed myself through the telephone line like an egg through a snake.

When I reached his office, Mr Murray invited me in and told me to sit down. He then passed me a thick document which obviously was a printout from his computer.

"Read the first page and then tell me what you understand of it," Mr Murray said.

I read the first page which was a list of certain points of law relating to the Seven Day Rule. I was familiar with much of it because it had been used in

Faisal's rejection letter. However, there were footnotes at the bottom of this page which provided exceptions to the Seven Day Rule. One of the footnotes explained that those who were granted a TPV before 27th September, 2001, were exempt from the Seven Day Rule.

I looked up at Mr Murray and he smiled.

"So, do you understand?" Mr Murray asked.

"If I rightly understand," I replied, "the Seven Day Rule should not apply to Faisal because he was granted a TPV on the 11th September, 2001, sixteen days before the Seven Day Rule came into force. Faisal is exempt from the Seven Day Rule and should already have his permanent visa because of the report from the RRT."

"You're an intelligent man," Mr Murray replied. "But have a look at this."

He then flicked the pages of the documentation.

"Let me show you something else. Let's just say that Faisal obtained his TPV *after* the 27th September, 2001."

Mr Murray then showed me pages of this extensive documentation. There was a section about exemptions to the Seven Day Rule. If a refugee resided in a second country and in that second country there was a real chance of persecution, or at least there was a failure to protect their human rights, the Seven Day Rule could be put aside.

I was delighted! Finally we had the law to cover us in the situation of this Seven Day Rule farce. This reminded me of a saying that a Russian student of mine once told me: "The law is like people walking past your window. One of them may even turn and smile at you". Finally there was a section of the law that worked in Faisal's favour.

But then my next question. Why hadn't Farqad used this documentation? He was Faisal's migration agent. That was his job, that was what he was being paid for. Yet, it required other people to actually do his job.

"Can I have these papers?" I asked.

"Of course you can. You can give them to Faisal to give to his case officer if you like."

I couldn't wait to give them to Faisal and I immediately raced around to his house to do so. Faisal was mystified as to the exciting news I had to give him. I brought along all the papers Mr Murray had given me and showed them to Faisal. Poor Faisal tried to read the first page but the wording was far too complicated than he could handle. So I explained the news to him, pointing to the relevant sections and then simplifying the language enough for him to understand.

"Where did your friend get this information?" Faisal asked.

"From an Internet website for lawyers, I guess."

Faisal sat on his haunches and sighed. "Then, why doesn't Farqad tell this to the case officer?"

"I have no idea. You should show this information to him when you see him next."

Faisal took this information to his lawyer and he explained to me that Farqad was overly excited to receive it. Subsequently, Farqad tried on many occasions to contact the case officer by phone but was unable to get through. So, he emailed the information. Mr Murray had earlier explained to me that as soon as the case officer saw this law, she would immediately give Faisal his permanent visa because she would immediately recognise she was breaking the law. How else could she explain why she had been delaying Faisal his permanent visa?

A day went by. Two days went by. A week went by. Two weeks went by. But we heard nothing. I sent Faisal an sms every day and was constantly ringing him. What news was there? Faisal told me that he had rung Farqad several times and Farqad answered that he had tried to ring the case officer but could not get through. That we did not have an answer to the email probably meant that the email had not been read by the case officer. The case officer was under no compulsion to open her email as far as we could see. But this only made the situation more serious for her when she finally read it.

I made Faisal ring Farqad every day to make Farqad ring the case officer. Each time Faisal rang, Farqad would say that the phone was engaged, or the case officer was not there or all sorts of what sounded like excuses. So, in exasperation, I decided that Faisal and I should pay a surprise visit to Farqad and ask him to ring the case officer while we sat in the office.

One afternoon, I went with Faisal to the centre of Auburn and marched into Farqad's office with the determination of a runaway locomotive, demanding Farqad to make the phone call to Faisal's case officer immediately. Farqad looked at me and Faisal who was behind me, stupefied by the sudden intrusion. However, he dutifully picked up the phone and made the phone call while Faisal and I invited ourselves to sit down. Miraculously, Farqad got through to the case officer. Faisal and I waited in suspense as Farqad hummed and haahed regarding the email. Once he got off the phone, Faisal and I were in suspense. What had happened?

"That piece of paper with those laws about the Seven Day Rule," Farqad commented, "apparently they no longer apply."

"What?" I screamed.

"There has been new legislation that overrides this law," Farqad replied cautiously. "That documentation you showed me says that those who got their TPV before the 27th September, 2001, were exempt from the Seven Day Rule. But this was not always the case. Originally, all refugees fell under the Seven Day Rule regardless of which date they entered Australia. Then, in 2003, an amendment was made to this law stating that anyone who obtained their TPV before 27th September, 2001, was exempt from the Seven Day Rule. However, this amendment has once again been overruled and all refugees come under the Seven Day Rule regardless of the date that they received their TPV."

"What?" I cried and stood up in indignation. "You mean to say that if Faisal's case had been presented to the case officer some time after 2003 until whenever the amendment was removed he would have his permanent visa now? It's a matter of bad timing?"

Farqad looked at his desk, then up at me.

"Well, it's not quite like that," he said rather defensively.

"Convince me otherwise. This means that there is someone up there who is chopping and changing laws due to some whim or fancy of the moment, putting exemptions in then taking them out. I mean, we are dealing with people here, for Christ's sake."

"Michael, this is the law."

"But the law is not constant. We are brought up to be law-abiding citizens as if this is a good thing and yet the law is not a constant. It can change. And I don't know the person who changes it, yet I can suddenly become a law breaker because something I do today could be, by some stroke of an anonymous pen, an infringement of the law tomorrow."

I had reached exasperation point and I felt the blood rush to my head. I didn't know what to do, laugh, cry, beat the wall, what. Really, what I wanted to do was walk into the case officer's office and let her have it. What did she really want anyway, what was her problem?

We left Farqad's office. I was exasperated and just didn't know what to do. When we arrived back at Faisal's place, neither of us said a word immediately. Faisal prepared tea while I paced up and down in the living room like a caged tiger.

Faisal came into the loungeroom and placed the tea tray on the floor. I stopped walking, placed my fist on the wall, leaned my forehead on my arm and stared out the window.

"So, I have to try to prove that I'm sick and that my sickness will last more than three years?" Faisal eventually said.

"It looks like that's what you have to do," I said, still staring out the window.

"But that's lying."

I turned to Faisal and then snorted with cynicism.

"You know, Faisal, I was brought up to believe that honesty is the best policy and all this 'you should always tell the truth' crap. I know Islam teaches it. I was taught it when I grew up in the church. Religious people and philosophers teach truth as if it were a sacred entity that should never be defiled. But in your situation right now, the truth will destroy you and your family. If you maintain that you are not sick, that you don't need medical attention in Australia for more than three years, you won't get a permanent visa. Who will look after your family for another three years then? What happens if during those three years, Pakistan forces all the refugees in Peshawar to return to Afghanistan? Who will protect them?"

I closed my eyes and banged my fist on the wall in despair and then continued.

"Faisal, I don't know how to tell you this in any other way but, for the love of God, if you want to save your family, tell this case officer what she wants to hear. Stuff the truth! She's not interested in it. Lie to save your family."

Faisal sat and looked at the ground and then at me.

"I don't know if I can do that. God loves those who tell the truth. I have always told the truth all my life. I don't want to stop that now."

I gave out an exasperated laugh.

"Tell the truth, then. Get knocked back. Watch all the Afghanis get their permanent visas, fly back to Pakistan to see their families and then organise to sponsor them to live here, while you spend another three years separated from your wife and children and allow this separation to torture you and most probably kill you. They are your choices."

There was a moment of silence. Suddenly we heard a noise at the door and then Sattar entered the flat accompanied by a few new Afghani faces I had never seen before. I was in no state to be social and so, after being polite and sharing a cup of tea with Sattar's guests, I excused myself and left.

That night, as I lay on my bed, I just couldn't hold back the tears. I felt completely frustrated with the situation. I felt bitter hatred towards all authority and felt absolutely helpless, unable to do anything to make the situation favourable for Faisal, fearing the absolute worst that could happen.

Chapter 16

When Khatyn heard the news, she seemed to know exactly what Faisal needed to do.

"Why don't you take it to the local Member of Parliament, the local MP?" Khatyn suggested.

"What's the local MP?"

"You know, the local representative of our government. If you have a problem or a complaint about something that you think is serious enough to be considered by the government, there are government representatives, that is, Members of Parliament, who you can talk to. They're in every electorate, you know, every area where we vote on Election Day."

"What can the local MP do?" I asked.

"The local MP can look into the case and at least write a letter to the Department of Immigration. DIMIA, by law, has to reply within three days."

"But how do I get to see the local MP?"

Because I had never needed to call on the help of my own government, I was of the impression that making an appointment to see the local MP was akin to asking for an audience with the Pope.

"Just ring them up, make an appointment. You have to remember that the local MP will be willing to help because you and Faisal are potential voters. Faisal is probably in a good situation because he will add to the MP seven other potential voters."

"Seven?" I asked bewildered, wondering where these seven other voters would come from.

"His family, you dummy! His wife and children. When they come out to Australia, if the local MP has done something for Faisal, I'm sure Faisal will explain this to his wife and children, and when they are all eligible to vote, they will make sure they return the favour to the local MP."

What Khatyn explained to me certainly was new information. But it was all I had left to help. Khatyn suggested that I make an appointment with the local MP in her electorate because she had heard that he was approachable. Khatyn rang on my behalf and I was granted an appointment two weeks later.

In the meantime, Faisal was sent on a paper chase to obtain reports and evidence which explained something to the effect that Faisal was suffering from some sort of psychological stress and this was affecting his physical body in particular ways. Faisal had to add that they did not have the appropriate facilities in Afghanistan to keep him in good health.

Faisal reluctantly went along with all this, probably because I was now urging him to do so. I was, in fact, abusing my position as his friend. Although I viewed Faisal and myself as equals, Faisal still considered me a little higher and with additional respect than he probably would normally give anyone else, simply because I had once been his teacher. Faisal couldn't even call me by my first name but still addressed me as Teacher. Because of this, Faisal was willing to go against his principles and do what I told him.

But I also was at a moral quandary. I was required to choose between two principles I held important in my life, telling the truth and protecting someone from harm. Whereas I usually believed in observing both, in this case, these two principles were acting against each other. Which was more important? I really did not reflect on it too much. Basically, I chose the latter, that it is more important to save a life than to tell the truth. Faisal still was coming to terms with the decision.

The day of our appointment finally arrived. I remember it was a terribly stormy day, windy and raining at the same time. The storm itself seemed to be a precursor of bad tidings.

The three of us, Faisal, Khatyn and I, arrived at the reception desk and were warmly received by the receptionist who told us to take a seat and wait. Finally, a very tall, rather plump but imposing man walked into the reception area. I could smell what seemed like a cloud of aftershave wafting off his body.

"Michael Farril. Is that you?" he asked as he turned towards me. I stood up to shake his hand.

"Yes, good afternoon. This is Faisal, the person I'm here to talk to you about. And a friend of mine, Khatyn."

"Please, come into my office," the MP said and extended his arm in the direction of a door where Faisal, Khatyn and I skulked in like three naughty students going to the principal's office.

The local MP's entire composure made me so nervous that I felt that I was not worthy to be there in his office. It took a few moments for me to compose myself enough to be able to articulate exactly why we were there.

Once I had mustered up enough courage to explain our presence in the MP's office, I began explaining Faisal's plight. The MP looked at me with an expression portraying a disinterested snarl which was very unsettling and caused my mouth to go dry. After a general introduction, the MP asked to look at some of Faisal's papers. When I turned to look at Faisal, I could see him sitting there with that blank expression I was familiar with when he first entered my class, and coupled with his beard, it really made him look as if he were Osama bin Laden's undersecretary. This picture of him made my heart sink and gave me the impression that our mission was already an outright failure before we had a chance to begin. I was sure that the MP thought, like I had thought, and the interviewer at the detention centre had thought, based simply on Faisal's overall appearance, that Faisal had to be a terrorist – it could not be otherwise.

The MP snatched the papers out of my hand abruptly in a manner which said more than words that he did not believe for a moment that Faisal was a refugee. I watched his eyes speed read through one page after another while letting out an audible, harsh breathing sound as if he were snoring. After this initial preview of the papers, the MP blurted out in a rather obtrusive manner, "I'm tired of these refugees complaining. We did not invite them here."

I was horrified and totally afraid to answer. I sat there motionless, not knowing what to do next. But I was so grateful that Khatyn had come along because she was not afraid to answer.

"I'm sorry but I really don't think this is correct," Khatyn replied calmly but pointedly. "Australia did, in fact, invite refugees to come here because Australia is a signatory to the 1967 Protocol relating to the Status of Refugees. This means that our country is advertising to the world that if you are a refugee, Australia will welcome you with open arms."

Khatyn's comment was followed by deathly silence from the local MP who then once again picked up the collection of papers I had handed to him relating to Faisal's case. This time he went through various pages much slower as if he were trying to find some evidence to dismiss Faisal from the office empty handed. Eventually he landed on a page which grabbed his interest.

"It says here that you are of Pashtun ethnicity," the MP said gruffly.

"Yes, he is Pashtun," I replied in defence.

"Then he doesn't need protection here. The Taliban was made up of the Pashtun tribe. Pashtuns aren't in difficulty in Afghanistan. If this man was of any one of the other tribes in Afghanistan, I could appreciate his claim that he was escaping problems in Afghanistan. But not as a Pashtun."

This comment about Faisal's racial background was like thrusting a sword into my soul. The general assumption that Pashtuns and Taliban were like the two sides of the same coin had certainly persisted in our mentality. I had originally accepted this as an axiom simply because of what my student, Mohammed, had said. This MP had no doubt accepted this information in much the same way as I had. But I felt trapped. How could I convince this MP during this short hearing that he was mistaken? I felt as if my heart was dissolving. But once again, Khatyn spoke.

"Hang on, sir. Don't you think that equating a nationality with a political party can lead to an unfair injustice?"

"Do you mean to suggest that I have my facts wrong, young lady?" the MP said in defence of this challenge. But I was amazed by Khatyn's self-composure.

"What I mean is that we should be careful that we don't draw hasty conclusions about Faisal's political involvements simply based on his ethnic background. Let's not make the same mistake we made during the Second World War when many Australians of German descent, that is, descendants of the Germans who had come to Australia in the mid-1800s, were put into camps simply because of the nationality of their ancestors. The Australian government did not separate nationality from political persuasion, thinking that 'German' and 'Nazi' were in some ways a description of the same thing, and so put Australians with German names and German heritage into camps. I'm sure that someone of your calibre would not like this mistake to be repeated."

Khatyn's comment was strong, direct and accurate. It was also like a big smack across the face of this MP. But although Khatyn stood up bravely against this important authority and put him in his place, this man had the power to do something, and undermining his position was likely to work against Faisal.

There was a moment of silence as the MP once more flicked through the papers. There was a thick silence in the room with only the sound of this MP breathing heavily as if he were suffering from sinusitis. Finally, the MP stumbled across another piece of information that he found worthy of note.

"It says here that this Faisal was a member of the Hezbe-Islami party. I'm sure you are aware that this party is against the current government in Afghanistan. The representatives of this party are also against the Australian and American governments."

There was utter silence. I had nothing to say in Faisal's defence. I knew Faisal had been a member of this party but I also knew why he had been drawn into this party in the first place. Even Khatyn remained silent on this issue. I knew that Khatyn was not at all acquainted with Afghani politics or Faisal's political history in order to counteract this statement.

The dauntless river of time felt as if it had transformed into a painfully slow moving glacier. I didn't dare look across at Faisal or Khatyn. Instead, I just stared at some benign object that occupied the local MP's desk, looking for a suitable reply to this statement. But I could think of nothing and so I looked up at the roof and prayed to whoever was listening in the other world to give us the information we needed to persuade the local MP that even this point about Faisal needed reconsidering. Suddenly, out of the silence, Faisal's voice was heard.

"Excuse me, sir," Faisal said almost whispering. "It is true that the Hezbe-Islami party is now against America and Australia. But this wasn't always true. During the war between the USSR and Afghanistan in the 1970s, America was friends with the Hezbe-Islami party. America and all the world fighting against Russia supported this party because they knew that the Hezbe-Islami party was the only party that could push Russia out of Afghanistan."

"Then why is Hezbe-Islami against America and Australia now?" the local MP retorted.

"Because, like they didn't like Russia, they don't want other countries controlling Afghanistan. They only want Afghanis to govern Afghanistan. They want Afghanistan to be free."

That was a blow below the belt. Although a decisive answer to the local MPs accusation, this was a statement that was more than likely to destroy the only hope that we had left in helping Faisal get his permanent visa. I felt completely shattered and was trying my utmost not to burst into tears.

Eventually the local MP terminated our meeting and buzzed his secretary to collect the papers and make a photocopy of them. When the secretary came in and collected the papers, the MP stood up and commented that there was not much more he could do for us. The case had been heard by DIMIA, then sent to the RRT where Faisal had obtained a favourable response, so it was really up to DIMIA to make a final decision. We were then dismissed and so we waited in the reception area for the receptionist to return the original papers back to Faisal.

At the end of the interview, I felt that we had not achieved anything. Rather, we had completely done the reverse. This was our last port of call to help Faisal out and it just did not work in his favour.

When we were outside of the building, Khatyn told us to stop. She had left her umbrella back inside the office and wanted to retrieve it. Faisal and I took the opportunity to have a cigarette while we waited.

While we puffed away, Faisal turned to me and said, "He won't do anything for me, will he? I am a Pashtun so I should not be here in Australia. But, Teacher, where can I go? I'm a person without a country. I cannot go back to Afghanistan. I cannot stay in Pakistan forever. And now I can't even stay in Australia. Tell me, where can I go?"

I had nothing to say to that. The entire experience with the local MP left me feeling completely empty with absolutely nothing left to offer Faisal as consolation. We stood there silently, contemplating the dismal weather, the wind and the rain, as if the weather itself were summing up how we felt inside. Eventually, Faisal turned to me and asked, "Where's Khatyn?"

I looked around me. Khatyn certainly had taken her time to retrieve her umbrella. I was about to return to the building in search of her but as the thought crossed my mind, Khatyn appeared with a look of embarrassment and in possession of her umbrella.

"What happened? Why were you so long?" I asked.

"I couldn't remember exactly where I had left my umbrella in the office so it took a bit of time to find it," Khatyn replied. With that, we set off.

One afternoon, a few days after the interview, I went round to Faisal's for a visit. Faisal went through the usual formulaic greetings and then the tea ceremony. At the end of all this ritual, Faisal then looked at me with a rather strange expression on his face.

"So, do you want to hear the good news or the bad news?"

I didn't want to hear any bad news. So, I just told Faisal to tell me the good news if there was any.

"Sattar got his permanent visa!" Faisal said almost with a cynical laugh.

"What?" I exploded. "When?"

"Yesterday. I have to go and pick up his visa on Friday from the post office."

"But didn't Sattar also fall under the Seven Day Rule like you?"

"Yes, but the Seven Day Rule was waived." There was a pause and then he continued.

"I mean, I'm happy for him. He got his PV."

Yes, I was happy too. I was happy for Sattar to get his PV but angry because Faisal was more deserving. Faisal spoke English, Faisal worked, Faisal integrated with Australian society and Faisal was very tolerant of alternative views.

"He's having a party this Friday to celebrate. We're having it here. Do you want to come?"

I could not really say that Sattar and I were chums. But because Sattar and Faisal lived in the same house, and because I saw Sattar often when I visited, I felt under compulsion to attend.

Faisal told me to be at his place at seven o'clock and I arrived punctually. I knocked at the door but there was no answer. I turned the door knob and realised that the front door was not locked so I made myself at home and walked down to the loungeroom. It was deserted. I then sent an sms to Faisal to find out where he was. Before I received a reply, I heard the crinkly noise of plastic bags and a male and female voice.

Suddenly two figures walked down the hall and into the living room. When they entered the room, there I saw Faisal with Khatyn.

"Hi, Khatyn," I said rather surprised. "What are you doing here? How did you get here?"

"I was out the front of my house when Faisal drove by. He stopped and asked if I wanted to come over for a party for Sattar and said that you were here. The children have both gone out so I decided to come over."

This was so admirable of Faisal. It was very striking because Faisal had broken with his own custom by accompanying a woman on his own. But Faisal knew how much a friend Khatyn was to me and so he did not shy from inviting her along when he saw her.

After all the appropriate greetings, the three of us went into the kitchen. Faisal took three glasses from the dish rack and asked me if I wanted a drink to which I replied in the affirmative.

"Sattar's party is tonight, isn't it?" I asked.

"Yes," Faisal replied.

"Well, where is everyone?"

"They will be here later. Sattar still hasn't finished work yet."

After Faisal had poured the drinks, he then said to me, "Do you want to know the good news or the bad news?"

"The good news, of course," I replied anxiously. "I don't want to hear any bad news."

"You remember my case officer? Well, she's not my case officer anymore," Faisal said elated.

I stood there stupefied for several moments while I tried to comprehend the news before I was able to say something.

"What do you mean?" I asked.

"Well, she said she was tired of my case and so she is giving it to someone else and she's going on holidays."

None of this made sense. Since when did case officers pass on their cases to another case officer so they could go on a holiday? I thought this was rather peculiar until Faisal provided me with the other piece of news.

"Oh, and can you explain what this means?" Faisal asked and pulled out a sheet of paper from his shirt pocket. I opened it up and saw that it was written from the local MP's office and was addressed, not to the case officer, but to the case officer's superior. The letter was firm.

As I read through the letter, a warm feeling of triumph passed through my body. Here in this letter, the local MP addressed the Department of Immigration in rather strong terms. The local MP began by pointing out that the RRT had abandoned the Seven Day Rule when giving a final pronouncement which meant the Department of Immigration should have also complied with this decision.

The letter then went on to say in very strong words that the findings of the RRT indicated that Faisal should have his permanent visa already which implied that DIMIA had unnecessarily delayed Faisal's acquisition of a permanent visa. The letter then went on to say that DIMIA should seriously consider Faisal's case because he has been separated from his family for such a long time now. The letter then ended with a rather firm statement to make the Department of Immigration act immediately.

It was a rather concise letter but it packed a punch. I looked at the letter and read it again and again to see if I really had been reading it correctly. The local MP had, in the end, done what was needed to be done.

"Your case officer didn't go on holidays," I said to Faisal with a smile. "I think she's been permanently removed!"

"Oh, and the Seven Day Rule has been waived by my new case officer. So, all I need is a police clearance and I can get my permanent visa."

"A police clearance?" I asked. "Haven't you already submitted a police clearance?"

"Yes, but it's only valid for six months. I now have to fill in a new police clearance form. While I was trying to get the doctor's report to say I was sick and I couldn't be treated in Afghanistan, my last police clearance form expired," Faisal explained.

Faisal then looked up to the ceiling and gave out an exasperated sigh.

"This means I have to wait even longer. You know, it takes a long time for the police clearance form to get processed."

"How long?" I asked.

"It could be a month, it could be two months. Who knows?"

I banged my fist on the bench.

"Damn your last case officer. She has completely stuffed up your life, you know."

There was a moment of silence and then Khatyn stuck her glass in the air in readiness to give a toast.

"Anyway," she said. "Faisal has a new case officer, no Seven Day Rule to worry about, so it will all be over soon. Here's cheers to our local MP and a better future."

The three of us clinked glasses as if we were the three musketeers.

I then turned to Khatyn.

"Khatyn," I asked. "You know when we went to see the local MP? While Faisal and I waited outside, you went back to get your umbrella. But you were gone a long while. What happened?"

Khatyn's face went as red as a tomato and she smiled embarrassedly.

"Goodness! You didn't!" I stuttered.

"I didn't what?" Khatyn said with a laugh.

"You didn't do something drastic with the MP in the office to help Faisal get his PV," I almost whispered.

Khatyn then laughed and laughed to choking point. It took her a moment before she was able to get her composure back to be able to speak.

"Michael, if I understand what you mean, then, no, I didn't do it with him in the office. I did it with him about 20 years ago. He's the father of my children. That was long before he went into politics. I just went back to the office and told him not to be so pigheaded like he was when we were much younger – which is why I left him – and to try, just for a moment, to swallow his prejudices and imagine Faisal as a decent human being who needs help."

When I heard that, I wanted to laugh and cry all at the same time. In this last, cold desperate moment, Khatyn was our angel of salvation.

That night, there was a small party of Afghanis of about eight to celebrate with Sattar. As usual, Faisal joined in with the celebrations in good spirits, despite no doubt the sadness that weighed in his heart and the frustration of waiting. We made a good night of it. During the festivities, all I could think of was Faisal's permanent visa party. I was hoping it would come soon.

But what made it difficult was knowing that Faisal had obtained his TPV at Woomera detention centre long before Sattar did and yet Sattar managed to get his permanent visa before Faisal. Sattar had two things in his favour, a better presented case and a more sympathetic case officer.

As the weeks passed, more and more Afghanis got their permanent visas. First Saber got his, then Jamal, then Parviz and then Qadus. What also made it even more difficult for Faisal was that each time someone got his permanent visa, they rang Faisal first. I could imagine that as much as these guys were happy to relate the wonderful news, each time they did so, it was like a smack in Faisal's face.

One afternoon, Khatyn rang me. I had just finished doing my swim and was in the swimming pool change rooms. As soon as I answered the phone, Khatyn asked if I was about to pay Faisal a visit. I had no real intention of going there at that time of day. I asked Khatyn why she had asked me this.

"I don't think Faisal is very well," Khatyn said rather earnestly. "We bumped into each other at the shops about an hour ago. I've never seen him like that before. He looked very depressed. He had no colour in his face and I think he's been crying."

A wisp of fear passed over me. My goodness, what has happened now? What could be the worst news we could hear?

"Did you ask him what the matter was?" I said almost in a whisper.

"I was unfortunately in a rush so I thought I'd get you to ring him and see if he's okay."

"Thanks, Khatyn," I replied. All I had left to do to get changed was put my shoes and socks on and then throw my swimming bag over my shoulder. Once outside the swimming pool, I nervously dialled Faisal's number. Faisal answered almost immediately with a croak in his voice.

"How are you?" I asked Faisal.

"I'm okay," Faisal replied in his normal, standard reply to this question.

"Are you *really* all right?"

There was a pause at the other end of the phone.

"No, I'm not," he finally replied.

It was like a knife thrust into my chest. Something was really wrong.

"Would you like me to come over now?"

There was once again a pause and then Faisal said that he wanted me to come over.

When I arrived at his place, his face was ashen white and his eyes were red. It appeared that he had been crying just as Khatyn had said.

I gave him a hug. Faisal then led me into his room and we sat down for tea.

"Is everything okay?" I whispered.

Faisal smiled and looked down and then looked at me.

"Well, yes and no. I mean, I'm okay," he said in a rather up and down way. "You know? When an Afghani gets his permanent visa, he rings me first, like I'm their father or their captain or something. I got a phone call today."

When he mentioned phone call, I was terrified. But he continued.

"You remember Salim? Well, he got his permanent visa today."

I must have had a perplexed look on my face.

"I know that other Afghanis have got their permanent visas and it didn't affect me that much. But this is like the straw that broke the camel's back."

I was amazed that Faisal actually used this expression! This diverted my attention momentarily from the issue at hand. Faisal then continued.

"The problem with Salim is this. I met Salim in the hotel at Karachi. We left Pakistan at the same time, we travelled all the way to Australia at the same time, we were in the detention centre for the same time and we left Woomera detention centre at the same time."

Faisal sat on his haunches and looked up at the ceiling. He then sighed.

"All this waiting is tiring me. I just want to see my family again."

It's moments like these that I wish I knew what to say but I was speechless. There were no words. I wanted to comfort him by saying that he was bound to get his permanent visa very soon but after all we had been through, we knew that there was no guarantee that this was the case. Although I didn't want to think it, I had this terrible gut feeling that Faisal was yet to get another phone call telling him that he now had to fulfil other criteria that we had not heard about and this would probably take another few months to be processed.

At least what was troubling him was not life-threatening. When Khatyn first rang me to tell me she had bumped into a depressed-looking Faisal, and then Faisal told me plainly that he was not okay and he wanted me to come over, I thought he was being sent back to Pakistan that very afternoon. As frustrating as the news was, at least it wasn't half as bad as I originally thought.

I spent the afternoon with him, drinking tea and chatting. This seemed to cheer him up. I couldn't stay all afternoon as I had to return to work that evening. But I was happy to leave him with the knowledge that he was okay.

It was some weeks after this event, during one of my classes, my mobile phone rang. I could see, flashing on the small screen, Faisal's name.

"Oh my God," I whispered. Faisal knew I was teaching and knew not to phone me during work hours. For him to be ringing me like this meant that it was more than just an emergency – it was a catastrophe.

I had to answer it. It may have been AELC teacher policy to turn mobile phones off while we were in the classroom but we were dealing with a life and death situation here. I excused myself and walked outside the classroom to answer the phone.

I pressed the button.

"Yes?" I asked hesitantly.

"Hello, Teacher? Are you busy?" I heard Faisal's voice say.

"Well, yes, I'm teaching at the moment. Why?"

"Then I'll tell you quickly. I got my permanent visa."

I think it took a minute before I registered what he had said. As soon as I realised, I screamed, "Yes!" and jumped in the air. I was sure that everyone who heard me thought I had won the lottery!

"Oh, Faisal, that's incredible news! But I have to go now. I'll ring you after class."

As soon as the class finished, I rang Faisal back to confirm the details. Yes, he had finally got his permanent visa. He had just picked it up from the post office. After our conversation, I rang my mother, my sister, and Khatyn. This was the greatest news.

I went straight to Faisal's place that afternoon. This was a sparkling, new Faisal. His face was shining as if he had taken a deep draught from the Fountain of Youth. As soon as he opened the door, I just hugged him so hard I thought he would never breathe again.

"We've done it! You're an Aussie, now!" I said full of jubilation. "You'll have to start eating meat pies and vegemite, singing Waltzing Mathilda and saying 'G'day' to everyone!"

We both laughed.

"So, where is your visa?"

Faisal brought me into his room and picked up an envelope from his side cupboard. He pulled out a piece of white cardboard that was folded into a passport-sized booklet. I opened it up. On the left hand side was Faisal's photo with two ink stamps overlapping the photo. On the right hand side was a description of the class of the visa and a statement saying that he was entitled to stay within Australia indefinitely but if he travelled, he must be back in Australia by a certain date.

"Is it really a permanent visa?" Faisal asked me. I looked up and laughed, thinking that Faisal was joking but in fact he was serious.

"You mean, you're not sure?"

"I'm never sure of anything when it has to do with my visa," Faisal replied. "You know all the trouble I went through. Promises and everything. Now I never know for sure."

My heart went out to him when he made this comment. He was so right. We had heard so many positive points about his case and still we ended up waiting and fighting. At no time was anything certain.

"Yes, Faisal, I can assure you. This document means that you can stay in Australia quote 'indefinitely' unquote. That means, forever."

"It means, then, that I can finally see my family?"

"Yes, you can finally see your family." This news made me both happy and sad. I was happy because Faisal would finally once more be reunited with his family, even if it was only for a time. But I was sad because he would be separated from me for a while. It was now that I realised how much the man had become a part of my life.

"I guess, then, that you will be going back to Pakistan, soon?" I asked.

"Yes, as soon as I can get enough money for the plane trip," Faisal replied.

"But isn't it dangerous for you to go back to Pakistan?" I asked worriedly.

Faisal looked at me with a deadpan, expressionless face.

"Yes, of course, it is. But my family is there and I want to see them."

I looked at Faisal, not knowing what to say. But then Faisal added, "Don't worry! If I don't stay too long in Pakistan, then it's not a problem. I will only go back for a couple of weeks. That will be short enough time for me to see my family and then get out of the country before anyone who wants to capture me knows I'm there."

I closed my eyes and squeezed Faisal's hands.

"You be careful, then!" I then said. "I would really like to see you back here again safe and sound."

It wasn't long after this that Faisal made all the arrangements for his flight back to Peshawar. I asked him how he was flying back. He had a flight from Sydney to Singapore, then a change of flight from Singapore to Islamabad. From there, a friend of his would pick him up and they would travel together by bus to Peshawar.

On the evening of his departure, I went around to Faisal's place. There was a crowd of about fifteen Afghanis. It was as if President Karzai was about to travel! Everything was packed and Faisal looked fresh and ready to go. In 24 hours, Faisal would finally see his family again, his family whom he had not seen for four years.

The trip to the airport was like a convoy. There were four cars travelling for one man to the airport. Faisal rode in someone else's car while I took some Afghanis in mine. These Afghanis chatted in Dari most of the way and I could actually participate in the conversation as if I were an Afghani.

When we arrived at the airport, Faisal went and checked in. Once all the formalities had been completed, Faisal came back to the Afghani crowd. Each of them hugged Faisal and then began to leave one by one. Finally, there was only Salim and I left. Faisal turned to Salim, hugged him and muttered something in Pashto.

Faisal then turned to me. There was a slight pause. Then Faisal and I were caught up in a strong embrace. I didn't want to cry but the emotion of the moment just welled up inside me and the tears poured out abundantly. I was sad but I was also very happy.

"Good-bye, my Pashtun," I said through my tears. "I will miss you terribly."

"Don't cry, Teacher. I will be back," Faisal said in a concerned tone.

I laughed through my tears.

"I'm crying because I'm happy for you, Faisal. This has been a long moment in our lives. We have finally made it."

"Yes, we have."

I knew the situation with Faisal was different to mine. I did not want Faisal to leave, but I knew he wanted to go. He had a family waiting for him at the other end of his trip.

I gave Faisal one more hug. It was a hug I wanted to last forever. But I knew it had to come to an end. As we separated, I held his shoulders and looked at him in the eyes.

"I wish you a safe trip. Give my regards to your family," I whispered.

Faisal nodded, smiled and then turned around. He walked to the departure gate and disappeared. Feelings of both sadness and happiness again caused tears to well up in my eyes. I felt as if I had now entered a vacuum. A large slice of me was now completely missing.

Salim and I went to the observation lounge to watch the planes come and go. It was some time before Faisal's plane finally taxied out onto the runway. His plane sped down the runway and began its ascent into the night sky. As I watched his plane disappear, I raised my hand and waved good-bye as if Faisal would be able to see.

"Farewell, my Pashtun," I whispered, allowing the tears to flow freely down my cheeks, "and may your God be with you."

The entire adventure between the two of us passed through my mind in a moment.

There had been so many times we thought he would be banished from the country.

I was comforted by the thought that, although he had now left, it would not be long before he would be back again.

www.ingramcontent.com/pod-product-compliance
Lightning Source LLC
Chambersburg PA
CBHW021117300426
44113CB00006B/184